Praise for Ray Raphael's

Mr. President

"In a time when many find themselves questioning the efficacy of the presidency (seemingly regardless of party affiliation), the eligibility of future candidates, and the efficiency of the election process, a look back at the origins of the highest office in the U.S. is particularly timely. In this engaging narrative, Raphael elucidates the goings-on of the Federal Convention. . . . Meticulously detailed and thoroughly researched—Raphael cites the papers of many icons of the nation's birth, such as Alexander Hamilton and Benjamin Franklin—this is a valuable read for Democrats and Republicans, as well as historians and those interested in contemporary American politics."

—*Publishers Weekly*

"Far from dryly legalistic, Raphael's presentation, with its context of the partisan 1790s, ensures the avid interest of early-republic buffs."

—*Booklist*

"Renowned historian Raphael delivers an authoritative biography of the Constitutional Convention and the herculean task faced by the representatives. . . . Raphael's exceptional history of the beginning years of the United States should be required reading, especially in an election year." —*Kirkus Reviews* (starred review)

"It's not easy to find something new to say about the most powerful office in the world. Ray Raphael succeeds through the ingenious expedient of taking us back to the time when we had a country but no president, and reminding us how much work it took to fill that void. All fans of presidential history will need this book."

—Ted Widmer, director, John Carter Brown Library, Brown University, and author of *Ark of the Liberties: America and the World*

"Ray Raphael's *Mr. President* presents to the reader a careful, lively, and in many respects, wholly surprising history of the origins and early development of the American presidency. His analysis of the years immediately preceding the Constitutional Convention of 1787 helps us understand better why the job of creating an American presidency was such a difficult one for the framers; and his meticulous examination of the records of the convention yields a wholly novel conclusion: the man who played the most important role in determining the character of America's executive branch was not James Madison or James Wilson, but the flamboyant, outspoken delegate from Pennsylvania, Gouverneur Morris. This book will command the attention of both professional historians and the general reader for decades to come."
—Richard Beeman, author of *Plain, Honest Men:*
The Making of the American Constitution

"Ray Raphael's *Mr. President* is a brilliant analysis of why our Founding Fathers thought a chief executive was necessary for the American democratic experiment to flourish. The shrill arguments between Adams, Jefferson, Hamilton, Mason (and other law wizards) are recounted in these pages in vivid detail. A classic work of history!"
—Douglas Brinkley, professor of history at Rice University,
author of *The Wilderness Warrior: Theodore Roosevelt*
and the Crusade for America

"This is a fascinating and fresh narrative that takes the reader from the fierce debates establishing the federal executive at the Constitutional Convention through Thomas Jefferson's election, which tested the framers' handiwork. It makes you wonder why it's never been told before." —Joyce Appleby, author of
The Relentless Revolution: A History of Capitalism

RAY RAPHAEL

Mr. President

Ray Raphael's fifteen books include *A People's History of the American Revolution: How Common People Shaped the Fight for Independence* (2001) and *Founding Myths: Stories That Hide Our Patriotic Past* (2004). He is also coeditor of *Revolutionary Founders: Rebels, Radicals, and Reformers in the Making of the Nation* (2011). Having taught at Humboldt State University and College of the Redwoods and all subjects in a one-room public high school, he is now a full-time researcher and writer. He lives in Northern California.

Mr. President

Mr. President

*How and Why the Founders
Created a Chief Executive*

RAY RAPHAEL

VINTAGE BOOKS
A Division of Random House, Inc.
New York

FIRST VINTAGE BOOKS EDITION, JANUARY 2013

Copyright © 2012 by Ray Raphael

All rights reserved. Published in the United States
by Vintage Books, a division of Random House, Inc., New York,
and in Canada by Random House of Canada Limited, Toronto.
Originally published in hardcover in the United States by Alfred A. Knopf,
a division of Random House, Inc., New York, in 2012.

Vintage and colophon are registered trademarks of Random House, Inc.

The Library of Congress has cataloged the Knopf edition as follows:
Raphael, Ray.
Mr. president : how and why the founders created a chief executive /
by Ray Raphael.— 1st ed.
p. cm.
Includes bibliographical references and index.
1. Presidents—United States—History—18th century.
2. United States—Politics and government—1783–1809. I. Title.
JK511.R36 2012
352.230973—dc23 2011033471

Vintage ISBN: 978-0-307-74238-4

Author photograph © Marie Raphael
Book design by Soonyoung Kwon

www.vintagebooks.com

Printed in the United States of America
10 9 8 7 6 5 4 3 2 1

Contents

Mr. President

A Pregnant Moment

They had been meeting together in the east chamber of the Pennsylvania State House for a week, and their time had not been wasted. The delegates were almost at full strength—forty-three men from eleven states—and they were working their way down the list of proposals suggested by Edmund Randolph, governor of Virginia. Having dwelled at some length on the first six items, which focused on the structure and purpose of a new national legislature, they set out to tackle the seventh. James Madison, who would chronicle this and every other moment for more than three months, recorded in his copious notes what happened next:

FRIDAY JUNE 1ST 1787

The Committee of the whole proceeded to Resolution 7th "that a national Executive be instituted, to be chosen by the national Legislature—for the term of _____ years &c to be ineligible thereafter, to possess the executive powers of Congress &c."

The first speaker to the resolution, Charles Pinckney of South Carolina, said he favored a "vigorous Executive," but not with powers that extended "to peace & war &c." That, he feared, "would render the

Executive a monarchy, of the worst kind, to wit an elective one." Other delegates no doubt shared this concern, yet before addressing what executive powers might be, they took up one essential question that was on all their minds. From Madison's notes: "MR. WILSON moved that the Executive consist of a single person." Charles Cotesworth Pinckney, Charles's cousin, seconded and clarified the motion— "*National* Executive," he said.

Then there was silence. For the first and only time during the Federal Convention of 1787, not one eminent statesman ventured even a passing comment, much less a reasoned position.

Not Gouverneur Morris, the flamboyant, peg-legged orator who spoke more than anyone else at the convention and had a particular fascination with the executive office. Morris was never at a loss for words—except this once.

Nor James Wilson, perhaps the sharpest legal mind in the room, who gave more speeches than anyone but Morris. Wilson undoubtedly hoped someone else would step forth to support his motion, but nobody did.

James Madison, the third-most-talkative delegate over the course of the summer, had an excellent excuse for not coming forth: he was genuinely perplexed. Six weeks earlier, before the convention, he had outlined a broad plan of government to his friend George Washington. The national legislature should have supreme power over the states, Madison stated boldly, and it should be composed of two branches, organized much as they are today. A central judiciary department should also exercise "national supremacy." On the other hand, "the national supremacy in the Executive departments is liable to some difficulty," he admitted. "I have scarcely ventured as yet to form my opinion either of the manner in which it ought to be constituted or of the authorities with which it ought to be cloathed."[1]

The three delegates next in line for the honor of most loquacious, Roger Sherman, Elbridge Gerry, and George Mason, also passed. Sherman, a veteran of the drafting committees for both the Declaration of Independence and the Articles of Confederation, undoubtedly had some ideas on the matter, but he didn't wish to share them just yet. Neither did Gerry, who voiced wildly unpredictable notions on almost every item discussed, nor Mason, Washington's neighbor and intellectual mentor, who had co-authored the Virginia Constitution in 1776 and who had preempted Jefferson's Declaration of Independence by declaring in Virginia's Declaration of Rights that "all men are born equally free and independent." All these great orators held their tongues.

Even Alexander Hamilton, who would soon hold the floor for an entire day and who would suggest at that time that a single executive serve for life, opted at this moment not to say what he really thought.

Two of the three superstars in the room, George Washington and Robert Morris, also remained silent. Washington, of course, was blessed with an excuse even better than Madison's, for as the convention's presiding officer, he was supposed to remain above the fray. Morris, the all-powerful "Financier" or "Great One," possessed exclusive firsthand experience as a national executive, for he had run the affairs of the United States virtually on his own not once but twice, first for a few weeks during the winter of 1776–77, and later for three whole years at the end of the Revolutionary War, from 1781 to 1784—but Morris, like the others, said nothing.

It fell to the oldest and wisest among them, Benjamin Franklin, to end the eerie quiet. Madison's notes continue:

> A considerable pause ensuing and the Chairman asking if he should put the question, Doctor FRANKLIN observed that it was a point of great importance and wished that the gentlemen would deliver their sentiments on it before the question was put.

"A point of great importance"—that was precisely the problem. Eleven years earlier, the United States of America had made a great to-do about rejecting the British monarch, in principle as well as in person. The new nation had buttressed its very existence with the cardinal principle that people can and must rule themselves, free and clear of any king or queen, so how could they now place one man above all the rest, in charge of executing the myriad affairs of government?

Yet most delegates believed their national government, which currently lacked an executive branch, had proved too weak. (Morris's three-year "reign" had been a temporary aberration, born of necessity to bring the struggling government out of bankruptcy.) Americans should be more realistic, they felt, or the new nation might not survive.

To explore their dilemma and its full implications, let us transport ourselves to that time and place, June 1, 1787, the Assembly Room of the State House in Philadelphia, with James Wilson's motion to create a one-man national executive suspended in the air, unsupported but also unchallenged, and as yet poorly defined. Stripping away our knowledge of what has transpired since, let us savor that moment of indecision. Would this really be such a good idea? Did the prospects for increased efficiency outweigh the manifold dangers?

Further, aside from theoretical concerns, how would Wilson's proposal play politically? Would the people "out of doors"—the politicized populace that had pushed the Revolution forward—ever allow a single person to rule?

PART I

Precedents

(for better and mostly worse)

CHAPTER ONE

"Little Gods on Earth": Monarchs and Their Governors

Most of the men who pondered James Wilson's motion in silence had been raised to honor and love their king. Benjamin Franklin spent his early years under a female monarch, Queen Anne, but for the rest the protector and benefactor whom they were taught to include in their prayers had been either King George I, who ascended to the throne in 1714, or his son, King George II, who succeeded him in 1727.

All but a handful of delegates were old enough to remember the death of King George II and the ascension of his twenty-two-year-old grandson, King George III. The date was October 25, 1760, shortly before the first hints of colonial unrest. The youngest, Jonathan Dayton of New Jersey, had been born just a week and two days before, while Benjamin Franklin, by far the oldest, was fifty-four years old. Respected internationally for his scientific achievements, Franklin was then in England, politicking on behalf of Pennsylvanians who were trying to limit the special privileges and power of the Penn family, the colony's proprietors. The British Crown was a likely ally in this endeavor, he reasoned. If Pennsylvania could be changed from a proprietorship to a royal colony, it would be freed from the Penns' grip. Thus, for the most practical of reasons, Benjamin Franklin on the eve of the Revolution was a Royalist. He broke off from vacationing with his son William to attend King George III's coronation.

George Washington, aged twenty-eight in 1760, and his neighbor George Mason, then thirty-four, had reasons of their own to seek the Crown's good graces. Mason held shares in the Ohio Company of Virginia, which needed the approval of the British king to stake claims in the North American interior. Washington, while serving as the company's surveyor back in 1753, had explored its alleged holdings west of the Appalachian Mountains, and the following year he led an assault on a small party of French scouts at Jumonville Glen, a minor skirmish that by 1760 had turned into a global war. Had the king's army not come to their aid, Virginia militiamen under Colonel Washington would have been no match for their French and Indian opponents. To acquire land and defend it, Washington, Mason, and all other colonial speculators were beholden to both the legal authority and the military might wielded by King George II or King George III or whoever else might sit on the British throne.

Robert Morris, aged twenty-six at the ascension of King George III, had spent the first half of his life in Liverpool, England. As a teenager he settled in Philadelphia, where he rose quickly to a partnership in a prominent mercantile firm, and by the time of George III's ascension the French and Indian War was treating this merchant prince well. By selling scarce and strategic goods, and also through state-sponsored piracy known as privateering, Morris was setting himself on a trajectory that would make him the richest man in America, but he could not possibly ply his trade across the high seas without the protection of HMS *Vanguard*, HMS *Sutherland*, HMS *Nightingale*, and all the rest of His Majesty's ships in the king's navy. Robert Morris had every reason to bless the power of the British monarch.

So it went, down the line.

In 1760, James Wilson, the delegate who offered the motion for a single executive, was an eighteen-year-old student living in Scotland. Five years later, when he immigrated to America, Wilson would not have to alter his allegiance to the British Crown, for he would still be living safely within the king's realm.

James Madison, aged nine, was being raised to believe that the British monarch was not only the head of state but also the embodiment of religious authority, the "Supreme Governor of the Church of England." Perhaps the lad was still too young to realize how closely his family's tobacco-producing plantation depended on the Crown's ability to hold the British Empire together, but that would come with time.

Gouverneur Morris, aged eight, had no reason to question his privileged position in the British social order. His father was in fact a titled aristocrat, the Lord of Morrisania, which comprised much of the present-day Bronx in New York City. Although Gouverneur was not the firstborn son and would never himself become a lord, he was still greatly privileged, thanks to the traditional British hierarchy, with a monarch at the top.

Of all the delegates other than Franklin, only Alexander Hamilton, aged three or five at the time (the record is unclear), was *not* imbued in his earliest years with reverence for King George I or II. An illegitimate child in the West Indies, Hamilton was tutored at home by his French Huguenot mother and by a local Sephardic Jewess, neither of whom was likely to have encouraged adoration of the British monarch. For all the rest, however, professing gratitude and pledging allegiance were taught early and renewed often, at every stage of their political education.

To our modern sensibilities, the hierarchical relationship between British subjects and their monarch in 1760 might appear overly submissive, but as people viewed the matter then, subjects received as much as they gave. Sir William Blackstone, the mid-eighteenth-century jurist who defined the British polity in his authoritative *Commentaries on the Laws of England*, explained that allegiance was "the tie, or *ligamen*, which binds the subject to the king, in return for that protection which the king affords the subject." The bond was symbiotic.[1]

Protection took two forms. Most obviously, as commander of armies and navies, the monarch was expected to shield subjects from any and all external enemies. This was particularly apparent for British colonials in 1760, who felt they had been "freed from the invasions of a savage foe" when the king's forces defeated the French in Canada.[2]

Equally important, however, was the guarantee against lawlessness or tyranny within the monarch's realm. The Crown was legally present in all courts; any violation of the law was an offense to his power and authority, to be punished accordingly. Further, the Crown was charged with guaranteeing the people's liberties. George II, in his first speech to Parliament in 1727, proclaimed that it was his special duty "to secure to all my subjects, the full enjoyment of their religious and civil rights."[3]

To protect the people from foreign foes and domestic disorders, a British monarch needed to possess formidable, across-the-board powers. The monarch was the commander in chief of the armed forces, the head of state, the pinnacle of the titled hierarchy, the wealthiest individual, and the largest landowner. When new lands were added to the empire, they immediately became the king's property, to be dispensed at his pleasure.

The monarch also headed the official state religion, the Church of England, and even with respect to the affairs of state he or she was said to govern by the divine grace of God. When King George II died in 1760, the governor, council, and house of representatives from Massachusetts welcomed his successor by "beseeching GOD (by whom Kings do Reign) to bless the Royal King George the Third with long and happy years to reign over us."[4]

But with power such as this, couldn't the Crown also *deprive* the people of their liberties?

Of course it could, and it had. King James I, who succeeded Queen Elizabeth in 1603, described kings as "little Gods on Earth." Parliament at that point in time held no force of law. It could pass bills, but it had no way of enforcing them. It was essentially an advisory body to the king, who could dissolve it at his will. Parliament did wield the power of the purse, however. Historically, it had been created to raise money for the Crown, and that was still the only real card it could play.

Throughout the 1630s, King Charles I, James's successor, tried to rule without convening Parliament at all. During the Eleven Years' Tyranny, as it was called by his opponents, Charles ruled with autocratic power. He arrested people who refused to comply with the increasingly doctrinaire policies of the Church of England, and he raised money by extracting archaic fees that were still on the books but hadn't been collected for centuries. By the time he reconvened Parliament in 1640, members there were prepared to challenge his power, and they did.

A century and a half later, this was all common knowledge for the educated men in Philadelphia who held their tongues when James Wilson introduced his motion. They knew the grisly details of England's catastrophic civil wars that stemmed from the fallout between Parliament and King Charles I: the beheading of the king in 1649, the rise of Oliver Cromwell, his conquest of Ireland and Scotland, and the transformation from a nominal republic to a dictatorship under his rule. They knew that British people had recoiled and reinstituted a monarchy in 1660, that the old rivalries between Parliament and the Crown continued, and that in 1688 the Glorious Revolution had affirmed forever Parliament's standing as a governing body.

They also knew that Parliament, to restore security and ensure continuity, placed a new pair of monarchs on the throne, William and Mary, even as it constrained royal authority with a Bill of Rights. Henceforth, Britain would be governed by Parliament and the Crown simultaneously. By distributing power rather than concentrating it, the revolutionaries of 1688 had inoculated the British polity against tyranny.

At least that was the plan. Over the next eighty-eight years, while the American colonies remained within the British realm, two emergent political parties—Whigs and Tories—squabbled over the meaning and operation of this mixed system. Broadly speaking, Whigs viewed themselves as the upholders of the Glorious Revolution, trumpeting individual liberties and pushing back against any hint of monarchical abuse, while Tories favored the stability that comes with established hierarchies, often siding with the Crown in its inevitable tugs-of-war with Parliament.

That's the simplistic picture, comprehensible to us today, but the men who gathered at the Pennsylvania State House in the summer of 1787 to establish a new set of rules for the fledgling United States, having been raised within this political matrix, had a much richer understanding of the complexities of Whiggism and Toryism. Although their ideas might differ on how to weight the elements, they all believed in the superiority of a mixed governmental system. Had they been asked to devise a constitution in 1760, before their quarrels with the mother country, they would no doubt have come up with a plan closely resembling the British model, which all agreed was the best in the world. Wilson's motion for a single executive would have passed by acclamation in a moment, and they would have haggled only over the particulars. They all would have wanted to fashion their government around both a monarch—whether selected by birth, appointment, or election—and a body representing the people, something akin to Parliament.

Much had happened between 1760 and 1787, however. When Charles Pinckney, the first speaker on the subject of establishing an executive office, warned against endowing that office with powers over "peace & war &c.," all he needed to do was utter the *m*-word—"monarchy." The term that had once inspired such reverence was now the kiss of death.

The tectonic shift in political philosophy did not come easily. In fact, the Revolutionary generation—the "rebels" of the 1760s and 1770s—were so deeply imbued with the notion of monarchy that they refused to renounce their allegiance to the British Crown until the bitter end, long after empirical evidence had proved the king an adversary. For more than a decade, colonists blamed all their troubles on Parliament, the king's ministers, and their "Tory" allies in America, while excusing the king himself.

On August 14, 1765, when a Boston crowd hung a straw man and a giant boot from an elm tree at the south end of town, they identified the figure with the initials "A.O.," signifying Andrew Oliver, the local official who would be collecting money for the stamps that Parliament required on all colonial court documents, contracts, licenses, newspapers, almanacs, and even playing cards. The boot needed no explanation; everyone knew it represented the Earl of Bute, nicknamed Jack Boot, the former tutor to King George III who had now become his chief adviser. The sole of the boot was painted green, an oblique reference to the British prime minister George Grenville, author of the infamous bill. Even in the most provocative street theater, the king was excused. In the minds of the protesters, the Stamp Act was thrust upon colonial Americans by his advisers and by Parliament, and it was to be executed by appointed officials, but King George III, who presumably had been duped into supporting the measure, lay blameless. Indeed, when the act was repealed the following year, colonial protesters sang his praises for releasing them from the burden imposed by Parliament. One New England minister told his congregation that when the king signed the repeal, he said that "if he had known it would have given his good subjects in America so much uneasiness, he never would have signed the former act."[5]

In 1767 John Dickinson, in his influential *Letters from a Farmer in Pennsylvania,* urged colonists to apply economic pressures to force the repeal of a new round of taxation, but he simultaneously entreated them to eschew any measures that would alienate them from their mother country, and in particular from their king. "We have an excellent prince, in whose good dispositions toward us we may confide," he wrote. Even if the king was momentarily deceived "by artful men," he would not become "cruel or unjust," and his "anger" would not be "implacable." "Let us behave like dutiful children who have received unmerited blows from a beloved parent," he concluded. "Let us complain to our parent; but let our complaints speak at the same time the language of affliction and veneration."[6]

Through the late 1760s and early 1770s, as Parliament continued to thrust taxes on American colonists, and as colonists continued to resist, not even the wildest rebel dared question the king himself. In part to prove they were patriots rather than traitors, protesters continued to profess allegiance, to celebrate the king's birthday and the anniversary of his coronation, and to begin all their raucous toasts with a drink to his health. Patriots believed that if the king would only cast away his devious advisers and listen to the colonists' complaints without prejudice, he would side with his American subjects. At least publicly, they *had* to profess that belief; otherwise, they would be challenging the very heart of British government and culture.

With each new round of repression, colonists selected appropriate scapegoats. In 1768, for instance, the villain of choice was Earl of Hillsborough, the newly elected secretary of state for the colonies, who ordered a clampdown on those resisting the Townshend duties. When crowds covered the doors of Tories with dung, they labeled it "Hillsborough paint."

In the Tea Act controversy of 1773, colonials directed their ire at Parliament, Prime Minister Lord North, the East India Company directors, and the agents who expected to sell tea in the colonies, whom they reviled as "political bombardiers." When thousands upon thousands of citizens met in Boston's Old South Church to protest the three boatloads of tea anchored in the harbor nearby, their angry speeches never tied King George III personally to the Tea Act, the East India Company, or any foul deed, even though he certainly had been a willing partner and active agent.

Even in September 1774, as citizens throughout Massachusetts cast off all British rule outside of Boston, and as they riddled their protests with such rancorous phrases as "ransack our pockets," "the parricide which points the dagger to our bosoms," "numberless curses of slavery upon us," and "unparalleled usurpation of unconstitutional power" (these quotations from the Suffolk Resolves), their resolutions always included a deferential disclaimer, offered at the beginning. Again, from the Suffolk Resolves:

> That whereas his majesty, George the Third, is the rightful
> successor to the throne of Great-Britain, and justly entitled to
> the allegiance of the British realm, and agreeable to compact,

of the English colonies in America—therefore, we, the heirs and successors of the first planters of this colony, do cheerfully acknowledge the said George the Third to be our rightful sovereign, and that said covenant is the tenure and claim on which are founded our allegiance and submission.[7]

The patriots' ability to engage in actual rebellion while professing deference appeared to have no bounds. A final caveat in the Suffolk Resolves offers a clue to their collective cognitive dissonance. Although "some unthinking persons" would understandably be tempted to engage in excess, patriots should at all costs abstain from rioting, for "in a cause so solemn, our conduct should be such as to merit the approbation of the wise, and the admiration of the brave and free." Virtually all documents produced during the Massachusetts rebellion of 1774 contained similar disclaimers against mobs and riots. Rebels were trying not to tear down society but to shore it up and reset its course. They were *good* people, not traitors, and to prove this, they continued to profess allegiance to the crown that embodied their nation and culture—even as King George III opposed their every move.

In November 1774, upon receiving the latest news from Massachusetts, King George III wrote to Lord North, his prime minister: "The New England governments are in a state of rebellion. Blows must decide whether they are to be subject to this country or independent." Both the king and Lord North resolved at that moment to squelch the uprising with additional troops. The following spring, the first wave arrived in Boston and was dispatched to Lexington and Concord, where they met armed resistance from people who considered themselves patriotic subjects of the British Crown. The war was on, yet colonial rebels *still* refrained from leveling verbal abuse at the king. Through the summer and fall of 1775, even George Washington, as he commanded an opposition army, blamed the British suppression on the "diabolical ministry" rather than on King George III, who, as commander in chief of the British forces, had actually ordered the military offensive. Routinely, Washington called his opponents on the battlefield "ministerial troops," in preference to the traditional "King's troops."[8]

Delegates to the Continental Congress, continuing the mental gymnastics, implored King George III, with the "utmost deference for your Majesty," to intervene with his ill-willed ministers. His Majesty's closest councillors, they informed him, were "artful and cruel enemies who abuse your royal confidence and authority, for the purpose of effecting our destruction." Unrealistically, they asked the king to renounce the people he had been trusting to administer his regime for more than a decade.[9]

Finally, on October 27, 1775, in front of a joint session of Parliament, King George III himself chided the rebels and vowed to suppress them. The Americans "meant only to amuse by vague expressions of attachment to the Parent State, and the strongest protestations of loyalty to me, whilst they were preparing for a general revolt," he told the MPs. Since "the rebellious war now levied . . . is manifestly carried on for the purpose of establishing an independent empire," the king vowed "to put a speedy end to these disorders by the most decisive exertions. For this purpose, I have increased my naval establishment, and greatly augmented my land forces." He also planned to make use of "foreign assistance" to squash the rebellion.[10]

How would Americans respond to this categorical affirmation of enmity from their beloved Majesty?

In Philadelphia, where the Second Continental Congress was meeting, news of the king's speech arrived on January 8, 1776. Moderates like James Wilson, refusing to accept the evidence at hand, thought that if Congress made an unequivocal denial of any proclivities toward independence, maybe *that* would finally convince the king to alter the course of his ministers. Others, however, reasoned that since the king himself had broached the subject of independence, that option could finally be placed on the table here in America. The next day, January 9, an anonymous pamphlet called *Common Sense* appeared on the streets of Philadelphia. In truth it was authored not by an American but by a recent English immigrant, Thomas Paine, who had arrived penniless scarcely a year before. Paine was unencumbered by the local patriots' fear of being labeled a traitor; in fact, because he had no reputation to lose, he didn't have to worry about any label whatsoever. He could just speak his mind, and that he did.

Paine's aim was to promote independence, but first he challenged the colonists' habitual support for the British monarch. Not only the king's ministers were at fault, Paine argued, nor even just King George III; the heart of the problem was the *institution* of monarchy, which was inherently destructive to the people's liberties. The very existence of a monarch, according to Paine, contradicted a fundamental tenet of the Enlightenment's natural rights philosophy, the basic equality of human beings. He opened his assault with a rhetorical question: "How a race of men came into the world so exalted above the rest, and distinguished like some new species, is worth inquiring into, and whether they are the means of happiness or of misery to mankind." This "inquiry" into the origin of kings led him to conjure the image of William the Conqueror in 1066: "A French bastard landing with armed banditti, and establishing himself king of England against the consent of the natives, is in plain terms a very paltry rascally original.—It certainly hath no divinity in it. . . . The plain truth is, that the antiquity of English monarchy will not bear looking into."

For Paine, "hereditary succession" offered final proof of the "evil of monarchy." Even if one man somehow convinced his contemporaries that he should serve as their king, this offered no assurance about the prowess of his descendants. "One of the strongest natural proofs of the folly of hereditary right in kings is that nature disapproves it, otherwise she would not so frequently turn it into ridicule by giving mankind an *ass for a lion*."

So a king was simply an ass? Here was an argument presented in the language of tavern-goers, who constituted a hefty proportion of adult male colonial Americans. For years, much of the political discussion had been taking place in taverns, so these made natural venues for public readings of *Common Sense*. Throughout the early months of 1776, patriotic men lubricated with hard cider and rum punch read, listened to, and discussed Paine's daring book, and by and large they embraced it. Imagine hearing Paine's closing argument against kings, in that setting and at that time:

> In England a k—— [the foul word "king," suddenly rendered too foul to write, was no doubt scornfully used in public readings] hath little more to do than to make war and give away places [lucrative governmental positions]; which in plain terms, is to impoverish the nation and set it together by the ears. A pretty business indeed for a man to be allowed eight hundred sterling a year for, and worshipped into the bargain! Of more worth is one honest man to society, and in the sight of God, than all the crowned ruffians that ever lived."

Then the jeers—from the same men who had shouted "Huzzah!" for the king a short while back.

Had Thomas Paine been writing in a historical vacuum, his words would hardly have had the impact they did, but during the early months of 1776, as Americans read and debated *Common Sense,* external events confirmed that the British imperial government, a mixed monarchy, was hell-bent on destroying the American struggle for liberty and equal representation. Late in February, patriots learned that Parliament, with George III's enthusiastic support, had prohibited trade with the rebellious colonies and declared all American vessels, even those anchored in port, to be property of the Crown. Warships from the Royal Navy were setting American ports ablaze, while the king's army had recruited mercenaries from small states in Germany—foreigners!—to fire on American freemen.

Suddenly Americans no longer spoke only of the "diabolical ministry"; now they placed the blame for all their troubles, openly and unabashedly, on "Kingly persecution." Almost in an instant, King George III was transformed from friend and protector to enemy. The British monarch, the ultimate symbol of national unity, became instead the devil incarnate.[12]

Colonists had not deserted their king, they claimed; their king had deserted them. He had violated the original bargain, for instead of protecting his people, as a king must do, he was waging war against them, and for his betrayal King George III would pay a price. Like jilted lovers, Americans turned with a vengeance on the man they had once revered as a "Patriot King."

In July 1776, when the splinter colonies made their final break from Great Britain, Congress declared its reasons to the world, and this time, in the Declaration of Independence, angry accusations against the British Crown replaced deferential posturing. The body of that document was a full-throated diatribe directed primarily against one man: King George III. "The history of the present King of Great Britain is a history of repeated injuries and usurpations, all having in direct object the establishment of an absolute Tyranny over these States," the Declaration of Independence stated boldly, and to prove its point, it listed seventeen specific grievances in venomous terms, each complaint starting with the simple pronoun "He"—referring to a king they now disowned. "He has plundered our seas, ravaged our Coasts, burnt our towns, and destroyed the lives of our people," the document read. "He is at this time transporting large Armies of foreign Mercenaries to compleat the works of death, desolation and tyranny, already begun with circumstances of Cruelty & perfidy scarcely paralleled in the most barbarous ages, and totally unworthy the Head of a civilized nation." By contrast, Congress made no mention of the wicked ministers who had served as whipping boys for patriot propagandists over the previous decade, nor of Parliament, certainly a full partner in the oppression of American interests and liberties. With contorted diction, Congress managed to blame even the laws passed by Parliament on the person of King George III: "He has combined with others to subject us to a jurisdiction foreign to our constitution, and unacknowledged by our laws; giving his Assent to their Acts of pretended Legislation."

The moment of independence became deeply engraved in American consciousness and, with it, the complete and total disavowal of the British monarch. In the six years of military struggles that followed, every time American troops faced off against the king's soldiers, and every time the king's soldiers ran roughshod over civilians in occupied territory, their antipathy toward the king, and by association all things royal, was reinforced. Antimonarchical sentiments became intrinsically linked to the nation's emergence, and therefore to its collective self-definition.

Any retreat to monarchy, in this context, was deemed a threat to the very existence of an independent nation. There was no turning back. Through the war years and beyond, the term "monarch" raised memories of dependency on a nation that had become the enemy, so to espouse it was akin to treason. The label had such clout that republicans hurled it with some frequency at any political opponent who espoused a greater concentration of power. Since a royal monarch was the supreme instance of concentrated power in the British political tradition, anything that leaned the slightest in that direction had to bear the extra burden of denial. Advocates of a stronger central government were forced into "I'm no friend of monarchy" disclaimers, much as rebels before the war felt the need to couple their protests with professions of loyalty to the Crown. The king, and all things kingly, had become an albatross.

Such was the legacy of the British monarch in America, up to and including the first week of June 1787. All delegates to the convention meeting in the Pennsylvania State House to devise a stronger government knew this. If they happened to favor James Wilson's motion to concentrate executive authority in a single individual, they would open themselves immediately to complaints and criticism. Better, perhaps, to let someone else speak and absorb the first blow.

On-the-ground executive authority in most colonies in British North America lay in the hands of royal and proprietary governors, by proxy from the king or queen. For the better part of two centuries, these governors had tried to exert and extend what they viewed as their prerogatives, and very often colonists resisted. While political players in the colonies were slow to oppose the British monarch, they willingly contested the men whom the monarch had chosen to execute the royal will.

The first colonial governors ruled as agents of commercial enterprises. A governor's job was first and foremost to turn a profit for his company, and to this end he provided for the orderly occupation of land and the development of resources. A governor was entitled to collect fees and quitrents from his subjects, while the company, which he represented, benefited by exporting whatever the settlers were able to extract or produce.

All of this required the displacement of Native people, whether through negotiation or war. Governors thereby ruled with military authority, and they expected military obedience. In 1612 the Virginia Company codified its martial law in a proclamation called "Laws Divine, Morall, and Martiall":

> No manner of person whatsoever . . . shall detract, slander, calumniate, murmur, mutinie, resist, disobey, or neglect the commandments, either of the Lord Governour, and Captaine Generall, the Lieutenant Generall, the Martiall, the Councell, or any authorized Captaine, Commander or publicke Officer, upon paine for the first time so offending to be whipt three severall times, and upon his knees to acknowledge his offence, with asking foregivenesse upon the Saboth day in the assembly of the congregation, and for the second time so offending to be condemned to the gally for three years; and for the third time so offending to be punished with death.[13]

This was only one of more than three dozen measures, each intruding deeper into the lives of the colonists. "Every man" was to take "especiall and due care, to keepe his house sweete and cleane . . . and set his bedstead whereon he lieth, that it may stand three foote at least from the ground, as he will answere the contrarie at a martiall Court." Any fisherman who caught a sturgeon was to "bring unto the Governour" all the fish's caviar "upon perill for the first time offending herein, of losing his eares." Subsequent offenses would warrant a year and then three years in the galleys.

Colonists who survived the first ordeals eventually raised their voices against military rule, so arbitrary and prone to abuse. As indentures diminished and the proportion of free citizens expanded, colonists demanded the rights of Englishmen, to which they were nominally entitled. Civil society warranted civil rule, and one by one the colonies evolved from commercial enterprises into political entities. Although Maryland and Pennsylvania, which included Delaware, remained proprietary, and Connecticut and Rhode Island maintained their original corporate charters to the eve of the American Revolution, the rest became royal colonies. This meant that citizens were subject only to the Crown, not to a private company, and that governors were no longer responsible to company shareholders.

The change simplified the line of command, but in itself it did not diminish the authority of colonial governors, who continued to exert executive, judicial, and legislative powers. Royal governors owed their primary allegiance to the Crown, which issued their orders, and only residual allegiance to the people they had been hired to rule. As Governor Benning Wentworth from New Hampshire told his assembly: "My firm attachment to his majestys person family & government challenges my first attention—my next pursuit shall be the peace & prosperity of his majestys good subjects of this Province." True, a royal governor had to contend with other foci of political influence—a council, usually appointed in England, and a locally elected assembly, which the governor needed in order to extract taxes from colonial inhabitants—but even so the governor, acting as viceroyalty, always had the last say. He could "negative" bills at his will, and anytime he so desired, he could prorogue or dissolve the assembly.[14]

The presumed authority of colonial governors suffered during the English Civil War in the middle of the seventeenth century, when authority in the mother country was up for grabs, but with the Restoration in 1660, King Charles II reasserted the power of the Crown over its dominions overseas. Colonial rule became the province of Privy Council members acting variously as the Committee for Trade and Plantations, Council for Foreign Plantations, or Lords of Trade. In 1696 these evolved into the Board of Trade, which tightened enforcement of trade laws. On behalf of the Crown, this powerful group appointed governors, issued their instructions, dispensed land, and sent legislation to Parliament that taxed and restricted colonial commerce. Men who wanted to become colonial governors, or those already in office who wished to remain in power, played up to these royal officials, their primary audience.

Ambitious lords and gentry in England sought colonial governorships to bolster their wealth, power, and prestige. Governors could expect to enrich their fortunes through a variety of perfectly legal channels. Anytime a colonial governor bestowed his blessing on an official transaction, he received personal compensation for sanctioning the affair. Fees for certification of vessels, letters of administration for probate, township patents, licenses to purchase land from Indians, marriage licenses, attorney's licenses, or any other granting of a governor's exclusive authority thus lined his pockets. So did a significant portion—generally one-third or one-half—of the fines and forfeitures paid for such infractions as bribery, practicing law without a license, derogation of courts, violation of the navigation acts, or ignoring quarantine regulations. While fines and forfeitures were set by law, fees were often determined only by "English custom," a wording open to interpretation and abuse.[15]

Increasingly, colonists grumbled at the practice of awarding governorships to favored clients so they might receive the perquisites of office. According to one report submitted to the North Carolina Assembly:

> Governments have bin sometimes given as a reward for services done to the Crown, and with design that such persons should thereby make their fortunes. But they are generally obtained by the favour of great men to some of their dependents or relations, and they have bin sometimes given to persons who were oblidged to divide the profit of them with those by whose means they were procured. The qualifications of such persons for government being seldom considered.[16]

Favoritism, nepotism, and kickback schemes—the system was not designed to win the hearts and minds of the colonists. Further, since most governors were dispatched from England, they had little familiarity with the people they were supposed to govern, the local geographies, or the political idiosyncrasies of their domains. Baron Thomas Culpeper governed Virginia for three years before venturing a brief trip there in 1680. In his absence, Culpeper's on-site agents extracted the quitrents, salary, fees, and fines that came with his post. During his token visit he browbeat the assembly to guarantee a permanent salary to all future governors, then hastened back to England bearing a handsome fortune, £9,500 of the provincial treasury. He also used the governorship to solidify his giant proprietary claims in the Northern Neck, between the Potomac and the Rappahannock Rivers.[17]

As stand-ins for the Crown, even absentee governors possessed sweeping powers. A governor appointed important colonial officials, including sheriffs and judges, so by tempting sycophants with his patronage, while cutting off those who opposed his will, he wielded great power. He possessed the authority to grant pardons, issue charters of incorporation to cities and towns, establish ports and markets, and engage in diplomatic relations with Indians. Although not directly authorized to make laws, he could exert considerable influence in the legislative arena by calling or disbanding the assembly and by negating bills it passed. As commander in chief of his colony's armed forces, he could appoint officers (another opportunity to profit from patronage), muster and arm the militias, and even command people to move their homes should he declare the need. There was no oversight, and the people had no recourse.

A governor's power, though, was not absolute. Erecting a fort or declaring martial law required the consent of his council. Colonial assemblies, meanwhile, held the power of the purse and often used it to their advantage. If a governor wanted money for military operations, he needed the assembly to provide funds through taxation. In some colonies, in order to receive his full salary, over and above the fees and fines that were his due, a governor first had to convene the assembly, which would pay him from the taxes it collected.

So although royal authorities and their appointed governors exerted an overarching reach over colonial affairs, significant enclaves of local power did develop. These were not ordinary colonials, of course, but prominent planters and men of commerce, the wealthiest and most ambitious, those with the most to gain and the most to lose. The colonial elite dominated not only the councils, as one would assume, but the assemblies as well, and they were not nearly so pliable and obedient as agents of the Crown would have liked.

Struggles for power between royal governors and colonials were legion. Witness Sir Edmund Andros, who for a short period of time wielded more authority than any other governor. In 1685, King James II unilaterally abolished the formerly distinct governments in Massachusetts-Bay, Plymouth, Maine, New Hampshire, Narragansett, Rhode Island and Providence Plantations, Connecticut, New York, East Jersey, and West Jersey. In their stead, he created a single jurisdiction, the Dominion of New England, to be ruled by Andros, a loyal supporter and former governor of New York, and a council of twenty-eight appointed by the Crown. Notably absent from this new governmental edifice were the colonial assemblies.

Andros tackled the job with the autocratic fervor James desired. He extracted quitrents that made freeholders feel like peasants. He imposed new taxes without the consent of the citizenry. (Previously, that had been the purview of the now-abolished assemblies.) He abolished town meetings. Yet the people had the last word: literally within moments of hearing that his mentor, King James II, had fled and abdicated the throne, Andros was captured, imprisoned under lock and key, and held for nine months before being shipped back to England.

The Dominion of New England was admittedly an aberration, but colonial distrust of British governors was widespread throughout the colonial era. Colonists viewed them as strangers intent on lining their pockets and ordering people around. Yet they had to be cautious in their resistance, since the governors were backed by the British Crown, so when they did go after a governor, they focused on his alleged personal shortcomings. In the first decade of the eighteenth century, Edward Hyde, better known as the Viscount Cornbury, made many local enemies with his high-handed style when he assumed the governorships of New York and New Jersey. Retaliating, his critics painted him as an effete courtier and fop, a derogatory stereotype that had riled up the populace since at least Shakespeare's day, a century past. Charges of corruption might be difficult to prove, but slander, gossip, and ridicule required no evidence. Political opponents spread the word that Cornbury was fond of dressing as a woman and prancing about, a burlesque caricature of high-toned European noblemen. This charge stuck. Half a century later, William Smith, in his seminal *History of the Province of New-York,* reported Cornbury's cross-dressing as fact. By 1787, when a group of well-educated Americans meeting in Philadelphia contemplated the nature of executive authority, the stereotype that Cornbury represented—a corrupt, decadent British governor preying on his colonial subjects rather than serving them—was deeply ensconced in the American experience.[18]

Each colony had its litany of past abuses, its list of notorious governors. Prior to 1765, any opposition to a royal governor remained primarily a local affair, with little impact in other colonies. With the pan-colonial resistance to imperial policies that started in the mid-1760s, however, local contests took on wider significance. Contests for power in one colony were noted elsewhere, and alleged abuses, such as dissolving assemblies that challenged Parliament, became linked within a single overarching narrative.

In New York on November 1, 1765, the day the hated Stamp Act took effect, protesters focused their wrath on the acting governor, seventy-seven-year-old Cadwallader Colden, who insisted he would enforce the measure. They hung Colden in effigy, broke open his coach house, removed his prized chariot, and committed the effigy and chariot alike to flames in a giant bonfire. Previously, most resistance to governors had been contained within legal channels; this time, the lower orders turned their backs on deference and opposed executive authority in the most forthright way they could. Opposition to Colden was only one battle in a wider war against imperial taxation, a war joined by British colonies from New Hampshire to South Carolina.

In 1767, upon the suggestion of Charles Townshend, Chancellor of the Exchequer, Parliament enacted duties on specified American imports. Colonists resisted these Townshend duties not only because they presented a new round of "taxation without representation," a complaint featured in all American textbooks, but also because the revenues were to be used to pay the salaries of royal governors, thereby stripping the colonial assemblies of their one significant check on executive abuse, the power of the purse. Further, the Townshend Acts, as this series of parliamentary bills was labeled, officially suspended the New York Assembly, which had refused to comply with an act requiring the quartering of British soldiers in private homes; by implication, Parliament could henceforth suspend any colonial assembly. This restructuring of colonial government, disempowering the assemblies and liberating governors from their only dependency on the people they governed, angered colonists as much as the actual taxes.

The Townshend Acts were repealed in 1770, but the British ministry instigated a new crisis two years later by ordering that salaries of superior court judges, in addition to those of governors, be paid through imperial revenues, not through funds raised by the assemblies. Henceforth, the executive *and* judicial functions of government would lie beyond the people's control. In Massachusetts, political activists used this latest threat to the people's autonomy to mount a new challenge to the sitting governor, Thomas Hutchinson. American born and bred, educated at Harvard, and of impeccable moral character, Hutchinson did not fit the mold of the corrupt, conniving Englishman out for his own good, and that created problems for his political opponents. In their attack on the governor's powers, however, Boston's aggressive patriots were aided by Benjamin Franklin, who managed to get hold of some letters that Hutchinson had sent to his friends in high places in London. Government had been "too long in the hands of the people of Massachusetts," Hutchinson had written. "There must be an abridgment of what are called English liberties" in the colonies, since it was impossible for people "3,000 miles distant from the parent state [to] enjoy all the liberty of the parent state." That was the end of Hutchinson's political career in Massachusetts, and it also closed the argument on colonial governors in general. Simply put, none could be trusted, ever.[19]

For southern delegates to the Federal Convention in 1787, there was one additional governor to vilify, a man so evil he had done the unthinkable. In November 1775, the last royal governor of Virginia, Lord Dunmore, had proclaimed freedom to all slaves who joined with the British to fight against their patriot masters. "That man," wrote George Washington at the time, "must be crushed before spring. . . . Nothing less than depriving him of life or liberty will secure peace to Virginia." Twelve years later, for the president of the convention and all other delegates representing states dependent on bonded labor, the memory of Dunmore and his "diabolical schemes," in Washington's words, still loomed large. They could not afford to vest any executive with powers so vast that he might, by decree, commandeer the (human) property of others. That was their bottom line.[20]

All this was basic history, long since internalized by each of the learned delegates gathered in the Pennsylvania State House in the summer of 1787. There must be no more Dunmores, no more Hutchinsons or Cornburys or any of the rest, just as there would be no more monarchs like King George III. For every bit of authority they wished to place at the executive's command, they would have to demonstrate they were not raising these ghosts from the dead. Just as the new executive office must include no features reminiscent of royal prerogatives, it must also be distanced from the unpopular royal governorships. The executive or executives must not be able to exert undue influence through patronage, nor should he or they possess the power to dissolve assemblies. If the executive office was given authority to negate particular acts of the legislature, that too would certainly arouse some suspicion and possibly serious resistance. The office should not provide an avenue for aggrandizement or facilitate personal ambition. Above all, any executive must in some manner remain responsible to the people, the only true source of governmental authority.

This was a tall order, to create an effective executive office that did not repeat past excesses. Was it even possible?

CHAPTER TWO

Revolution and the Retreat from Executive Authority

In the beginning there were committees. When rebellious colonists first exchanged British rule for homegrown governance, they entrusted executive tasks to nobody but themselves.

Nascent patriots started to use committees as agents of executive authority in the late 1760s. Hoping to force the repeal of taxes on paper, glass, lead, paint, and tea, merchants in several seaports mutually pledged not to import any nonessential items from Britain, and to enforce these agreements, they formed committees. In Philadelphia, for example, a special Committee of Merchants was charged with determining who had violated the nonimportation agreement of March 10, 1769. Miscreants were to be dragged to the London Coffee House, where they had to confess their sins and promise to mend their ways.

In Charleston, patriots gathering under the city's Liberty Tree elected thirteen merchants, thirteen planters, and thirteen mechanics (whom we today call artisans) to a committee with similar enforcement powers.

In Boston, the enforcement committee morphed from a merchants-only affair, the Boston Society for Encouraging Trade and Commerce, into the Body of the Trade, known simply as the Body, which welcomed virtually every citizen in town. Since "the Town itself subsists by trade," explained *The Boston Gazette*, "every inhabitant may be considered as connected with it." The people themselves, all of them, would enforce the nonimportation agreement in an orderly but forceful manner. In numbers sometimes upwards of one thousand, they visited merchants accused of selling banned items and frightened them into compliance. These Bostonians raised the concept of "committee of the whole" to a new level.

Starting in 1774, in the wake of the Boston Tea Party and in response to the punishing Coercive Acts, committees not only challenged British authority but also replaced it. The committees varied in name and function—Committees of Correspondence, Committees of Observation and Inspection, Committees of Safety—but they all assumed some sort of executive function.

Tracking the various committees requires a scorecard. In 1774, Philadelphia patriots formed the Committee of Nineteen. A few months later, to deal with the heightening tensions created by the closing of Boston's harbor, a mass meeting of several thousand citizens selected the Committee of Forty-Three, and that in turn led to the Committee of Sixty-Six, charged with local enforcement of a pan-colonial nonimportation agreement called the Continental Association. Continuing in numerical ascension, the Sixty-Six evolved into the First Committee of One Hundred, formed in response to the bloodbath at Lexington and Concord, and finally the Second Committee of One Hundred, which pushed for independence. All these committees, created by popular elections, were instructed to execute the will of the people, as determined at mass open-air meetings in the State House Yard.

The Continental Association, the supreme achievement of the First Continental Congress, called for enforcement committees not just in the major cities but in communities throughout the colonies:

> That a committee be chosen in every county, city, and town, by those who are qualified to vote for representatives in their legislature, whose business it shall be attentively to observe the conduct of all persons touching this association; and when it shall be made to appear, to the satisfaction of a majority of any such committee, that any person . . . has violated this association, that such majority do forthwith cause the truth of the case to be published in the gazette; to the end, that all such foes to the rights of British-America may be publicly known, and universally condemned as the enemies of American liberty; and

thenceforth we respectively will break off all dealings with him or her.[1]

These local committees, the voice and force of Revolutionary America, exerted their authority in an ancient manner—community ostracism—that combined judicial and executive functions. Without this committee structure, the Association would have been no more than an idle plea, lacking any enforcement procedures.

The First Continental Congress, which initiated the Association, was itself an outgrowth of local committees and conventions. In eight of the twelve colonies that sent delegates, congressmen were selected by special conventions of delegates chosen at the county level. Massachusetts was one of only four colonies to select its representatives in the legislature, but that body had just been officially dissolved by the governor, and the real authority in the province resided in the town committees of correspondence, the county conventions they created, and eventually the Massachusetts Provincial Congress. The entire edifice, particularly in Massachusetts but also elsewhere, was heavily weighted at the bottom. Local committees came together in county conventions, which organized province-wide conventions and congresses, and these, in turn, created the Continental Congress, conceived at the time not as a governing body per se but as "a meeting of Committees from the several Colonies on this Continent" or as a "congress, or convention of commissioners or committees of the several colonies."[2]

When delegates from twelve colonies convened in Philadelphia's Carpenters' Hall in early September 1774, one of their first tasks was to select a presiding officer. The choice was not in the least contentious:

> Mr. Lynch arose, and said there was a gentleman present who had presided with great dignity over a very respectable society, greatly to the advantage of America, and he therefore proposed that the Hon. Peyton Randolph Esqr., one of the delegates from Virginia, and the late Speaker of their House of Burgesses, should be appointed Chairman and he doubted not it would be unanimous. The question was put and he was unanimously chosen. Mr. Randolph then took the Chair.[3]

There followed a brief discussion as to "what shoud be the stile [title] of Mr. Randolph & it was agreed that he should be called the President." There was no debate, nor even any talk, concerning Randolph's job description, for it did not differ from that of hundreds upon hundreds of presiding officers—called variously presidents, chairmen, or moderators—of myriad meetings, conventions, and congresses held throughout the colonies during the previous decade. His tasks, like theirs, were to keep order, facilitate the flow of deliberations, and funnel communications. Letters to Congress were addressed to him, and letters from Congress bore his name. Beyond these basic functions, he had no power or authority. He was to initiate no program, favor no position, and indeed not even speak his mind. When debates heated up, he was to mediate between rival factions. In today's parlance, we might call him a facilitator.

Peyton Randolph was well suited to perform his circumscribed role. His personal aspect, like Washington's, commanded respect. John Adams described him as "a large, well looking man." Silas Deane, another delegate, wrote, "Mr. Randolph our worthy President may be rising of sixty, of noble appearance, & presides with dignity." (He would in fact turn fifty-three on his fifth day in office.) Politically, the first president was a moderate. Back in 1765, he had opposed the most radical measures in Patrick Henry's Stamp Act Resolutions. In his personal communications, but not on the floor of Congress, he favored "the gentlest methods" in enforcing the Continental Association. When patriots mobilized for a military assault on Williamsburg the following spring, he warned that "violent measures may produce effects, which God only know the consequences of." Yet he was certainly a resolute patriot. In both 1769 and 1774, when the royal governor dissolved the House of Burgesses, Randolph, the Speaker of that body, presided over an extralegal convention that met in its stead. Virginia, the largest of the colonies, was the most vociferous opponent of British imperial policies south of New England—"These Gentlemen from Virginia appear to be the most spirited and consistent of any," John Adams wrote in his diary—and Randolph, a former attorney general, agent for the colony in London, and twenty-five-year veteran of the House of Burgesses, was that colony's most esteemed elder statesman. He was the natural choice, the only one considered.[4]

Most significantly, Peyton Randolph understood when to hold his tongue, even though he might favor this side or that. For all the respect he enjoyed from other delegates, Randolph did nothing in his capacity as president to affect the outcome of any debate, and that's exactly what the delegates wanted from him. While Patrick Henry, Richard Henry Lee, Christopher Gadsden, John Adams, and Samuel Adams pushed Congress toward radical actions, and Joseph Galloway, John Jay, and James Duane argued for more conciliatory measures, Randolph played no special card. As delegates debated the several hot topics before them—the question of representation, what items to include and exclude in the Continental Association, Joseph Galloway's controversial plan for reconciliation (he wanted two Parliaments, one in London and the other in America), whether to recompense the East India Company for the tea destroyed in Boston Harbor, and whether to urge the colonies to prepare for a military conflict with the mother country—they did not want an advocate of any particular position to sit in the chair. That's why they liked Randolph: their honored leader knew his place, which was not to "lead" in the sense we think of today but to serve as a steadying influence, lest the debates get out of hand.

Given the rhetorical training and large egos of the men who spent the better part of two months in Carpenters' Hall wagging their tongues, this in itself was no easy task. As John Adams noted famously to his wife, Abigail, on October 9:

I am wearied to death with the life I lead. The business of the Congress is tedious, beyond expression. This assembly is like no other that ever existed. Every man in it is a great man—an orator, a critic, a statesman, and therefore every man upon every question must shew his oratory, his criticism and his political abilities. The consequence of this is, that business is drawn and spun out to an immeasurable length. I believe if it was moved and seconded that we should come to a resolution that three and two make five we should be entertained with logick and rhetorick, law, history, politicks and mathematicks, concerning the subject for two whole days, and then we should pass the resolution unanimously in the affirmative.[5]

It might be argued, perhaps, that President Randolph should have been more aggressive in moving the debates along, but delegates would no doubt have balked if he had applied too heavy a hand. To cut off debate was not within his authority. He could convene the body or adjourn it, that was all.

On October 24, as Congress was wrapping up its business so delegates could return home for the winter, Randolph suddenly left his post to preside over Virginia's House of Burgesses, which had been called back into session. Nobody doubted that the House of Burgesses, an official governing body, took precedence over this ad hoc convention, which had run its course in any case. Two days later Congress dissolved itself. Although it resolved that another Congress should convene the following May "unless the redress of grievances, which we have desired, be obtained before that time," it did not provide for a central executive body to deal with the crises over the ensuing six months. The First Continental Congress was not a government but just a convention, and its job was over.[6]

By contrast, the First Provincial Congress in Massachusetts, meeting simultaneously in October 1774, did attempt to establish executive authority. It had to. Unlike the convention in Philadelphia, this body was facing an imminent military invasion from British regulars. In the previous two months, patriots from all of Massachusetts outside Boston had overthrown British authority, both politically and militarily. In the "shiretown" of Worcester, for instance, 4,622 militiamen from thirty-seven townships—half the adult male population of the entire county—had lined both sides of Main Street on September 6 and forced two dozen British-appointed officials, hats in hand, to walk the gauntlet, reciting their recantations thirty times apiece so all the militiamen could hear. Everyone knew that British leaders, sooner or later, would send an army into the countryside to reassert control, so the Provincial Congress needed to raise, train, arm, and supply a military force of its own. That was a far tougher task than passing resolutions and writing letters. It required *execution*.

Fearful of ceding any authority, however, delegates formed themselves into committee after committee to perform these executive functions; they even formed committees to appoint other committees. Only one job required a single individual to serve in an executive capacity, and that's how Receiver General Henry Gardiner, tax collector for the Province of Massachusetts, became the first executive officer in the future United States to be empowered separately from, and in opposition to, British authority. Whereas President Randolph, like the moderators of countless town meetings, county conventions, and provincial congresses, possessed no powers beyond the meetings he led, Henry Gardiner was instructed to solicit and receive tax moneys from every town in Massachusetts, a delegated executive task.

A new Continental Congress did in fact convene on May 10, 1775. The "redress of grievances" had not been "obtained"; instead, British soldiers had marched on Lexington and Concord, and blood had flowed. Delegates to the Congress in Philadelphia, like those in Massachusetts, found themselves with a war on their hands. Upon the request of the Massachusetts Provincial Congress, the Continental Congress assumed "the regulation and general direction" of the army gathering around Boston.[7]

Now in the business of managing an army, the Second Continental Congress had no choice but to assume executive functions, and like their fellow patriots in Massachusetts members insisted on performing all these by themselves. They formed new committees, a host of them, almost daily. Anytime delegates faced a problem, they appointed an ad hoc committee to address it. On one day alone, June 3, Congress created seven new committees: one to prepare a response to Massachusetts, one to borrow £6,000 for the purchase of gunpowder, one to provide an estimate of further sums that needed to be raised, one to write a petition to the king, and three distinct committees to write separate letters to the people of Great Britain, Ireland, and Jamaica. Once each committee had performed its isolate task, it automatically dissolved.[8]

Congress had a new president this time, John Hancock, the wealthy Boston merchant who had funded many of the revolutionary activities there. On May 10, delegates had reelected Peyton Randolph, but two weeks later President Randolph left once again to head the House of Burgesses. Hancock, his ambitious substitute, became attached to his prestigious position, and when Randolph returned to Congress in September, Hancock refused to step down. Yet despite the new president's ambitions, Congress gave him no more powers than it had given Randolph. He couldn't issue orders of any sort, make purchases, borrow money, or even contact foreign emissaries without the express consent of Congress. When not presiding on the floor, he sent, received, and transmitted countless communications. While the president inscribed his fabled "John Hancock" on letter after letter, regular delegates, in their floating committees, ground out the work of coordinating and supplying a fledgling army.

Slowly, the hodgepodge array of ad hoc committees evolved into a lesser and more manageable number of standing committees, each one dealing with all matters within its specified field: the Maritime Committee, Treasury Committee, Board of War and Ordnance (actually a committee), Medical Committee, Committee of Secret Correspondence, and the Secret Committee of Commerce, charged with keeping the supply train flowing. The surfeit of committees reflected Congress's continuing rebellion against the abuses made possible by the concentration of executive authority. For a century and more, British officials, often holding multiple offices, had profited at the colonists' expense. Now the people themselves vowed to control their own government, and this meant distributing executive tasks as widely as possible.

That was the idea, at any rate. In reality, a few men did more than their share, and these ardent delegates emerged with disproportionate power. Most prominent was a merchant-prince from Philadelphia, Robert Morris, who had amassed a fortune during the French and Indian War by supplying military wares to the army, profiting from wartime shortages of consumer goods, and privateering. As chairman of the Secret Committee of Commerce, he issued contracts for the procurement of supplies, often to his own firm. Other contracts went to his trading partners. If this sounds corrupt, it was not universally treated that way at the time. Morris chaired the Secret Committee of Commerce precisely because he possessed the contacts, credit, ships, and merchandise to keep the Continental Army in the field. He could access the goods, and that's what counted.

With Benjamin Franklin, Morris also anchored the Committee of Secret Correspondence, which communicated, sometimes using invisible ink, with foreign merchants and diplomats. He served too on the Marine Committee, charged with creating an American navy and distributing the goods obtained by American privateers. This committee dovetailed with both secret committees, for all three had as their primary goal the procurement of necessary goods from abroad. The entire matrix centered on Robert Morris. In October 1776, when members of Congress wondered why they were not better informed about certain business of the Committee of Secret Correspondence, the committee, in the persons of Franklin and Morris, replied: "We are . . . of opinion that it is *unnecessary* to inform Congress of this intelligence at present because Mr. Morris belongs to all the committees that can properly be employed in receiving & importing the expected supplys."[9]

When Congress fled to Baltimore on December 12, 1776, fearing that advancing British forces might soon invade the city, three members stayed behind to carry on critical transactions: George Clymer, George Walton, and Robert Morris. When Clymer and Walton vanished into their private lives, Morris was left on his own to perform all the tasks required to keep an army in the field and the nation solvent: requisitioning supplies and paying bills, keeping the books, dispatching vessels, arranging deliveries, and so on. To Silas Deane he wrote: "It is well I staid as I am obliged to set many things right that would otherways be in the greatest confusion. Indeed I find my presence so very necessary that I shall remain here untill the enemy drive me away." Morris kept wagons loaded with his valuable possessions, ready for an emergency escape in the event of a surprise attack.[10]

Morris's work did not go unappreciated by Congress, which on December 21 formally approved the "care of the public business as signified in Mr. Morris's letters." On one day alone, Congress read on the floor twenty-three of his letters. More significantly, it transformed the team of Morris, Clymer, and Walton into an emergency committee with the broad and unprecedented power "to execute such continental business as may be proper and necessary to be done at Philadelphia," and it gave this committee immediate access to $200,000, along with the authority to borrow as much "as the continental use there may demand." Since Clymer and Walton disappeared from public service during this time, one man, Robert Morris, now possessed the power to run the fledgling nation by himself. He could (and did) order salt to be removed into the country, purchase clothes for soldiers, rig boats with guns, commandeer wagons to evacuate the city, and make myriad on-the-ground decisions with no oversight, no check on his deeds.[11]

Previously, Congress had guarded its powers jealously, fearing that a grant of executive authority to one or a few individuals might start the new nation on the road to tyranny. With the new nation struggling for survival, however, delegates relented by forming an ad hoc executive branch that was empowered to take independent action. If the exigencies of war demanded a distinct executive, so be it, republican principles be damned—at least for the time being, in this state of emergency.

The immediate crisis ended when Washington's army crossed the Delaware and forced a British retreat. Then, when Congress returned to Philadelphia, it resumed business as usual, which meant government by committees, but there was no template for this, no rules or codes. Without a constitution or firm precedents, the confederation of thirteen states that had declared independence from Great Britain remained under interim management.

The embryonic nation could not go on forever like that, ruled by Congress's seat-of-the-pants committees. To be accepted by the world as a legitimate state and, more pointedly, to attract foreign assistance in its fight against Great Britain, former colonists required a governing body that a nation such as France could reasonably do business with. This, in turn, required a more formal definition of the relationship between Congress and its component parts, thirteen diverse states that still considered themselves sovereign.

The resultant Articles of Confederation turned out to be just what its name implied, a confederation, not a government per se. The states, as sovereign entities, allocated few tasks to Congress beyond those required for coordinating the war effort and engaging with foreign countries. Yes, there would be a federal post office, but no, Congress could not raise its own funds. Even to fight the war, it would have to appeal to the states for money. Yet Congress was still expected to support and administer an army, and this required it to function in an executive capacity.

The closest thing to an executive body in the Articles was a "Committee of the States," composed of one delegate from each state, to carry on business "in the recess of Congress." That committee could only deal with matters that Congress, in advance, had specified, and it could "never"—a key word—tackle a wide range of the most important matters of state:

> engage in a war, nor grant letters of marque or reprisal in time of peace, nor enter into any treaties or alliances, nor coin money, nor regulate the value thereof, nor ascertain the sums and expences necessary for the defence and welfare of the United States, or any of them: nor emit bills, nor borrow money on the credit of the United States, nor appropriate money, nor agree upon the number of vessels of war to be built or purchased or the number of land or sea forces to be raised, nor appoint a commander in chief of the army or navy.[12]

The confederation's only executive body, in short, was instructed in no uncertain terms not to take action on any matter of policy or great consequence.

Although the Articles of Confederation did not formally take effect until they were ratified by the last of the thirteen states, Maryland, on March 1, 1781, Congress used the document as a guide as it fought off the British imperial army and navy, but the Articles were of no great help. Waging a war required a host of on-the-ground executive actions that Congress and its committees, with no funds of their own and little authority over the states, were in a poor position to take.

The states, unlike Congress, had access to money through the power to levy taxes. They also had clearly defined authority and powers and were therefore in a better position to provide for executive administration. Still, with the excesses from colonial times still fresh in their minds, the state constitution makers used various mechanisms to curtail executive power. Massachusetts, the first to cast off British rule and therefore the first to need a new governmental arrangement, addressed the problem by eliminating the governorship entirely. In 1775, in the immediate aftermath of Lexington and Concord, it decided to resume its old charter in all respects—minus a separate and distinct executive. All functions formally performed by the royal governor were assumed by a council elected by members of the assembly.

New Hampshire, likewise, abolished the office of governor in the provisional new government it created early in 1776, and it made no alternative arrangement for executive functioning. Although it established a council with an elected president, it defined that body only as a "separate branch of the legislature" and assigned it no specific executive duties.

South Carolina's provisional new government did provide for a chief executive, but it did not call him a "governor," one who governs or rules. Instead, like New Hampshire, South Carolina called its most prominent leader a "president," one who presides, a lesser term carried over from its Provincial Congress. Two other states, Pennsylvania and Delaware, also adopted the title "president" over "governor."

The states devised various mechanisms for holding executive officers closely accountable. Six of the ten states that formed new constitutions within a year of independence elected their governors or presidents annually. Two states had biennial elections, the remaining two triennial. Five of the annual-election states permitted no more than three successive years in office, and only three states failed to require rotation in office, as they said at the time, or term limits, as we call it today. "A long continuance in the first executive departments of power or trust is dangerous to liberty," the Maryland Constitution of 1776 declared. "A rotation, therefore, in those departments is one of the best securities of permanent freedom."[13]

Executive officers were not granted authority to "prorogue, adjourn, or dissolve" the legislatures. In some states this prohibition was made specific; in others the power was simply absent. One state, New York, allowed its governor to prorogue (suspend) the legislature for no more than sixty days within the period of a year, but he still could not adjourn or dissolve it. All Revolutionary-era Americans could recall, or had heard about, the many times royal governors had seized power from the people by preventing elected representatives from gathering, and they wanted none of this in their new governments.

Eight of the ten states established executive or privy councils to lessen the authority of their chief executives. Although colonists had suffered much grief at the hands of His Majesty's Privy Council, these junior versions would help diffuse the concentration of power in the new state governments. No single executive should be empowered to act on his own will alone, they believed. An elected council, not personally beholden to a chief executive officer, would keep him from using patronage for political or economic gain.[14]

Finally, and most definitively, all but two of the new constitutions denied their governors or presidents the power of the veto. Recalling how royal governors once ran roughshod over colonial assemblies, most Americans opposed giving executive officers any influence in legislative matters. The two exceptions, New York and Massachusetts, had extenuating circumstances. Governors in these states, unlike in the others, were popularly elected, so their veto was viewed as the people's check on the legislature, and the veto was not absolute, as in colonial times. In both states, the legislature could override a gubernatorial veto with a two-thirds vote.[15]

New York (1777) and Massachusetts (1780) were the last two states to adopt constitutions, and the fact that both provided for the popular election of governors and then granted these officers a limited veto power signaled an evolution in public attitudes. Couldn't the myriad difficulties of a prolonged war be lessened by the efficient administration of a stronger governor? Particularly in states torn by fighting, proponents of executive power, once a distinct minority, finally gained some traction.

In South Carolina in 1780, with British forces staged to take over Charleston, the legislature granted its chief executive, John Rutledge, the "power to do everything necessary for the public good except the taking away the life of a citizen without legal trial." When the British then made advances into Virginia, Governor Thomas Jefferson called the legislators together and asked for additional powers, such as the authority to draft slaves to build military fortifications. His proposals were modest, however, when compared with others'. Under attack and very nervous, Virginia's assemblymen seriously debated whether to "have a dictator appointed," with the "power of disposing of the lives and fortunes of the citizens thereof without being subject to account." Although legislators rejected the notion of an all-powerful executive, they did grant Jefferson's successor, Thomas Nelson, the authority to impress food and supplies, call forth militias and dispatch them at his will, and imprison or banish suspected Tories.[16]

The desperation of war placed similar pressures on the confederated quasi-government in Philadelphia. Back in December 1776, as he struggled to keep Washington's army in the field to defend the young nation's capital, Robert Morris had proposed that Congress "pay good executive men to do their business as it ought to be & not lavish missions away by their own mismanagement. I say mismanagement because no men living can attend the daily deliberations of Congress & do executive part of business at the same time." The following year Congress gave a tentative nod to Morris's ideas by establishing a few key "boards" and appointing some men who were not delegates, but the boards possessed little money or authority, and like Congress itself they depended ultimately on the state governments.

Increasingly, as the war lengthened and deepened, Robert Morris's call for full-time executive officers, however repugnant to republican ideals, received serious consideration. In 1780, Alexander Hamilton, Washington's aspiring aide-de-camp who had taken upon himself the study of politics and government, presented a comprehensive plan to strengthen the confederacy and reorganize Congress. In a letter to James Duane, an influential delegate to Congress, Hamilton reiterated Robert Morris's basic complaint—"Congress is properly a deliberative corps and it forgets itself when it attempts to play the executive"—and then outlined distinct executive departments with individuals at the helm. He even suggested which individuals would be best at these new posts: General Philip Schuyler (his soon-to-be father-in-law) as president of war, Alexander McDougall as president of marine, and Robert Morris as financier. Here was a structure that emphasized efficient management, but even Hamilton at this point stopped short of the ultimate centralization of power, a single man above the department heads, a chief executive.[17]

Hamilton's timing was perfect, for Congress was in a collective state of despair. The war, with no apparent end, was only part of the problem; equally significant was the total collapse of the economy. The value of currency issued by Congress, backed by nothing in particular, spiraled downward. By the close of 1780 a Continental dollar could not even buy a penny's worth of goods. Few sensible investors were willing to loan money or advance goods to Congress, a body that had no viable way to raise funds other than begging from its constituent states.

Lacking both money and credit, Congress had to act decisively. On February 7, 1781, delegates resolved to create three "civil executive departments" that would be headed, as Alexander Hamilton and others had suggested, by individuals, not committees or boards. The first office listed was "Financier," followed by "Secretary at War" and "Secretary of Marine." The priority was clear. Without a workable financial system, nothing else was possible.[18]

Less than two weeks later, Congress unanimously elected Robert Morris, who had ushered Congress through hard times back in the winter of 1776–77, to serve as financier. When Morris expressed reluctance, Congress enticed him with the offer of extraordinary powers. He could make all his own appointments, with no input from Congress. Everybody in the government who handled money in any capacity would serve at his pleasure. He could borrow money from foreign governments and import or export goods, all on the nation's tab. He could deal with foreign ministers, thereby running his own department of foreign affairs. Without congressional oversight, he could issue private contracts to supply the army. Soon, he also assumed control of the Marine Department. *The* Financier, as he was called, accepted the powers and used them, and he produced results. He stimulated the flow of money through a national bank, and he restored confidence in governmental notes by backing them with his own personal credit, which people still trusted.

If the Financier's powers sound to us today dangerously close to one-man rule, that's how many at the time viewed it as well. Late in 1781, Joseph Reed commented wryly to Nathanael Greene:

> The business of that august body [Congress] has been extremely simplified, Mr. Morris having relieved them from all business of deliberation or executive difficulty with which money is in any respect connected, and they are now very much at leisure to read dispatches, return thanks, pay and receive compliments, &c. For form's sake some things go thither to receive a sanction, but it is the general opinion that it is form only.[19]

The Financier's "reign" (as some called it) ended in 1784 for two reasons. First, despite all his powers, Morris was never able to achieve his primary goal, giving Congress the power to tax. Without that, the federal government could never rest on a firm and lasting financial footing. Second, the war had come to an end, and with it people's tolerance for allocating exceptional powers to any executive officer. In the words of the Financier's outspoken assistant, Gouverneur Morris (no family relation to Robert), peace was "not much in the interest of America," for it lessened the need for strong government. "War," on the other hand, "is indeed a rude, rough nurse to infant states."[20]

The coming of peace shifted the political tide back toward the pure republicans, those who opposed any centralization of political authority. The focal points of power and politics in the postwar years were the states, not Congress. With the disappearance of an immediate military threat, a lack of funds, no clear mandate, and scant authority under the Articles of Confederation, congressional delegates felt they had more important business to transact, both public and private, back in Virginia, Massachusetts, or wherever they resided. Sometimes Congress could not even convene for lack of a quorum. "Congress continue to be thin, and of course do little business of importance," James Madison, a congressman from Virginia, wrote to George Washington on April 16, 1787.[21]

Madison penned these words four years after the war officially ended and three years after the Financier left office. In the interim, Congress's influence and reputation had continued to slide. In the fall of 1786, when authorities in Massachusetts appealed for federal help to suppress what they labeled a domestic insurrection, Congress, without money and lacking the authority to call up a peacetime army, came up empty. Yet ironically, as weak as it was, Congress was vilified for failing to cure the nation's ills, while those wanting to strengthen its hand were accused of power mongering. So Congress was caught in a bind, too feeble to act yet suspected of being too strong.

There was a way out, people like James Madison, Alexander Hamilton, Robert Morris, and Gouverneur Morris reasoned. If Americans overhauled the existing rules of the confederation, they could form a stronger union that was better equipped to govern at home and attain influence abroad. To give that government more "vigor" and "energy," as these men and others said at the time, they would need to reverse the retreat from executive authority, but they had to tread lightly. Even the faintest hint of monarchy, or the least resemblance to the hated royal governorships, could jeopardize any plan to create a new government.

PART II

Conjuring the Office

CHAPTER THREE

First Draft

Shortly before 10:00 on the first morning of June, forty-three astute statesmen, seasoned by the tumultuous Revolution that had dominated political life over the previous two decades, filed into the east chamber of the Pennsylvania State House, normally occupied by the state assembly. The room was large and airy, forty feet on a side, more than twice the height of a man, and generally bright unless the shutters were closed. Tall multipaned windows dominated the walls flanking the entrance. On cool days, and there were still a few of these, the room was warmed by two fireplaces on the paneled wall facing the door.[1]

Since the convention had opened a week before, delegates now approached seats they had already claimed, comfortable Windsor chairs arranged around small writing tables, each with quill and ink at the ready. The secretary, Major William Jackson, a former member of Washington's staff and agent for Robert Morris, took his place at the front, just below and to the side of the president's chair, while James Madison, who was recording a more personal and detailed account than Jackson's, sat as usual "in front of the presiding member, with the other members on my right & left hands." This was the most "favorable position for hearing all that passed," Madison explained in the preface to his invaluable *Notes of Debates in the Federal Convention of 1787*. George Washington assumed his seat in a mahogany Chippendale chair, topped by a frieze of the sun and its rays, which had been fashioned by a local craftsman during the Revolutionary War. The doorkeeper closed the entryway. A lagging delegate from Georgia came forward to present his credentials. Then Washington read the order of the day, which was quite simple: the convention would transform itself into a committee of the whole to resume discussion of a working draft to reshape the federal government.

This would be their sixth session and their third day of active deliberations. To understand the dramatic events of June 1, the day the American presidency was first discussed by a public body, we need some familiarity with the terrain they had already explored.

The previous Friday, May 25, delegates had convened and unanimously chosen George Washington as their president. They presented credentials from the eleven states they represented, chose a committee to prepare the rules, and then retired for the weekend to settle into their temporary lodgings.

On Monday, May 28, they decided on some rules. Since the delegates were hardly strangers to deliberative bodies, they had little difficulty agreeing on the customary blend of democracy (no member would be permitted to speak a second time "upon the same question" before every other member had been given a chance) and deference (upon adjournment, "every member shall stand in his place, until the President pass him").

Then, on Tuesday, they imposed one more behavioral regulation: "That nothing spoken in the house be printed, or otherwise published, or communicated, without leave." Enforced secrecy, unlike the other rules, defied the prevailing ethic of the times. Throughout the Revolutionary era, Americans had insisted on transparency in their deliberative bodies, but these men wanted to speak their minds freely, without regard to how their words might be portrayed, understood, or misunderstood by the public.

The convention then began to address substantive matters. Edmund Randolph, governor of Virginia, the largest state in the confederation, announced that since Virginia had been the first to call for a convention, its delegation would lay matters on the table for proper consideration. Randolph and his colleagues had arrived in Philadelphia earlier than the rest, and while waiting for the others, they had drafted a coordinated list of proposals for altering the Articles of Confederation.

Randolph, as head of the delegation, then read aloud fifteen resolutions, known collectively as the Virginia Plan, to be accepted, rejected, or amended as the convention might see fit.

On Wednesday, May 30, delegates started discussing Randolph's resolutions, item by item. The first proposal set out its basic premise, "that the Articles of Confederation ought to be so corrected & enlarged as to accomplish the objects proposed by their institution; namely, common defence, security of liberty and general welfare." Hold it right there, Gouverneur Morris said. The convention should come right out and state its true intention: to transform the confederation into a genuine government. Randolph, in agreement, moved to delete the words "the Articles of Confederation ought to be so corrected & enlarged" and substitute in their stead: "A national government ought to be established consisting of a supreme Legislative, Executive & Judiciary."

The key words here, "national" and "supreme," differentiated the new government sharply from the old one. According to Morris, the confederation was "a mere compact resting on the good faith of the parties," not a government per se, which must involve a "compulsive operation." "In all communities there must be one supreme power, and one only," he argued, and that power should be a supreme, national government.

Six states voted with Morris and Randolph, one against, and one divided. The consequences of the decisive vote, taken so early in the proceedings, were monumental. Having abandoned the Articles of Confederation, delegates would no longer have to bow to any of its provisions; instead, they could create a new government on an open slate. Morris and his fellow "nationalists"—delegates favoring a unitary national government rather than a confederation of states—had just staged a revolution in favor of strong government.[2]

With this new framing, delegates proceeded to tackle items two through six of the Virginia Plan, which addressed the composition, selection, and authority of a proposed national legislature. Some issues, such as the small-state/large-state debate over representation in Congress, were deemed too divisive and hence tabled, but the convention did settle the matter of who should be allowed to vote for representatives to the lower house of the legislature. This was tricky. Most delegates agreed with Elbridge Gerry, who held that "the evils we experience flow from the excess of democracy," and Roger Sherman, who proclaimed,

"The people immediately should have as little to do as may be about the government. They want information and are constantly liable to be misled." Yet they also understood that in any republic the people must have *something* to do about their government. James Madison, searching for a broad consensus, managed to synthesize these views in a manner the convention could accept. In several states, he noted, the first branch of the legislature appointed the second, which in turn appointed a governor or council, and these made still further appointments. This process of "successive filtrations" could be adapted to the national government. If delegates allowed people to vote directly for their representatives, the delegates would then be able to leave the people out of the mix in selecting higher officials—including executive officers.

That's where matters stood on Friday, June 1, when Secretary Jackson read to them Randolph's seventh resolution:

> Resd. that a National Executive be instituted; to be chosen by the National Legislature for the term of ___ years, to receive punctually at stated times, a fixed compensation for the services rendered, in which no increase or diminution shall be made so as to affect the Magistracy, existing at the time of increase or diminution, and to be ineligible a second time; and that besides a general authority to execute the National laws, it ought to enjoy the Executive rights vested in Congress by the Confederation.

Pennsylvania's James Wilson, hoping to give the incipient executive office a personal face, immediately moved "that the Executive consist of a single person," and Charles Cotesworth Pinckney of South Carolina, seconding the motion, added "National" before "Executive." Wilson's motion brought the convention, which was just reaching its stride, to a sudden standstill. "A considerable pause ensuing"—that's how Madison denoted the embarrassing silence that followed Wilson's motion. The delegates to the "grand federal convention" had been chosen at least in part for their ability to deliberate and communicate, but just this once all communication ceased.

At first glance, we might think these seasoned statesmen held their tongues because the notion of a single executive departed so radically from the Articles of Confederation, which had kept all executive authority within Congress, but the Articles had been tossed out two days before, so that was not their major concern. They hesitated to speak because Wilson's motion magnified a host of other sticky issues, each a land mine in its own right.

Who would elect a chief executive?

How long would he serve?

What authority would he exercise?

Who could check his power?

Such questions would surface even if executive authority was shared among several individuals, but the very hint of one-man rule raised the stakes across the board. Each question suggested a range of possible solutions, and further, all fields were interconnected; a single executive imbued with extensive powers, for instance, might need greater checks or shorter terms. The problem, then, was where to start.

Perhaps the executive(s) should be selected by the national legislature, but why not by the state legislatures, or state governors, or some assemblage of judges or special electors, or even the people themselves?

Should he/they be elected annually, as was the custom for most officers in the Revolutionary era, or should he/they serve for longer terms—two years or four, seven or even more?

Should he/they be eligible for reelection, or would that place the new government on a slippery slope toward monarchy?

Most critically, what would be the province of this new office, with no direct historical precedent? Should the executive officer(s) have powers of war and peace? Foreign diplomacy? Coining money? Patronage? Where would his/their powers start—and end? Who might serve as a check on the possible abuse of those powers?

Each of these related to the question James Wilson had placed on the table. Perhaps there should be one man at the top, but why not three or even more, to distribute the burden and limit the potential for abuse?

Each delegate arrived at the convention with preexisting views, based on his particular situation and experience. Certainly the six men who had served as presidents or governors of their states had developed opinions on whether executive functions would best be accomplished by one man or several. So did the two who had been presidents of Congress, and also the Financier, Robert Morris, well accustomed to giving orders from the top. Most of the delegates had been members of Congress at one point or another, while all had served on deliberative bodies. Each and every one had confronted issues dealing with the implementation, or execution, of acts and resolutions. All these would come to bear in due time.

Connecticut's Roger Sherman, for instance, was unlikely to trust *any* independent authority to the executive. He was a legislature man through and through, having participated in the Continental Congress for more days than any other member. Sherman had been blessed with neither pedigree (his father was a farmer who had lost more than half his land) nor charisma. "Mr. Sherman exhibits the oddest shaped character I ever remember to have met with," wrote William Pierce, a delegate from Georgia fond of producing thumbnail sketches of his colleagues. "He is awkward, un-meaning, and unaccountably strange in his manner." Yet Sherman did possess ambition. A farmer and cordwainer (shoemaker) in his early years, he became in rapid succession a surveyor, shopkeeper, and almanac publisher—more or less in the Ben Franklin mold, without the flash. Upwardly mobile, he studied law, passed the bar, and was elected to the Connecticut Council in 1766 and the Continental Congress in 1774. For twenty-one years, Sherman's major contributions in the public arena had come from service in the legislative arena, where government by committee prevailed. In his view, since the legislature was the sole "depository of the supreme will of society," executive authority was an oxymoron.[3]

John Rutledge, on the other hand, had resigned from the presidency of South Carolina back in 1778, in protest over the new state constitution that terminated his veto power. Less than two years later he once again became the state's chief executive, assumed extraordinary powers to counteract the British invasion, and was dubbed "Dictator." As much as anyone in the room, and that included many a powerful figure, he felt perfectly at ease with a system of government that featured top-down command, notwithstanding the many challenges to that political orientation throughout the Revolutionary era. As a plantation owner who had commanded the labor of hundreds of slaves, as a leader of the low-country elite that dominated South Carolina's political life, and as president and then governor of the state, he had always been at the top of the chain of command and resisted legislative restrictions on his authority.

Gouverneur Morris, formerly of New York but now representing Pennsylvania, had both legislative and executive experience. In 1775, at the age of twenty-three, he served as a delegate to New York's Provincial Congress, but two years later he helped write the state's first constitution, which allowed the people, not the legislature, to choose their governor. He represented New York in the federal Congress in 1778, and then, after moving to Pennsylvania because of a political dispute in New York, he became Robert Morris's assistant superintendent of finance, making him the second most powerful executive officer in the brief history of the young nation. Morris, like Rutledge and unlike Sherman, came from a class that was accustomed to exercising personal authority. The youngest son of the Lord of Morrisania (the present-day Bronx in New York City), he had both the lineage and the demeanor of an aristocrat, and he was not likely to have scruples about granting extensive powers to the fledgling executive department. Yet Morris was known to be "fickle and inconstant," in the words of William Pierce. Politically, he could play the field. (He played the field romantically as well, not in the least slowed down by the loss of one leg.) So despite his privileged standing, nobody could predict with any certainty where his affinity for executive command might lead him on any specific issue.

James Wilson, Morris's colleague from Pennsylvania, had been fighting for a strong executive at the state level for more than a decade. The radically democratic Pennsylvania Constitution of 1776 placed all authority in the hands of a single-house legislature, which was elected by a greatly expanded franchise and which held a weak executive under its sway. For Wilson and other moderate-to-conservative men of the "better sort," this was no way to run a government, but their repeated attempts to overturn the Pennsylvania Constitution failed. Wilson had reason to expect a better reception from the present assembly. When this esteemed lawyer and scholar moved for a single executive, "single" implied strong and independent. That was his agenda.

All delegates, like these men, arrived with their own personal inclinations, but how would these translate to positions on specific issues? Even Wilson's proposal for a single executive did not *necessarily* imply a strong one. Some might argue, conversely, that vesting executive authority in multiple hands would make it stronger.

The concept of a national executive office was raw and undefined. It was up for grabs, but nobody reached forward to grasp it. Any opening gambit would undoubtedly provoke a round of responses, some perhaps rather harsh, and everybody shied off. Not until Benjamin Franklin, the folk philosopher turned elder statesman, chided delegates for their failure to "deliver their sentiments" on a point of so "great importance" did John Rutledge finally break the ice.

Rutledge opened strategically by echoing Dr. Franklin, always a safe bet. He "animadverted on the shyness of gentlemen" for not "frankly disclos[ing] their opinions," according to Madison's notes. That, of course, gave Rutledge permission to frankly disclose his: "He said he was for vesting the Executive power in a single person, tho' he was not for giving him the power of war and peace. A single man would feel the greatest responsibility and administer the public affairs best."

If Rutledge had hoped to end the silence, he certainly succeeded. He was immediately challenged, and the battle was on:

> Mr. SHERMAN said he considered the Executive magistracy as nothing more than an institution for carrying the will of the Legislature into effect, that the person or persons ought to be appointed by and accountable to the Legislature only, which was the depositary of the supreme will of the Society. As they were the best judges of the business which ought to be done by the Executive department, and consequently of the number necessary from time to time for doing it, he wished the number might not be fixed but that the Legislature should be at liberty to appoint one or more as experience might dictate.

So much for the desirability of *any* independent executive, let alone a single one. The president or presidents (whichever Congress might choose, at its discretion) should continue to function as they always had under the Articles of Confederation, mere administrators of the acts of legislators.

With the parameters set—a single, strong, and independent executive versus a loose conglomerate subservient to the legislature—James Wilson weighed in on his own behalf, trying to strike some sort of balance between the first two speakers. With Rutledge, he "preferred a single magistrate, as giving most energy dispatch and responsibility to the office," but to appease Sherman, he agreed that the executive should not interfere in legislative matters. Politically, Wilson's strategy was to disassociate the new executive office from any monarchical associations; this would be a totally new type of executive office, without the historical baggage of European regimes. Wilson "did not consider the prerogatives of the British Monarch as a proper guide in defining the Executive powers"—an argument meant to allay popular fears, and one that would reappear in the ratification debates.

Wilson's disavowal of monarchy didn't work on Virginia's governor, Edmund Randolph. According to Madison's notes, Randolph "strenuously opposed a unity in the Executive magistracy," which he regarded "as the foetus of monarchy." As a sitting governor, Randolph favored a strong executive but not a single executive. "The fixt genius of the people of America," he observed, was set against any imitation of the British monarchy. The only way to sell a strong and independent executive department was to vest authority in more than one person.

For all the plausibility of a single executive, this was hardly the proper time to go that route, not with Edmund Randolph so adamantly opposed. Randolph was the chief executive of the largest state, grandson of Virginia's only knight (Sir John Randolph), and nephew of Peyton Randolph, longtime leader of the House of Burgesses during the prewar protest years and president of both the First and the Second Continental Congresses. When Peyton died suddenly in 1775, Edmund administered his estate and inherited at least some of his political clout. Now, twelve years later, there was a Randolph once again atop the patriots' hierarchy. Edmund Randolph had been chosen by a delegation that included such luminaries as George Washington, George Mason, and James Madison to present the plan currently under consideration, and to buck him at the outset, with so little consideration, was unthinkable.

On the other hand, delegates were not ready to cede to Randolph and opt for multiple executives, an unconventional and unproven construct that lacked definition. What might a plural executive look like? Would it comprise the heads of separate departments, like the secretaries of finance, war, and marine in the early 1780s, each administering his own realm? That system had not received rave reviews, and the office of finance, which was key to all the rest, had been abandoned. Or would it be more like an executive council, some group of three or five or a dozen men deciding matters in concert? That system was currently in effect in Pennsylvania, where a popularly elected twelve-man council was charged with all executive functions, but this had little appeal for Pennsylvania delegates James Wilson, Robert Morris, and Gouverneur Morris, who had been trying for years to overturn it. Before even considering Randolph's preference for a multiple-executive office, delegates would have to figure out what that meant, and even if they devised a scheme that appeared to work on paper, they would be on uncharted territory. Better just to move on and leave this thorny issue for later. Madison's concise notes convey the tone: "Mr. Wilson's motion for a single magistrate was postponed by common consent, the Committee [of the Whole] seeming unprepared for any decision on it."

Seizing the moment to start anew, James Madison examined the broader picture, as he would often do over the following weeks and months. Wouldn't it be "proper," he asked, "before a choice should be made between a unity and plurality in the Executive, to fix the extent of the Executive authority"? What the executive was empowered to *do* might shed important light on this and related matters, such as who should select him/them and how long he/they should serve. Madison then proposed to imbue the executive with powers "to carry into execution the national laws" and "to appoint offices in cases not otherwise provided for." With little dissent, the delegations agreed. Executive powers were to be derived from the legislature, save only for some unnamed appointments "not otherwise provided for."

This loose definition clarified little, but because executive powers would be minimal, delegates found it easier to broach troublesome issues. A single executive with limited and derivative power would not be that dangerous after all. Perhaps he could remain in office longer, and his selection, although still important, was not quite so pivotal as before.

In any case, delegates willingly moved on to the blank left in Randolph's opening outline: "for the term of ___ years." Wilson opened the bidding with three years, and Charles Pinckney countered with seven. Sherman, for a change, agreed with Wilson. George Mason argued "for seven years at least" with one term only, but Gunning Bedford of Delaware warned against seven, since the nation might be "saddled" with a first magistrate who was not up for the job. Three and seven were the only numbers presented. The day was wearing on. Debate was limited. On a hasty vote, the longer term prevailed by five states to four, with one divided.

Late in the afternoon, delegates turned their attention to the manner in which the executive(s) would be chosen. Sherman argued in favor of appointment by the national legislature, as suggested in Randolph's initial draft, but then James Wilson shocked the convention by raising the possibility of election by the *people*—a very radical concept in the minds of most men in the room. That Wilson would be the one to offer this alternative was indeed strange, for he was no great friend of the masses. In 1779, Philadelphians had boiled into a rage at Robert Morris and other "monopolizers," whom they accused of withholding scarce goods to drive up prices. An angry crowd came after Morris, his lawyer Wilson, and a few of their gentry friends, who barricaded themselves within Wilson's three-story brick house and fired into the throng, killing five people. Then, in the aftermath of the infamous Battle of Fort Wilson (as it has been called ever since), Wilson cringed in the attic of Morris's country mansion to escape the wrath of the populace. Wilson had real and concrete reasons to fear the unfettered power of the people, yet theoretically, as an astute lawyer and legal scholar, he understood that all republican government must be built upon the construct of popular sovereignty. More than most others in the room, Wilson allowed reason to trump his personal inclinations, and that allowed him to become the convention's most outspoken proponent of popular elections. He alone among the delegates believed that representatives, senators, and the president should all be elected directly by the people. If a national government was to possess "vigorous authority," he reasoned, its power must "flow immediately from the legitimate source of all authority, . . . the people at large."[4]

Even Wilson, however, admitted that election by the people was "chimerical," since it was unlikely to win the support of other delegates. Mason, like Wilson, favored the idea in theory but pronounced it "impracticable." These two, Wilson and Mason, were the only delegates who even flirted with democratic election of the executive in this discussion. John Rutledge, on the other extreme, argued that the executive should be selected by the upper house of the legislature, because it was furthest removed from the people.

Wilson's suggestion of popular elections, and its summary rejection, revealed a seemingly insurmountable dilemma. All delegates wanted the government they created to be philosophically grounded in the people, yet not one of them wished to place the operations of that government under the people's direct control. So who else, if not the people, should select the executive(s)? Not the state legislatures; that would highlight regional jealousies, inhibit national allegiances, and open the new government to the same sorts of allegedly pernicious schemes currently under consideration in several states, things like paper money and debtor relief. The national legislature was the only other viable body, but as Wilson aptly observed, and several of his colleagues agreed, executive(s) chosen by the legislature could not be expected to remain independent of it.

This matter would not be settled in a few brief moments in the late afternoon, any more than the matter of a single versus a plural executive. The meeting adjourned for the day. It would be a long summer.

The second day, June 2, opened with a surprise. James Wilson announced he had solved the delegates' dilemma. From Madison's notes:

> Mr. WILSON made the following motion, to be substituted for the mode proposed by Mr. Randolph's resolution, "that the Executive Magistracy shall be elected in the following manner: That the States be divided into districts: & that the persons qualified to vote in each district for members of the first branch of the national Legislature elect ___ members for their respective districts to be electors of the Executive magistracy, that the said Electors of the Executive magistracy meet at ___ and they or any ___ of them so met shall proceed to elect by ballot, but not out of their own body ___ person in whom the Executive authority of the national Government shall be vested."

Even in embryonic form, we can recognize in Wilson's innovative proposal that strange institution we know today as the Electoral College. The concept was simple, even if the mechanisms were not. The people would remain in the picture, but others would make the final choice. Wilson was clearly excited by his ingenious solution.

Others, though, were not so taken. Elbridge Gerry of Massachusetts doubted "that the people ought to act directly even in the choice of electors, being too little informed of personal characters in large districts, and liable to deceptions." This comment surprised nobody. Two days earlier, Gerry had even opposed popular election of members of the lower house. This political veteran of Revolutionary struggles, an early proponent of independence who had served often and vigorously in the Continental Congress, confessed then he had been "too republican heretofore," but he "had been taught by experience the danger of the levelling spirit" by "the popular clamour in Massts."

Only one other delegate bothered to comment on Wilson's scheme. Hugh Williamson of North Carolina "could see no advantage in the introduction of Electors chosen by the people who would stand in the same relation to them as the State Legislatures, whilst the expedient would be attended with great trouble and expence." This simple rebuttal seemed to suffice. Wilson's measure suffered a resounding defeat, with only his own Pennsylvania delegation, along with that of neighboring Maryland, voting for it.

So Wilson's "electors" would not choose the executive(s). Nor would the state legislatures, since the convention was conceived in large measure to take power from those bodies. Nor would the people themselves, whom the illustrious delegates simply did not trust. The last option standing was the one first suggested in Randolph's draft. Without further ado, delegates voted "on the question for electing the Executive by the national Legislature for the term of seven years." This time the long-term option, coupled with the simplest method of selection, passed decisively, 8 to 2; again, Pennsylvania and Maryland were the sole dissenters.

The selection of the executive(s) by the national legislature, as Wilson pointed out, placed the executive office in a subservient relationship, which gave the lie to the delegates' frequent calls throughout the convention for independent branches of government. All these learned men were familiar with the concept of separation of powers, put forth by "the celebrated Montesquieu," as Edmund Randolph referred to the French author of *The Spirit of the Laws*. As a body, they agreed with Montesquieu's precept that republican government depended on the diffusion of authority, yet in this case they left Montesquieu by the wayside. Their willingness to do so speaks to the continued strength of a "tradition" they had pioneered in their governmental and quasi-governmental bodies before, during, and after the Revolutionary War. Since 1774, within their confederation, Congress *was* the government. The executives in eight of the thirteen states remained under the sway of the legislatures that appointed them. Although delegates knew that legislative rule by committee was a major factor in the breakdown of government, that mode of governing had come to feel *familiar*. A handy default, it would remain in the plan unless supplanted by some better scheme.

Now that both the manner of selection of the executive(s) and his/

their term in office seemed settled, Benjamin Franklin thought it might be time to address a matter very much on his mind: executive compensation. Given the history of executive abuse in colonial times, all agreed that the office should not be used for private gain. Randolph's seventh resolution had provided a reasonable safeguard—the executive(s) would receive a "fixed compensation for the services rendered," and that amount could not be altered during his/their term in office—but Franklin favored a tougher stance. The executive(s), he proposed, "shall receive no salary, stipend fee or reward whatsoever for their services." He had prepared in advance a lengthy paper defending his motion, and pleading infirmity, he asked James Wilson, his colleague from Pennsylvania, to read it in his stead. As Wilson did so, delegates no doubt cast occasional glances toward the author himself, the eldest of all elder statesmen, his voice too weak to talk at length but with a mind as clear as any. The Doctor, as people respectfully and affectionately called him, had a lifetime of experience in the affairs of the world, including more proximity to real power—the seats of European empires—than all the rest combined.

Franklin's paper opened with a rhetorical question: Who would be attracted to an executive office that was not only a "post of honour" but also a "place for profit"? To which he answered, "It will not be the wise and moderate; the lovers of peace and good order, the men fittest for the trust. It will be the bold and the violent, the men of strong passions and indefatigable activity in their selfish pursuits. These will thrust themselves into your Government and be your rulers." Such men would soon find ways to turn their "fixed" salaries into more lucrative pay. "Reasons will never be wanting for proposed augmentations. And there will always be a party for giving more to the rulers, that the rulers may be able in return to give more to them." He then continued this dismal train of thought to its logical conclusion:

There is scarce a king in a hundred who would not, if he could, follow the example of Pharaoh, get first all the peoples money, then all their lands, and then make them and their children servants for ever. It will be said, that we don't propose to establish Kings. I know it. But there is a natural inclination in mankind to Kingly Government. It sometimes relieves them from Aristocratic domination. They had rather have one tyrant than five hundred. It gives more of the appearance of equality among citizens, and that they like. I am apprehensive therefore, perhaps too apprehensive, that the Government of these States, may in future times, end in a Monarchy. But this catastrophe I think may be long delayed, if in our proposed system we do not sow the seeds of contention, faction & tumult, by making our posts of honor, places of profit.

Delegates listened attentively as Franklin, via Wilson, played the monarchy card, but they did not respond. "No debate ensued," Madison wrote, "and the proposition was postponed for the consideration of the members. It was treated with great respect, but rather for the author of it, than from any apparent conviction of its expediency or practicability." Judging by the lack of attention to the matter, not just at this moment but throughout the summer as well, we can infer that most delegates believed Randolph's idea of a fixed compensation would suffice. Still, Franklin's speech was a rallying cry for disinterested governance. Virtue, not avarice and ambition, must motivate the new rulers, and the job of the convention was to provide a framework whereby this would happen.

With Franklin's sermon over, work resumed. Having decided the executive(s) would serve for seven years—and this at a time when annual elections were the norm—delegates naturally wanted to devise a plan whereby a man (or men) who proved inadequate could be removed from office before his/their term had expired. The most logical body to impeach the executive(s) was the national legislature that had appointed him/them. John Dickinson, whose *Letters from a Farmer in Pennsylvania* was the first Revolutionary must-read back in 1767, thought impeachment should be initiated with the state legislatures to keep state governments involved, but nobody else agreed. The rest reverted to the fallback option, allowing the national legislature to impeach the executive(s) for "mal-practice or neglect of duty."

That was one way to preclude an executive from becoming a monarch. There was a more direct way as well: disallowing a second term. This passed seven states to two, with Pennsylvania divided.

With the executive office now tightly circumscribed, John Rutledge and Charles Pinckney of South Carolina moved once again that the executive should be "one person." Since he exercised only minimal powers, he served but a single term, and he could be removed from office for no more than "neglect of duty," the dangers of investing executive power in a single individual had been minimized. The practical expediency of a unified executive, meanwhile, was never even challenged. It was a cut-and-dried case, Rutledge and Pinckney believed. They "supposed the reasons to be so obvious & conclusive in favor of one [executive] that no member would oppose the motion."

No member except Edmund Randolph, that is. Virginia's leading delegate took immediate offense to the presumptuous none-dare-oppose-us declaration of the South Carolinians. Even in Madison's flat prose, the passion comes through:

> Mr. RANDOLPH opposed it with great earnestness, declaring that he should not do justice to the Country which sent him if he were silently to suffer the establishment of a unity in the Executive department. He felt an opposition to it which he believed he should continue to feel as long as he lived.

Substantively, Randolph's arguments were not exactly overpowering. A single executive, he conjectured, would appoint only people "near the center of the community" to serve in the government. Offering neither evidence nor logical reasoning, he stated that three executives would be "equally competent to all the objects of the department," but his argument from a political slant bore some weight. "The permanent temper of the people was adverse to the very semblance of Monarchy," so "the necessary confidence would never be reposed in a single Magistrate." Framers beware: a single executive could fuel the flames of discontent and doom the entire project.

So ended day 2. If the nation were to have a single executive, it would have to be against the strong advice and ardent wishes of the chief executive of its largest state.

On Sunday, the Sabbath, the delegates rested.

Come Monday, June 4, they resumed without missing a beat. Still on the table was the motion for a single executive, and still damping down the enthusiasm was Edmund Randolph's declaration that this was not only wrongheaded but dangerous and his views on the matter were forever set.

Nobody jumped to Randolph's side, while several delegates spoke against him. Multiple executives would lead to "uncontrouled, continued, & violent animosities." Each would protect the interests of the region he represented, jeopardizing the good of the whole. In "military matters," three heads instead of one would prove "particularly mischievous." Addressing Randolph's supposition that monarchical connotations would make the plan a hard sell, James Wilson saw "no evidence of the alleged antipathy of the people." As confirmation, he marshaled forth the new state constitutions, which provided for a single chief executive in one form or another. The analogy was weak—people who did not fear a king of South Carolina might well fear a king of the United States—but it still made Randolph's argument appear conjectural.

A majority view, albeit not a consensus, seemed to be coalescing. The limitations imposed on the executive had lessened the trepidation that the man holding that office would turn into a tyrant. Further, this person would not possess the critical "power of war and peace," which several delegates had vigorously opposed. So when the matter finally came to a vote, seven states favored a single chief executive, while three states opposed the idea—a clear victory although short of a landslide. One key state, Virginia, was hotly contested. George Mason, who still resisted, was absent, but so was George Wythe, a proponent. These two canceled each other out. Edmund Randolph was joined in opposition by John Blair, while James Madison, who had come to support a single executive, was joined by James McClurg and, yes, George Washington. The sitting president of the convention and odds-on favorite to become the nation's first chief executive cast the deciding vote within the Virginia delegation. Should the job ever be offered to him, and should he accept, he would exercise executive authority alone, not with others.

On the surface, it would seem a *single* executive was a victory for those who favored a *strong* executive, but in fact it was not, for now delegates had to work even harder to allay fears of a regression toward monarchy. This became immediately apparent as they pondered the executive's authority to review and possibly overturn acts of the legislature—what the delegates called bluntly a "negative" or more politely the power of "revision," and what we call today a veto. Here were the options:

The executive could have an absolute negative.

The executive could negative an act, but a supermajority of the legislature could overturn this; just how "super" the majority must be was open to question.

The executive would possess no authority to interfere with acts of the legislature.

Arguing for the most extreme form of the veto, James Wilson and

Alexander Hamilton contended that "the Executive ought to have an absolute negative. Without such a self-defense the Legislature can at any moment sink it into non-existence." Pierce Butler of South Carolina vigorously objected. He had voted in favor of a single executive, but he never would have done so had he suspected that one man would be granted such power. Benjamin Franklin declared "he had had some experience of this check in the Executive on the Legislature" under the proprietary governor of Pennsylvania. There, "the negative of the Governor was constantly made use of to extort money. No good law whatever could be passed without a private bargain with him. An increase of his salary, or some donation, was always made a condition." Not a single state delegation voted in support of an absolute veto.

On the other extreme, Roger Sherman, devotee of legislative power, argued predictably "against enabling any one man to stop the will of the whole. No one man could be found so far above all the rest in wisdom." Delaware's Gunning Bedford also felt the executive should stay out of legislative matters: "The Representatives of the people were the best judges of what was for their interest, and ought to be under no external controul whatever." This position, like Wilson's, failed to garner much support. Most delegates had bought into the general notion of checks and balances, and they wanted somebody, somehow, to exert some sort of check on the legislative branch.

Save for the Wilson-Hamilton and Sherman-Bedford extremes, there was nearly a consensus. The legislature should be checked, but it should also be able to override that check with a supermajority. From Madison's notes: "On a question for enabling two thirds of each branch of the Legislature to overrule the revisionary check: it passed in the affirmative sub silentio."

Delegates had taken up the matter of a national executive on Friday morning, June 1; by noon the following Monday, after two-plus days of debates and deliberations, they had sketched the outlines of a new office. A single executive, appointed by Congress, would serve a seven-year term but be ineligible for reappointment. He would have the authority to negative a congressional bill, but two-thirds of each legislative branch could override his negative. Congress, which had appointed him, could also remove him for "mal-practice or neglect of duty." His scant powers were loosely stipulated—"to carry into execution the national laws" and "to appoint offices in cases not otherwise provided for"—but even so, delegates had created and defined the broad parameters for a "chief magistrate," as they referred to the office.

But wait: Were these matters really settled?

Not according to George Mason, who had missed the critical vote on a single executive. The day following that decision, Mason announced he was not ready to abide by it, and his tirade against a single executive was at least as passionate as Edmund Randolph's had been. Mason "never could agree to give up all the rights of the people to a single Magistrate." An American chief executive, no less than the British monarch, would be tempted to use "bribery and influence" to augment his powers. The American version would be an even "more dangerous monarchy, an elective one."

People out of doors feared this, and they were the ones with the final say. "Notwithstanding the oppressions & injustice experienced among us from democracy, the genius of the people is in favor of it, and the genius of the people must be consulted." Further, the "genius of the people" would certainly reject one-man rule, thereby dooming the entire plan "not for a moment but forever." Eventually, Mason predicted, his colleagues would realize the disastrous consequences of their decision. Then, so as not to offend the people, they would strip the unitary executive of all significant powers. Finally, seeing that they were undermining their goal of a stronger government, they would reverse their decision, "increase the number of the Executive," and grant the office the powers it needed.

We have no record of how delegates received George Mason's lecture, but we know they could not summarily dismiss it. Mason had all the key characteristics of convention delegates, but in the extreme. Land and slave rich, he was wealthier than most. Although all delegates were learned to a degree, Mason was recognized and respected as among the best read of the lot. He had been at the inner core of Virginia's intellectual leaders for more than two decades. His neighbor George Washington had looked to him as a mentor during his politically formative years before the Revolution. With Washington, Mason had spearheaded the Virginia Nonimportation Resolves of 1769, and he had helped author the Fairfax Resolves of 1774. He had contributed to the Virginia Constitution of 1776, which opened with his trendsetting Declaration of Rights, a document that became a model for several state constitutions and the eventual Bill of Rights. Mason served only rarely in elective office, despite repeated badgering from numerous compatriots, but that only seemed to heighten his status as the ultimate political philosopher. William Pierce summed up his standing: "Mr. Mason is a Gentleman of remarkable strong powers, and possesses a clear and copious understanding. He is able and convincing in debate, steady and firm in his principles, and undoubtedly one of the best politicians in America." We can be sure that Mason's vehement opposition to a single executive, although a minority view at that point, was duly recorded in the minds of his fellow delegates.[5]

Immediately following Mason's harangue, the venerable Dr. Franklin added some cautionary words of his own, more casually presented than Mason's but no less effective. He started with a rambling tale of executive abuse, from the Netherlands this time, then came abruptly to the moral. "The first man put at the helm will be a good one," he said flatly. Nobody had a problem with that; the presence of George Washington in the room, and the shared assumption that he would become the first executive officer, did ease people's apprehensions to some extent. But then Franklin observed, "No body knows what sort may come afterwards." True, all too true. Delegates should not be seduced into thinking all executives would be of Washington's caliber, so they had better take care. Could they ever be careful enough? Perhaps not, Franklin feared, and he closed with a stinger: "The Executive will be always increasing here, as elsewhere, till it ends in a Monarchy."

That was precisely what nobody wished to hear. All the votes on this particular matter or that—three years versus seven, manner of selection, and so on—paled by comparison with the meta-issue the delegates could not escape: If they created a single executive, and made him in any way independent of Congress or the people, were they in danger of sowing the seeds of another monarchy?

CHAPTER FOUR

Second Guesses

The best argument for a new and independent executive branch of government was the extreme inefficiency of the competition—administration by deliberative bodies. A case in point was the current convention.

On June 15, after delegates had discussed, debated, and amended the fifteen resolutions in the Virginia Plan, working in earnest day after tedious day, New Jersey's William Paterson took the floor and announced that he and some colleagues wanted to throw out everything and start anew. This categorical dismissal could be defended, if necessary, by pointing to a recent precedent. On the very first day of deliberations, prodded by Gouverneur Morris, the convention had dismissed the Articles of Confederation in their entirety.

Paterson's caucus—the majority of delegates from New Jersey, Delaware, Connecticut, and New York, plus one from Maryland—proposed a return to the Articles, resolving only that they "be so revised, corrected & enlarged, as to render the federal Constitution adequate to the exigencies of Government, & the preservation of the Union." Word for word, this was what the states had charged them to do. Speaking on behalf of those states, they refused to cede all authority to a unitary body. Under the New Jersey Plan, the United States was to remain a confederation. There was no mention of a supreme national government.

The central reason for calling the convention was that Congress depended on the states for all its funds and was therefore perennially broke. In its second resolution the New Jersey Plan did speak to that need by granting Congress the right to raise its own money through import duties and postage fees, but it would remain a unicameral legislature. Each state would have one vote, as before. There would be no Senate. The underlying structure would not change.

To provide greater efficiency, the New Jersey Plan included an executive but referred repeatedly to the "persons" filling the office. So it was back to a multiple executive, as if James Wilson had never offered his motion, the convention had never discussed it, and no decision had been made.

The following day, a Saturday, delegates considered whether or not to revisit the myriad decisions they had made when pursuing the Virginia Plan. Old arguments resurfaced, with resolution nowhere in sight.

At 10:00 Monday morning, June 18, Alexander Hamilton entered the fray. A longtime proponent of centralized authority, he took the floor, and he held it for five or six hours, uninterrupted by any other speaker. With the help of William Pierce, we can imagine the youthful military man, only thirty years old, "of small stature and lean," his "manners tinctured with stiffness," holding forth to his peers, "sometimes with a degree of vanity that is highly disagreeable," and remaining "highly charged" for the better part of a day, nonstop.

Hamilton's speech would prove by far the longest of the convention, and also the broadest in its intent and scope. For every step taken by Paterson and company away from national government, Hamilton took two steps toward it, insisting, "We ought to go as far in order to attain stability and permanency as republican principles will admit." That was Madison's generous rendition. Hamilton himself jotted down notes to organize his speech, and his extant words reveal a deep disregard for the republican notions that had shaped political dialogue during the Revolutionary era: "It is said a republican government does not admit a vigorous execution. It [republican government] is therefore bad; for the goodness of a government consists in a vigorous execution."[1]

Fearing rule by the untutored masses, several delegates grumbled freely about democratic government, but republican government, in which educated men like themselves deliberated on public affairs, was not to be so readily dismissed. Almost to a man, they had been reared on a steady diet of republican virtue. Hamilton had not. He was a child in the West Indies during the Stamp Act and Townshend Act crises and did not become politically active until late in 1774, just as resistance was turning into revolution, so he never did internalize a commitment to the progressive ideals that pervaded those times. Within two years he was a professional soldier, an experience that shaped his thinking along very different lines. He pegged his career to his mentor, George Washington, and adapted readily to the military's top-down chain of command. Now, a decade later, he showed no special attachment to the notion that people must freely and frequently choose their own leaders.

Hamilton admitted that republicanism could not be entirely abandoned, but he would limit its reach as best he could. He started with a frontal assault on confederations, which could not produce viable governance. All confederations were doomed to fail, he asserted. He produced numerous examples from history, he leaned on political philosophy, and, most significantly, he pointed to human nature, to people's timeless pursuit of power, influence, and their own parochial interests. Judging from the proportion of notes that Madison and three other delegates took on this subject, Hamilton spent a good two hours demolishing New Jersey's plan for continuing the confederacy.

Did Hamilton think the Virginia Plan was any better? A little, perhaps, but not much. The states still retained some degree of sovereignty, which would hamper the national government. Worse yet, its solution to the "excess of democracy" (here Hamilton echoed the words of Elbridge Gerry) was yet more democracy. From Hamilton's own cryptic notes: "Gentlemen say we need to be rescued from the democracy. But what the means proposed? A democratic assembly is to be checked by a democratic senate, and both these by a democratic chief magistrate. The end will not be answered—the means will not be equal to the object. It will, therefore, be feeble and inefficient." And from notes taken by the delegate Robert Yates: "What even is the Virginia plan, but *pork still, with a little change of the sauce.*"[2]

To find a better way, Hamilton proclaimed, delegates need look no further than the government they had rejected eleven years earlier. "British constitution best form," he wrote cryptically in his notes. According to Madison, Hamilton stated "he had no scruple in declaring . . . that the British Government was the best in the world; and that he doubted much whether any thing short of it would do in America."

At the outset, delegates had promised to share their thoughts, even if unpopular, and Hamilton, with heightened drama, indulged liberally, even gleefully, in that permission.

Ironically, Hamilton was the only delegate not taught obedience to the British Crown as a child; he came to this view not from nostalgia but by some combination of reason and taste. The House of Lords was "a most noble institution." As to the executive branch, "The English model was the only good one." A hereditary monarch possessed so much power, privilege, and influence that he was above corruption. "See the excellency of the British executive," he said according to Yates's notes. "He can have no distinct interests from the public welfare. Nothing short of such an executive can be efficient." Only the House of Commons failed to receive any praise.

There was no place in a strong government such as Great Britain's for shared sovereignty, as proposed in both the New Jersey and the Virginia Plans. The individual states of the confederacy only added to the expense of government and made administration less efficient. If state governments "were extinguished," Hamilton argued, "he was persuaded that great œconomy might be obtained by substituting a general Govt." States were simply "not necessary for any of the great purposes of commerce, revenue, or agriculture."

Hamilton said he was not *advocating* a return to monarchy and abolition of the states, even though those were his preferences. He understood he might have to modify his wishes to suit "public opinion," or what Mason and others referred to as "the genius of the people." Still, he argued that public opinion was changing and might soon conform more closely to his views. He also reminded his fellow delegates that they were duty-bound to seek the optimal form of government and then come as close to that as they could. That is why he formulated his own schema, which he presented not as a "proposition" like the others but "to give a more correct view of his ideas, and to suggest the amendments which he should probably propose to the plan of Mr. R. [Randolph] in the proper stages of its future discussion."

In Hamilton's plan, the lower house of the legislature, representing "the mass of the people," would fight incessantly with the upper house, modeled after the British House of Lords and representing "the rich and the well born." To prevent this incessant conflict from immobilizing the government—to provide a "mutual check" on the two competing branches of the legislature—he called for a strong executive, very strong indeed. His notes labeled the executive a "monarch":

> The monarch must have proportional strength. He ought to be hereditary, and to have so much power, that it will not be in his interests to risk much to acquire more. The advantage of a monarch is this—he is above corruption—he must always intend, in respect to foreign nations, the true interest and glory of the people.[3]

In his speech, Hamilton elaborated. Any finite term of office—even seven years, as in the working draft of the Virginia Plan—would be insufficient to guard against an executive's power lust. Being ambitious, as men are, the executive would wish to "*prolong* his power." To this end he might even use the excuse of a war to create an "emergency to evade or refuse a degradation from his place." Only a monarch who already possessed all the power he could ever hope to obtain would be impervious to the pursuit of more. It was Hamilton's eeriest and most dangerous argument, and strangely naïve. The notion that the lust for power could be satiated, that some absolute ceiling would satisfy all monarchs, had already been disproved countless times in history. Hamilton himself could have torn his argument apart, had he been inclined to do so.

In the formal outline for his plan of government—written out in advance and read from the floor—Hamilton refrained from the use of the term "monarch," even though he had used it liberally in his speech. Instead, he used the term "governour," one who governs, still a step up from "president," one who merely presides. The governour would be selected by special electors, not by the people, and once elected he would serve for life if not impeached, entirely free from popular influence. Once in a generation, people would choose electors, who would in turn choose their governour; this one slender thread, which tied the people with their leader in the most tenuous manner, permitted Hamilton to label his plan "republican."

Hamilton's governour would possess the absolute negative over all laws passed by the legislature, a power that had been resoundingly rejected two weeks earlier by a vote of ten states to none. He would also possess powers not specified under the Virginia Plan:

to have the direction of war when authorized or begun; to have with the advice and approbation of the Senate the power of making all treaties; to have the sole appointment of the heads or chief officers of the departments of Finance, War and Foreign Affairs; to have the nomination of all other officers (ambassadors to foreign nations included) subject to the approbation or rejection of the Senate; to have the power of pardoning all offences except treason; which he shall not pardon without the approbation of the Senate.

Senators, who also served for life, were the only check on the governour. They had the "sole power of declaring war," and their consent was required for treaties and all appointments not allocated specifically to the governour. Hamilton gave no special powers to the lower house, undeniably the stepchild in his plan.

Hamilton's extreme concentration of power at the top was not the only shocking feature of his scheme. While other delegates were arguing over what role to reserve for the states, Hamilton stripped the states of any vestige of power. The national government, not the people of Virginia or Massachusetts or New York, would select the "Governour or president" of each state. This, he said, would help ensure state compliance with national laws, and just in case that failed, all state acts conflicting with national ones were automatically declared "utterly void." Equally heretical, by the standards of Revolutionary-era Americans, was the placement of state militias "under the sole and exclusive direction of the United States." At the time, simply calling up state militias to meet a national emergency remained controversial. For a powerful central government to commission all officers and take over militias entirely would produce outrage, if revealed to public view.

How did delegates receive Hamilton's plan?

Nobody spoke when he at long last finished his speech—perhaps because they were stunned, and certainly because Hamilton had worn them out. They were done for the day.

The following morning, June 19, a Tuesday, delegates said nothing of Hamilton's plan. It was Paterson's they discussed and Randolph's, which they reprinted, as revised thus far, so they might compare the two. James Wilson did make one oblique reference to Hamilton's dismissal of the states, causing Hamilton to respond that he "had not been understood yesterday." Virginia and Massachusetts would remain as "subordinate jurisdictions," he explained, but "as *States*, he thought they ought to be abolished."

In truth, other delegates had understood him perfectly well, and they also understood that following his lead would not only doom their entire undertaking but also end their political careers. Not surprisingly, they continued to disregard Hamilton and his ideas. At day's end, they reaffirmed their commitment to Randolph over Paterson by seven states to three, with one divided.

Although Hamilton's plan was not addressed, it did produce a potent backlash. On Wednesday, Oliver Ellsworth of Connecticut moved that the term "national government" in the opening resolution of the Randolph plan be changed to the more neutral "government of the United States." The motion passed by unanimous vote. Three weeks earlier, Gouverneur Morris had engineered a nationalist revolution within chambers; now, after seeing how far one man at least would take the concept of "national," the delegates, running scared, backed off. George Mason followed the vote on Ellsworth's motion with a diatribe against national usurpations, stating "he would never agree to abolish the State Governments or render them absolutely insignificant." Maryland's Luther Martin followed in kind, and Roger Sherman piled on.

On Thursday, June 21, three days after Hamilton's speech, William Samuel Johnson of Connecticut, in his opening remarks about the fundamental differences between the New Jersey and the Virginia Plans, included this passing comment: "A gentleman from New-York, with boldness and decision, proposed a system totally different from both; and though he has been praised by every body, he has been supported by none." (Yates's account.) Historians over the years have vested this parenthetical aside with momentous import. Radicals, attempting to demonstrate the reactionary thrust of the convention, have assumed "praised by every body" meant that other delegates shared Hamilton's extreme views, including his espousal of monarchy, while "supported by none" meant they were embarrassed to admit it. Hamiltonians, similarly, have used this passage to suggest that their man was not such an outlier after all, but in the mainstream. If others failed to spring to his defense, that was only for political reasons, not because they didn't admire the man and his ideas.[4]

These readings misinterpret Johnson's ironic intent. Johnson was juxtaposing Hamilton's ideas, particularly the annihilation of state power, which were "supported by none," with his performance, which was "praised by every body." This is clear from the other firsthand accounts of the proceedings. From Madison:

> Docr. Johnson. . . . One Gentleman alone (Col. Hamilton) in his animadversions on the plan of N. Jersey, boldly and deci-sively contended for an abolition of the State Govts. Mr. Wilson & the gentlemen from Virga. who also were adversaries of the plan of N. Jersey held a different language. They wished to leave the States in possession of a considerable, tho' a subordinate jurisdiction.

And from Rufus King:

> Johnson—The Gentleman from NYk is praised by every gentleman, but supported by no gentleman—He goes directly to ye abolition of the State Governts. and the erection of a Genl. Govt.—All other Gentlemen agree that the national or Genl. Govt. shd. be more powerful—& the State Govts. less so.

"One Gentleman alone," in Madison's rendering of Johnson, advocated the abolition of state governments. "All other Gentlemen," according to King, disagreed with Hamilton's scheme. Even Gouverneur Morris, also an outspoken proponent of an independent executive and a strong national government, thought Hamilton had gone too far. "General Hamilton had little share in forming the Constitution," Morris later recalled. "He disliked it, believing all Republican government to be radically defective."[5]

Hamilton, at this point in time, was indeed an outlier. If his speech influenced the convention at all, it was by establishing the boundaries of acceptable discourse. When he suggested a monarch for life and the abolition of state power in any form, he lost every other man in the room. Those who were old enough to remember the hated royal governors no doubt recoiled when he suggested they place state governorships in national hands. Not one man present could have shown his face back home if word got out that he favored the total commandeering of local militias, the last resort of free men, by a distant national government. Hamilton had gone where they dare not tread. True, some of his particular suggestions were more acceptable, and several of the powers he outlined for the presidency found their way into the final document, but at that moment no delegate wished to discuss even these, lest he be seen as supporting the rest. Delegates must have deemed these features reasonable since they later incorporated them, but any suggestion Hamilton made at that time had to be tabled, tainted as it was by his overarching philosophy.

Yet Hamilton was "praised by every body." To understand why, we need to appreciate the importance of oratory at the time. Giving speeches, arguing points, offering and debating resolutions—these were sport, and contestants were judged by style as well as content. William Pierce, who in his thumbnail sketches often commented on the delegates' oratorical skills, noted that despite Hamilton's "feeble" voice, "he enquires into every part of his subject with the searchings of phylosophy, and when he comes forward he comes highly charged with interesting matter, there is no skimming over the surface of a subject with him, he must sink to the bottom to see what foundation it rests on." Pierce was a tough critic, and Hamilton in this account fared much better than most. He dazzled his audience not only with his brilliant mind but also with his stamina. From personal experience, they all knew how difficult it was to go on as Hamilton did, always cogent, connecting thought after thought, always on target—even if the target was his, not theirs.[6]

So they marveled—and then continued with their business. In the following week, they considered the terms for legislators in the lower branch (one, two, and three years were the options) and the upper branch (four, five, six, seven, and nine years were placed on the table). They argued too over who, if anybody, should pay these public servants—the states (which would make them subservient to local interests) or Congress (which meant they would be paying themselves)—and of course they returned, time and again, to the potentially disastrous matter of proportional versus state representation. Day after day, issue after issue, they continued, and on June 28, late in the afternoon, Benjamin Franklin, not prone to religious excess, called upon a higher power to settle their differences:

In this Assembly, groping as it were in the dark to find political truth, and scarce able to distinguish it when presented to us, how has it happened, Sir, that we have not hitherto once

thought of humbly applying to the Father of lights to illumi-
nate our understandings? . . . I therefore beg leave to move that
henceforth prayers imploring the assistance of Heaven, and its
blessings on our deliberations, be held in this Assembly every
morning before we proceed to business.

But the delegates couldn't even agree on that. Without voting on God's
assistance, they adjourned.

All this round-and-about was anathema to Alexander Hamilton,
the very proof that democratic ways lead to chaos. In the days following his speech, he reaffirmed his commitment to his extreme views
time and time again. June 21: the states should indeed be abolished.
June 22, in support of monarchy: people undervalued the true worth of
royal corruption, "an essential part of the weight which maintained the
equilibrium of the Constitution." June 26, as recorded by Madison: "He
[Hamilton] acknowledged himself not to think favorably of Republican Government; but addressed his remarks to those who did think
favorably of it, in order to prevail on them to tone their Government as
high as possible." His ideas, though, were not receiving serious consideration. Even his vote had become meaningless, effectively overridden
in the three-man New York delegation by John Lansing and Robert
Yates, who remained opposed to the very idea of a central government
and voted against all attempts to strengthen it.

So why stay? On June 29, frustrated and restless, Alexander Hamilton took his leave and headed back to New York. With his departure,
the convention lost its most unapologetic advocate of executive power.
Whatever the chief executive was to become in later years, this group
of statesmen did not wish him to be an almost king, as Hamilton would
have preferred.

On July 17, a month after Hamilton had proposed an elective monarch,
delegates resumed their discussion of the executive. By then, six weeks
had elapsed since they had settled on the outlines of the new executive
branch of government. It was a good time to revisit that first draft,
evaluate it in light of later decisions, and see if it still looked sound. One
by one, they took up the resolutions they had already passed.

Should they stick with a single executive? Yes, by acclamation of
the state delegations. This did not mean that certain individuals, nota-

bly Edmund Randolph, George Mason, and William Paterson, had changed their minds, but they were no longer making a fuss over the matter.

Should the single executive be charged with executing the national laws? Of course, by definition. No dissent there.

Make appointments to offices not otherwise provided for? That too was just fine.

Possess the negative over acts of the legislature, subject to override by a two-thirds vote? Somewhat surprisingly, delegates had made their peace with a limited veto. There was no opposition to this either.

Should the single executive be chosen by the national legislature? Here was a point of contention. Gouverneur Morris predicted this would render the choice of the executive "the work of intrigue, of cabal, and of faction." James Wilson argued it would destroy the executive's independence and make it impossible for him "to stand the mediator," but the alternative—selection by the people—still seemed frightening. "It would be as unnatural to refer the choice of a proper character for chief Magistrate to the people," George Mason pronounced, "as it would, to refer a trial of colours to a blind man." Morris's motion to have the executive chosen by "citizens of the United States," instead of the "National Legislature," failed, receiving only the single vote of Pennsylvania, Morris's and Wilson's state. In some manner yet to be determined, Congress would choose the chief executive.

Should the executive be ineligible for a second term? This too was back in play. Gouverneur Morris offered a simple but strong argument against ineligibility: "It was saying to him, make hay while the sun shines." After some debate, six states voted to allow more than one term, while four stood firm—hardly a convincing result, but at least for the time being, the chief executive could be reelected.

If the executive could be returned to office, however, was seven years still an appropriate term? Many delegates thought not. A few, like Morris and Dr. James McClurg of Virginia, reasoned that reelection eliminated the need for *any* specified term; the legislature that appointed him could also remove him whenever it wished. The executive would therefore serve "during good behavior"—nothing more need be stated. Yet "not more than three or four" delegates saw it that way, according to Madison's notes. A stronger challenge to seven-year terms came from those now wanting shorter spans, but these differed as to the preferred length, and no specific number garnered enough votes to unseat "seven."

That was the confused state of affairs when Gouverneur Morris, the first speaker on the morning of July 19, took charge. Like Hamilton, Morris was an extremely effective debater—so gifted, in fact, that William Pierce gave him five stars in that regard:

> Mr. Governeur Morris is one of those genius's in whom every species of talents combine to render him conspicuous and flourishing in public debate. He winds through all the mazes of rhetoric, and throws around him such a glare that he charms, captivates, and leads away the senses of all who hear him. With an infinite stretch of fancy he brings to view things when he is engaged in deep argumentation, that render all the labor of reasoning easy and pleasing. . . . No man has more wit, nor can any one engage the attention more than Mr. Morris.[7]

Unlike Hamilton, however, Morris could not only capture the attention of this assembly but also change its direction.

Morris tended to play large, and he certainly did so now. "It is necessary to take into one view all that relates to the establishment of the Executive," he commenced, "on the due formation of which must depend the efficacy & utility of the Union among the present and future States." Prior debates had focused on particular aspects, he said, but the enormity of the task required they all be considered together. "Our Country is an extensive one. We must either then renounce the blessings of the Union, or provide an Executive with sufficient vigor to pervade every part of it"—and vigor, at the very least, required independence. Although all delegates gave lip service to an "independent" executive, they would be contradicting that principle if they gave the power of his appointment, and worse yet the power of his impeachment, to the legislature. Morris had been arguing this point all along, but now that the chief executive could repeat in office, his dependence on the legislature was more apparent than ever. To gain reelection, he would have to court legislators—the exact reverse of how it should be. "One great object of the Executive is to control the Legislature," Morris pronounced, as both he and Wilson had done before, but this time he went a step further. The executive must be "guardian of the people, even of the lower classes, against Legislative tyranny, against the great and the wealthy who in the course of things will necessarily compose the Legislative body."

Was Gouverneur Morris, son of a lord, really crying out against "the great and the wealthy," his own class? Back in 1774, during the height of popular resistance to imperial authority, Morris happened to be watching a large meeting in front of New York's Fraunces Tavern: "I stood on the balcony, and on my right hand were ranged all the people of property, with some few poor dependants, and on the other all the tradesmen . . . who thought it worth their while to leave daily labor for the good of the country." Identifying with the men of property, he had expressed his feelings about those beneath him:

> These sheep, simple as they are, cannot be gulled as heretofore.
> In short, there is no ruling them; and now, to leave the meta-
> phor, the heads of the mobility grow dangerous to the gentry;
> and how to keep them down is the question. . . . The mob begin
> to think and to reason. Poor reptiles: it is with them a vernal
> morning, they are struggling to cast off their winter's slough,
> they bask in the sunshine, and ere noon they will bite, depend
> on it. The gentry begin to fear this.[8]

Yet now he vowed to create an executive strong enough to protect those "poor reptiles" from men like himself.

This was part of Morris's larger scheme, an extreme variant of the "checks and balances" strategy that served as the foundation for much of the discussion at the convention. While most delegates believed that the two branches of the legislature should represent somewhat different interests and serve as checks upon each other, Morris, like Hamilton, thought the branches should be taken to their extremes: a "democratic" branch to represent the masses, offset by a consciously "aristocratic" one to serve the interests of the very top rung of society. Both democratic and aristocratic interests presented grave dangers, but by keeping them separate and distinct, the framers could ensure they curb each other's "excesses." "Vices as they exist must be turned against each other," he had said back on July 2. Yet while he once had seemed most fearful of the lower orders, now he expressed an equal concern that "the rich will strive to establish their dominion & enslave the rest. They always did.

They always will. . . . Wealth tends to corrupt and to nourish its love of power, and to stimulate it to oppression."

The popular branch alone could not check this drive for power. "The rich will take advantage of their passions & make these the instruments for oppressing them," he stated. That's why delegates needed to create a truly independent executive who could function as "the great protector of the mass of the people." He could hardly protect the people against legislative usurpations if he owed his job, and his continuance in office through reelection, to the very legislators he was supposed to hold in check.

There was an alternative. If the executive was to be "the guardian of the people," why not "let him be appointed by the people"? Delegates had long distrusted this concept, Morris not the least among them, but suddenly, driven by pure logic, he overcame his aversion—at least for the moment. If the people themselves chose their "protector," and if they were the only ones empowered to keep him in office, he would be free to curb legislative abuse. That was the circuitous route that turned Gouverneur Morris, an even less likely democrat than James Wilson, into a champion of popular election of the executive.

Further, Morris warned that if the legislature held the power of impeachment, the executive's independence would be even more seriously undermined. In that case, when the chief executive tried to check the legislature, legislators would simply remove him from office. But if impeachment by the legislature was not a desirable option, who could hold an inept or corrupt executive in line?

Morris's reasoning here led him to uncharted terrain. If the executive was eligible to repeat in office, and if each term was short enough, the people themselves, by refusing to return him to office, would hold what amounted to the power of impeachment. That's why Gouverneur Morris, who only two days before had argued that the executive should remain in office "during good behavior," possibly for life, suddenly suggested that his term be only *two* years—a shorter period than any of the delegates had yet suggested. If an executive misbehaved or failed to perform his functions, he would simply lose the next election. Reeligibility and frequent elections, taken together, supplanted the need for impeachment and the problems it created. Unlike impeachment, Morris's system would not subject the president to the whims of Congress, nor would it turn changes of leadership into cataclysmic events.

Orderly transfers of executive authority, when necessary, would be built into the very fabric of the system.

Here at last was a plan that was totally interconnected, with each component—popular election, reeligibility, short terms, and "impeachment" only by the people through the electoral process—logically pinned to the others. Morris's schema, radically more democratic than anyone but James Wilson had dared envisage, gave the people themselves a prominent place in the electoral process. Would this assembly of gentry dismiss it as out of the mainstream, as they did with Hamilton's?

No, they took Gouverneur Morris seriously. When Morris moved at the end of his presentation "that the whole constitution of the Executive might undergo reconsideration," the state delegations unanimously consented.

Something remarkable was happening. Through many of the prior debates, the delegates' vested interests had shaped their positions to an embarrassing degree. They had been not disinterested leaders, as good republicans should be, but obedient representatives from small states or large, "carrying states" or those with less trade, states that depended on slave labor or those that did not, yet quite unexpectedly Gouverneur Morris, as aristocratic as any of the delegates, and as haughty in his demeanor, was moving in a direction that ran counter to his class interests. He challenged some of his very own prior notions. Openly, he was changing his mind, and following his lead, others granted themselves permission to do likewise.

As delegates reconsidered their prior positions, the arguments crystallized. With cold, hard logic, Morris had demonstrated how legislative selection required ineligibility for a second term, lest the executive saddle up to Congress to gain reelection, and ineligibility, in turn, required longer terms in office, so the executive would have enough time to become proficient at his job before being forced out. These elements belonged in a single package, while Morris's proposed alternatives—popular election, reeligibility, and short terms—belonged in another. On the very first day of debating the executive office, James Wilson had suggested the very measures Morris was now presenting, but he did not fully demonstrate their interconnection. Now Morris showed there were two *sets* of choices, and delegates would have to select one of them.

The strongest argument remaining for the legislative-appointment rubric was the weakness of its chief alternative, popular election. While Morris, at least for the moment, appeared ready to accept Wilson's radical concept, few others thought the people were capable of making a wise choice. Most delegates, though, were willing to entertain *indirect* election through intermediate electors. This idea had been presented by Wilson on June 2 but defeated soundly, and by Hamilton on June 17 but ignored. Now it fared better. By a vote of six states to three, with one divided, the convention decided the chief executive should be "chosen by Electors." Then, eight states to two, the convention determined that those electors would be chosen by the state legislatures.* That still put the people themselves two steps removed from the chief executive, a safe enough distance.

Then, since the national legislature no longer chose the chief executive and he would not have to curry its favor, reeligibility did not appear so controversial. Two days earlier, reeligibility had squeaked through with a six-to-four vote; now, upon reconsideration, it passed by eight states to two, with Delaware and the key state of Virginia having changed their minds. Only the Carolinas resisted the tide.

Finally, with reelection possible, delegates decreased the seven-year term, which had been written into the plan on the first day of debating the executive office. They didn't reduce it much, however, settling quickly on a six-year term, nine states to one; Morris's idea of biennial elections was more than they could bear.

In a single day, delegates had altered the fundamental way they viewed the executive office. If we judge a speech by the votes taken soon afterward, Gouverneur Morris's performance on July 19 was among the most effective of the summer. While he didn't get his exact wish on all counts, he had reversed the thrust of the convention.

With hindsight, some of Morris's ideas, echoing Wilson's, were also the most "modern": frequent elections of the chief executive by the people themselves. Within this convention of men who knew they

---

* Only ten states voted during this round. Rhode Island sent no delegates to the convention; New Hampshire's had still not arrived; New York's had all departed, Hamilton first, then Yates and Lansing, who disapproved of the convention's direction.

needed to include "the people" yet hoped to keep the people's role in the new framework tightly constricted, Morris's and Wilson's notions stand as democratic anomalies, stranger yet because of the standings and proclivities of their authors.

. . .

The next morning, July 20, delegates considered how many electors to allocate to each state. Elbridge Gerry presented a scheme whereby each of the three largest by population (Virginia, Pennsylvania, and Massachusetts) would select three electors, the next six in size two each, and the four smallest only one apiece. Was that really fair? Shouldn't New Hampshire have two instead of one? Connecticut's Oliver Ellsworth wondered. (A large number of New Hampshire residents had come from Connecticut.) Then Georgia should have two as well, said Georgia's William Houstoun. Gerry's formula was affirmed, although four small states, unhappy with their share, voted against it. The elector scheme was taking on a definite shape.

With the allocation of electors determined, Gouverneur Morris, along with Charles Pinckney, tried to continue along the lines taken the previous day by removing the provision on impeachment from the working draft. Now that an orderly process was in place for periodic reevaluation of the executive, impeachment was no longer necessary and should be dispensed with. Impeachment in any form, Morris argued, "will render the Executive dependent on those who are to impeach," thereby undermining his independence and authority.

This time Morris met immediate resistance. North Carolina's William Richardson Davie, who spoke only rarely at the convention, predicted that if the only way to remove a president from office was through an election, the chief executive "will spare no efforts or means whatsoever to get himself re-elected." Impeachment was "an essential security for the good behavior of the Executive," he concluded.

James Wilson, previously allied with Morris, broke their bond and sided with Davie. George Mason asked rhetorically, "Shall any man be above Justice?" Then Benjamin Franklin turned Morris's argument on its head. Impeachment, the clever sage noted, was "favorable to the Executive" because without it the clearest path to removal was assassination. In that sad event, an executive "was not only deprived of his life but of the opportunity of vindicating his character." Impeachment of the chief executive, on the other hand, would lead to appropriate punishment when "his misconduct should deserve it" or to "his honorable acquittal when he should be unjustly accused." Franklin spoke the language of his colleagues, who professed to value honor above all else.

Edmund Randolph, who had favored a multiple executive and was still wary of concentrating power in the hands of a single executive, offered a convincing corollary to Franklin's argument. Legal impeachment procedures, he said, would promote justice while preventing civil unrest:

> Guilt wherever found ought to be punished. The Executive will have great opportunitys of abusing his power; particularly in time of war when the military force, and in some respects the public money will be in his hands. Should no regular punishment be provided, it will be irregularly inflicted by tumults & insurrections.

Some process for impeachment, Franklin and Randolph demonstrated, was necessary to the orderly functioning of government. This was precisely the sort of argument that would convince Gouverneur Morris, and it did. He had been outflanked, and to his credit he acknowledged as much. First he backed off mildly, admitting that "corruption & some few other offences . . . ought to be impeachable" but insisting that "the cases ought to be enumerated & defined." Then, as the debate continued, he realized his prior stand against impeachment had depended on staging elections every two years, but the convention had settled on six-year terms instead. Noting that his "opinion had been changed by the arguments in the discussion," he was now "sensible of the necessity of impeachments, if the Executive was to continue for any time."

Still, the nuts and bolts of impeachment had to be worked out. How should impeachable offenses be defined? What should be the punishments? Who should initiate and conduct the trials? Morris weighed in on each of these. Bribery, treachery, corruption, and incapacity should be "causes of impeachment," he stated. The executive "should be punished not as a man, but as an officer, and punished only by degradation from his office." While these ideas closely approximated the final Constitution, Morris's final suggestion did not fare so well. "We should take care to provide some mode that will not make him dependent on the Legislature," he reiterated—but to no avail. The resolution to make the executive "removable on impeachment and conviction of mal practice or neglect of duty" passed easily, eight states to two. The resolution did not state specifically *who* was to do the impeaching, but the default mode was Congress, as was implicit in the original Virginia Plan that allowed Congress to choose the executive.

Other delegates, like Morris, hesitated to grant the power of impeachment to Congress, but what were the alternatives? Impeachment and trial by the Supreme Court? By a special panel of judges? By an executive council of some sort? No matter what particular body was granted the authority to remove the chief executive from office, the executive's supremacy would be challenged and his independence undermined. The only group that legitimately outranked the chief executive was the people, as Morris had stated so clearly in his speech the previous day. America's executive officer, he now proclaimed, "is not the King but the prime-minister. The people are the King."

Having "settled" the issues of the executive's selection, length of term, reeligibility, and possible impeachment, delegates discussed other matters for the better part of three days. Then, late on Monday afternoon, July 23, William Houstoun and Richard Dobbs Spaight moved "that the appointment of the Executive by Electors chosen by the Legislatures of the States, be reconsidered." Houstoun, from Georgia, and Spaight, from North Carolina, had no great philosophical concerns. They worried only about "the extreme inconveniency & the considerable expense, of drawing together men from all the States for the single purpose of electing the Chief Magistrate." Eight state delegations agreed "that tomorrow be assigned for reconsideration." Only Pennsylvania and Connecticut dissented; Morris and Wilson, having finally prevailed four days earlier, would have preferred to let matters stand.

When "tomorrow" arrived, the backsliding began. Pleading hardship of the "more distant states," which would bear the expense of dispatching electors, Houstoun moved that the "National Legislature" reclaim the job of choosing the executive. Here again was the same old debate. Four delegates spoke to Houstoun's motion for "going back to the original ground," as Hugh Williamson of North Carolina put it, and it was Williamson who probably carried the house, if any of the speakers did. Reelection was to be avoided at all costs, he said. The

"Magistrate" would see himself as "an elective King, and will feel the spirit of one. He will spare no pains to keep himself in for life, and will then lay a train for the succession of his children." Only ineligibility would protect against that. Further, ineligibility would make legislative appointment once again feasible, since the executive, after assuming his office, would have no vested interest in pleasing Congress.

Houstoun's motion passed by seven delegations to four. Five states that had favored electors less than a week earlier now changed their votes.* So the legislature would select the executive, as in Randolph's original plan and as reaffirmed several times since, save only for the day of Gouverneur Morris's persuasive speech. Few delegates were thrilled with this option, but that was the way it would be.

Immediately, Elbridge Gerry and Maryland's Luther Martin moved "to re-instate the ineligibility of the Executive a second time." That went with the territory, and so did a longer term—perhaps much longer. The motion for ineligibility thus led to a bidding war on term length:

William Davie of North Carolina: eight years.

Elbridge Gerry: fifteen years.

Rufus King of Massachusetts: twenty years. "This is the median life of princes," he explained. (Madison, in his notes, hints that King might not have been serious.)

James Wilson, who opposed legislative appointment and ineligibility, was depressed by his defeat but would not surrender. If the executive could not be reelected, perhaps he should serve during "good behavior." That would be better than cutting him off prematurely, he mused. Older men make better leaders—just look at the age of popes, he suggested, perhaps with a wink. Of course he didn't really want to go that route; instead, in all earnestness, Wilson urged his fellow delegates to reconsider their reconsideration and reverse the previous vote.

Which prompted Gerry to give up. "We seem entirely at a loss on this head," he confessed. Maybe, if they sent the matter to committee, people there will be able "to hit on something that may unite the various opinions."

Right at that moment, James Wilson hit upon the answer. This had

---

* A delegation from New Hampshire had arrived the day before, bringing the number of voting states to eleven.

happened to him before, on June 2, but few others shared his excitement about that solution, the first proposal for special "electors," which they deemed too confusing. His solution this time was stranger yet. The problem with legislative appointment, and particularly with reelection by the legislature, was that the executive would have to please the very fellows who elected him—but what if the executive could not determine who those fellows might be? "Not more than 15 of the National Legislature" could be selected, "not by ballot, but by lot," and these would "retire immediately and make the election without separating." No possibility of "intrigue" there, and hence less dependence. This was not yet "a digested idea," Wilson admitted, but he threw it out there anyway.

By lot! Imagine the mockery from people out of doors when they heard that the very wise men at the convention, after months of deliberation, had determined that the head of state for the nation should be elected by a small cadre of individuals who had been selected through mere chance. No appeal to the example of Athenian senators in ancient times would prevent the ridicule. James Wilson, by all acclaims one of the finest and most precise minds in America, was flirting with the bizarre.

So too was Gouverneur Morris, another great but desperate mind. Wilson's idea "deserved consideration," he said. "It would be better than intrigue." Buttressed by Morris's apparent support, Wilson fashioned his bright idea into a motion, but in the brief discussion that followed, other delegates revealed they were not overly thrilled. "We ought to be governed by reason, not chance," Rufus King stated bluntly, affirming one of the cardinal principles of the Enlightenment. Wilson then admitted that this was hardly his preferred choice. "We ought to resort to the people for the election," he said yet one more time, as if mere repetition might win the day.

Dreamlike, the convention was turning into a dramatic farce, in which each character recites the same lines over and over. A cacophony of voices. Make a motion, talk, vote, reconsider, adjourn, vote again, affirm, postpone, resume debate, reverse, reaffirm, reverse again, and so on, without apparent end. Late in the afternoon of July 24, the move to postpone yet one more time won by acclamation.

Two days later George Mason tried to redirect the debate, as Morris had done a week before. Like Morris, he offered definitive positions on all three strands, but his views leaned in the opposite direction. First, on the method of selection: "election by the National Legislature, as originally proposed, was the best," not because it had anything special to commend it, but because "if it was liable to objections, it was liable to fewer than any other." That seems to have been the winning hand, albeit a low one. Legislative appointment was still the default mode, adopted only in the absence of anything better. In conjunction with this, Mason offered two motions in one: "that the executive be appointed for seven years, & be ineligible a second time." There was nothing new in this, but Mason took the offensive by giving his argument a new twist. Ineligibility, the cornerstone of his approach, was also the touchstone of republican government:

> Having for his primary object, for the pole-star of his political conduct, the preservation of the rights of the people, he [Mason] held it as an essential point, as the very palladium of Civil liberty, that the great officers of State, and particularly the Executive should at fixed periods return to that mass from which they were at first taken, in order that they may feel & respect those rights & interests, which are again to be personally valuable to them.

Mason's speech—a grand but innocuous acknowledgment of the people's supremacy, unencumbered by any measure that would actually grant them power—was perfectly suited to his audience. He had taken command of the high moral ground. Immediately, Benjamin Franklin, as committed to republican virtue as any man in the room, proceeded to fortify this territory with his customary wit:

> It seems to have been imagined by some that the returning to the mass of the people was degrading the magistrate. This he thought was contrary to republican principles. In free Governments the rulers are the servants, and the people their superiors & sovereigns. For the former therefore to return among the latter was not to degrade but to promote them. And it would be imposing an unreasonable burden on them, to keep them always in a state of servitude, and not allow them to become again one of the masters.

Mason and Franklin made a vote for the single-term limitation seem virtuous and patriotic. Delegates could feel good about themselves by favoring that. Perhaps even more important, by returning to their original track, before Gouverneur Morris had steered them off, they could feel as if they were finally done with the matter. We have no way of assessing whether it was republican virtue or fatigue that determined the results on Mason's motion, but in any case it carried handily if not overwhelmingly, seven states to three.

Delegates were tired. They were done. They had just appointed five of their number—James Wilson, Edmund Randolph, John Rutledge, Nathaniel Gorham, and Oliver Ellsworth—to a workforce they called the Committee of Detail, which they instructed to flesh out matters that had not been fully defined. While that group hammered out a more complete draft, the rest of the delegates could take a ten-day breather. They would not meet again till August 6.

Here's the draft delegates handed to the Committee of Detail, the sum total of what they had decided over the course of two months about the new executive department:

> Resolved, That a national executive be instituted, to consist of a single person; to be chosen by the national legislature, for the term of seven years; to be ineligible a second time; with power to carry into execution the national laws; to appoint to offices in cases not otherwise provided for; to be removable on impeachment, and conviction of malpractice or neglect of duty; to receive a fixed compensation for the devotion of his time to publick service; to be paid out of the publick treasury.
>
> Resolved, That the national executive shall have a right to negative any legislative act, which shall not be afterwards passed, unless by two third parts of each branch of the national legislature.

Sound familiar? Delegates had made no changes to the office of the executive since June 4. They had entertained many alternatives, some seriously; a few of these had made their way briefly into the working plan, only to be removed later. We can infer two things from this. First, for many delegates, several of these measures created serious problems, for they kept getting challenged. Second, since they had withstood the challenges, the measures had staying power. They were on course, at that point, to become part of the final document and ultimately the law of the land.

Imagine if they had. President Buchanan and President Lincoln each serve a seven-year term (assuming no assassinations in this scenario). John Tyler, never elected to the presidency and known today as the junior partner in "Tippecanoe and Tyler too," serves for six years, eleven months after William Henry Harrison falls ill on Inauguration Day and dies one month later. Franklin Pierce, Benjamin Harrison, Herbert Hoover all enjoy seven years in office, as does Franklin Delano Roosevelt, who is limited, like the others, to a single term. Strong presidents or weak, effective leaders or not, all would serve lengthy identical terms.

Very possibly, the office would have been allocated to a very different set of characters, politicians who, in today's parlance, were "Washington insiders." If members of the legislature chose the president, they probably would have selected power figures who had made their way up through the ranks of Congress, not men who were born in log cabins or otherwise presented themselves as "of the people." Meet President Thomas Hart Benton and President Thaddeus Stevens. Presidents Sam Rayburn and Tip O'Neill. Or try President Tom DeLay and the sitting president, Nancy Pelosi, secure in her office from 2007 to 2014, unless impeached and convicted "of malpractice or neglect of duty."

Well, maybe not. Probably, when the majority party in Congress selected one of its own, it would have paid some attention to national popularity, since one unofficial role of the president would be to attract voters to his political party. Heavy hitting on the inside would have to be balanced by appeal to the electorate, and who knows how that might have played out. In any case, though, the presidency would certainly have been launched on a very different trajectory, with powerful consequences for the subsequent history of the United States.

Try to imagine, too, what a man selected by Congress to serve as president would actually have *done*, had there been no guidance from the framers beyond what appeared in the working draft on July 26. Would he have been commander in chief of the military forces? Not necessarily, no word on that. Could he have engaged in international diplomacy? Not unless he went beyond the strict construction of his office. Propose a budget, place an agenda before Congress, or argue for laws he preferred? He was not empowered to do any of those things. Appoint judges? No. That authority, just five days earlier, had been granted to the upper house of the legislature.

Some of these powers had been suggested, but none enacted. The New Jersey Plan granted the executives (note the plural) the authority "to direct all military operations," but the authority was granted to multiple executive officers, not to one man—and it didn't matter in any case, since the New Jersey Plan was rejected four days later. Hamilton's schema gave to the executive, with consent of the Senate, the power to appoint ambassadors and negotiate treaties. He would possess the "sole" authority to appoint "chief officers of the departments of Finance, War and Foreign Affairs" and also take charge of "the direction of war when authorized or begun." Yet Hamilton's proposals, tainted by the politically dangerous views of their author, were quickly discarded. Further, regardless of who suggested them, they had been highly controversial.

Charles Pinckney, at the very outset, had feared the powers of the executive "might extend to peace & war &c., which would render the Executive a monarchy." For men of the Revolutionary generation, whose nation had fought the king's army during seven grueling years, allocating any authority over "peace & war" to a single individual still raised concerns. Virginia's James McClurg, in a postscript to the deliberations of July 20, "asked whether it would not be necessary . . . to determine on the means by which the Executive is to carry the laws into effect, and to resist combinations against them. Is he to have a military force for the purpose, or to have the command of the Militia, the only existing force that can be applied to that use?" A good question, and as yet unaddressed.

The only specific power delegates had handed the executive was a limited veto, and that was actually legislative in nature, not an executive matter per se. Instead of allocating powers, they had focused their attention on questions of access to the office, not the office itself. Who chose the executive and how long he might remain in office had a lot to do with politics but little to do with governance.

To grasp why delegates, somewhat illogically, debated issues of access before determining, or even outlining, what the access was *to*, we have to understand how nervous they were about what they were doing. The driving force of the convention, the very reason for its existence, was to grant additional powers to a central government, but who, within this new construct, would be exercising the augmented powers? Therein lay the problem.

The legislative branch was prone to division and open to intrigue, many delegates felt, and yet throughout the admittedly short history of the nation the legislature *was* the central government. This created considerable confusion. On the one hand, delegates wanted to load new powers on Congress, the heart of the government; on the other hand, they had little trust for legislatures of any sort, with their incessant wrangling, partisan interests, and thirst for power. The contradiction caught the eye of George Mason. "It is curious to remark the different language held at different times," he said on July 17, nine days before the recess. "At one moment we are told that the Legislature is entitled to thorough confidence, and to indefinite power. At another, that it will be governed by intrigue & corruption, and cannot be trusted at all."

The executive branch, for very different reasons, was also suspect. There, the negative examples dated from colonial times and from British history, which was still in a sense their history. Delegates were stretching to their political limits by urging centralization, which perforce would lessen the power of the states. If they centralized power even more by placing it in the hands of one person, the political repercussions could doom the project.

Wary of amassing too much authority in either branch, delegates embraced the notion of separation of powers espoused by "the celebrated Montesquieu." Since the premise of the convention was to concentrate power within a new central government, Montesquieu's admonition to disperse powers among separate components of that new and stronger government became an absolute imperative.

But this impeded progress. Any allocation of power to one branch raised fears of imbalance, causing delegates to back off, reconsider, and sometimes revoke the powers they had just granted. So the convention proceeded cautiously, too cautiously perhaps. The new powers of a national government, if they were to exist at all, needed to find their proper homes. And time was passing.

CHAPTER FIVE

Gouverneur Morris's Final Push

The American "president" was formally christened in the early days of August 1787, after a laborious birth. We have three extant drafts from the five-man Committee of Detail, which had been instructed to turn the convention's broad outline for governance into a preliminary version of a constitution.

The first draft, in the hand of Edmund Randolph, referred generically to a "National Executive," who was "to consist of a single person."

In his reworking of Randolph's draft, John Rutledge called the chief executive "Governor of the united People & States of America." The only delegate who had served as both "president" (1776–78) and "governor" (1779–82) of his home state, Rutledge opted for the term implying that a leader should not merely *preside* but actually *govern*. That appealed to advocates of a strong executive, but when Alexander Hamilton had suggested the national "governor" should serve for life, he scared off his fellow delegates and perhaps tainted the very word. A more modest yet still respectful appellation was called for.

It was James Wilson, author of the original motion for a single executive, who once again prevailed. According to Wilson's final draft of the Committee of Detail's report, "The Executive power of the United States shall be vested in a single person. His style shall be 'The President of the United States of America,' and his title shall be, 'His

Excellency.'" The convention accepted the "style" but not the "title." ("His Excellency," though never formalized, did remain in common usage until Andrew Jackson's administration. A common term during Revolutionary times, it was applied not just to George Washington, as is generally assumed, but to state governors.)[1]

The term "president" struck just the right chord. In late colonial and Revolutionary times, a president was one who presided over a convention, congress, or almost any type of meeting; sometimes he was called a moderator. The Continental Congress had a president, as did this very meeting, the Federal Convention. Typically, the rules governing the body stipulated that to minimize personal discord, speakers must address the president rather than each other. "Mr. President," a member would say, and then he would make his point. The rules of the convention, passed on May 28, stated: "Every member, rising to speak, shall address the President; and whilst he shall be speaking, none shall pass between them, or hold discourse with another, or read a book, pamphlet or paper, printed or manuscript."

A president, as moderator, was not to take sides but to stand over and above, a man apart. That was how orderly meetings worked, and couldn't this serve as a model for the leader of a nation? "The President of the United States of America," by remaining above the fray, could serve as a moral compass and limit conflict. Political strife, always a threat to civil well-being, would be held in check by "Mr. President," a man respected by all yet not a monarch, just a citizen.

That was the basic idea, reflected in the name. The draft of the Constitution emerging from the Committee of Detail meshed well with this ideal. Carefully, the committee restrained the president from governing his people with a strong hand, as a monarch would do. He was permitted to "recommend" legislation, but not to push for it or vote on it. He could write letters to state governors, but he was not empowered to force their hands, supersede their authority, or, on his own authority, suppress insurrections within their states. Although he could commission officers and receive ambassadors, the authority to *appoint* ambassadors and judges lay with the Senate, as did the power to make treaties with foreign nations. He could command military forces but not raise them. He could neither declare war nor negotiate peace. Always under close supervision, he could be removed from office through "impeachment by the House of Representatives, and conviction in the supreme Court, of treason, bribery, or corruption." Only once, to check the judiciary, did the committee use the word "power": "He shall have power to grant reprieves and pardons; but his pardon shall not be pleadable in bar of an impeachment."

Although all five members of the Committee of Detail—Wilson, Rutledge, Randolph, Gorham, and Ellsworth—had previously expressed support for a strong executive, the office they outlined was tightly reined in. By contrast, they gave to Congress a very imposing array of new powers, many of which had been the province of the Crown when Americans had lived under the British constitution. In addition to the Senate's authority to negotiate treaties and appoint ambassadors and judges, Congress could collect taxes, regulate commerce, coin money, borrow money, establish courts, negotiate controversies between states, make war, raise armies, build and equip fleets, call forth the militia, suppress insurrections, and "make all laws that shall be necessary and proper" to accomplish these and other tasks.

The new office of the president remained but a stepchild within this government in the making. The retreat from executive authority, so pronounced in the Revolutionary years, had slowed but not reversed. This did not satisfy Gouverneur Morris. He would not quit until the convention gave the president of the United States full and equal standing.

It rained in Philadelphia on Monday, August 6, the day delegates reconvened after their brief break. John Rutledge, as chairman of the Committee of Detail, read aloud its report. Then the session quickly adjourned, each man returning to his home or lodging with a printed copy to ponder. Confidentiality was a paramount concern, but the convention had trusted John Dunlap, who had published the first copies of the Declaration of Independence eleven years earlier, to print a very limited edition.[2]

The brief document that went into committee on July 26 had tripled in length. It looked more like a constitution than an outline, a promising outcome. Due to the draft's expansion, however, there was so much more to discuss, and because it appeared definitive, the stakes were higher yet. The next morning, August 7, delegates started to make their way methodically through the draft's twenty-three articles. They adopted Article I, "The style of the Government shall be, 'The United

States of America,'" and Article II, "The Government shall consist of supreme legislative, executive, and judicial power," with neither discussion nor dissent. Those were the easy parts; the rest would take time. Over the next week, at the height of summer and through a muggy Philadelphia heat wave, the pace of debate intensified. There were more motions than ever before, more votes, more changes to specific clauses, phrases, and individual words.

Gouverneur Morris had much to say on many counts. In the four days following the committee report, he offered a dozen motions to alter the committee's version; in the same time span, no other delegate presented more than four. He also used the occasion to bring up matters that had already been decided. On August 7, with George Read, he pushed once again for an absolute executive veto, but only Delaware, Read's home state, supported this. Morris then tried to limit the national franchise to freeholders, but again, only the delegation from Delaware voted his way.

The following day, in an impassioned speech, Morris insisted that counting three-fifths of the enslaved population when apportioning representation was an absolutely terrible idea. From Madison's notes: "He [Morris] never would concur in upholding domestic slavery. It was a nefarious institution—It was the curse of heaven on the States where it prevailed. . . . He would sooner submit himself to a tax for paying for all the Negroes in the U. States than saddle posterity with such a Constitution." This time only New Jersey agreed. During the summer's proceedings, no other member of the convention came out so forcibly against slavery.

On August 15, Gouverneur Morris repeated yet again his argument for an absolute veto. The resounding defeat of this idea eight days earlier, by a vote of nine states to one, fazed him not the least. Back on July 19, he had convinced the convention, at least momentarily, to reverse its decision on legislative appointment of the executive. Now he was trying to replicate that performance by promoting another twice-defeated idea. His central argument—"Encroachment of the popular branch of the Government ought to be guarded against"—was not new and won no additional converts, but recent developments were beginning to raise a new fear. Was the *upper* branch of the legislature also taking on too many powers? The Committee of Detail had granted the Senate treaty-making authority. Then, on August 8, upon Morris's urging, the clause prohibiting the Senate from initiating money bills had been withdrawn. This caused Hugh Williamson to comment bitterly, "We have now got a House of Lords which is to originate money-bills." Who, then, could check both the lower house *and* the upper house simultaneously? The president, if he received the power to "negative" any bill.

Delegates had been through this discussion before and arrived at a compromise—an executive veto that could be cast aside by two-thirds of each branch of Congress—but that would not check a runaway legislature, Morris thought. This time, he tackled the veto issue from a slightly different angle. Knowing he didn't have the votes, he suggested there might be "some more effectual check than requiring ⅔ only to overrule the negative of the executive." Following Morris's lead, Williamson proposed a new compromise: a three-fourths override instead of two-thirds. This higher hurdle would make the veto more powerful, but not absolute. Five states that had opposed Morris's absolute veto the week before agreed now to make an override more difficult, and the motion passed six states to four, with one divided.

The vote on the three-fourths override followed no discernible pattern. Large states and small, southern states and northern, came down on both sides of the issue. With no special interests at stake, delegates were seriously considering the delicate balance of power in the distinct branches of government, and the executive, outdone in the Committee of Detail draft by the legislative, was on a slight upswing. The convention strengthened the president's position not by granting him new powers per se but by increasing his ability to check Congress. The Committee of Detail's draft had included a similar change: the president could check the judiciary by issuing pardons. While the president himself exercised few special powers, delegates were creating for him a meta-role of referee.

Two days later, on August 17, the jockeying for authority among the branches resumed. On the table was Congress's power "to make war," as stipulated in the Committee of Detail's draft. Charles Pinckney thought "the House of Representatives would be too numerous for such deliberations." It met "but once a year," and "its proceedings were too slow." So who should be empowered to make war? "The Senate would be the best depositary, being more acquainted with foreign affairs, and most capable of proper resolutions," Pinckney said. Since the Senate, through its authority to make treaties, already possessed the "power of peace," it should have the "power of war" as well.

Pierce Butler, Pinckney's colleague from South Carolina, countered that "the objections against the legislature lie in great degree against the Senate." The president, on the other hand, would always be on the job. He could work quickly. He "will have all the requisite qualities, and will not make war but when the Nation will support it." Butler was likely recalling the problems he faced as adjutant general for South Carolina in 1779, when his state struggled to mobilize against an imminent British invasion. Surely, a single leader at that point would have performed more efficiently than any deliberative body.

Butler's proposal for vesting the president with the power to "make war" drew immediate and heated responses. Elbridge Gerry was shocked and dismayed. From Madison's notes: "Mr. GERRY never expected to hear in a republic a motion to empower the Executive alone to declare war." At the outset of the convention, Gerry admitted he had been "too republican heretofore," but Butler's retreat from republican values was going too far even for him. Only the people, through their representatives, could ever possess the power of war.

For Oliver Ellsworth, allowing one man to lead the nation into war made war too easy: "There is a material difference between the cases of making war and making peace. It should be more easy to get out of war, than into it. War also is a simple and overt declaration, peace attended with intricate & secret negociations." George Mason followed up on this theme: "Mr. MASON was against giving the power of war to the Executive, because not safely to be trusted with it; or to the Senate, because not so constructed as to be entitled to it. He was for clogging rather than facilitating war; but for facilitating peace."

No delegate supported Butler. Gouverneur Morris, whom we might expect to have at least commented on such an increase in presidential powers, remained uncharacteristically silent on this provocative suggestion. Like Alexander Hamilton, Butler had established an outer limit to acceptable discourse. Indeed, Hamilton himself, in the plan he offered two months earlier, had granted the executive only "the direction of war when authorized or begun." Despite his own disclaimers on republicanism, Hamilton had ceded that only Congress could take the monumental and irreversible step of initiating a war.

Still, Butler did pose one valid question. How could the nation defend itself against an invasion while Congress was not in session?

Madison and Gerry offered a solution. Congress would be granted exclusive authority to "declare" war, not "make" war, thus "leaving to the Executive the power to repel sudden attacks." Rufus King explained the differences in word connotations. To "make" war could be construed as to "conduct" war, and that was the province of the president, the commander in chief of the armed forces. To "declare" war, on the other hand, was to set the nation on a course of action that included the expenditure of blood and treasure, and nobody but the people's direct representatives should be authorized to do that. Only one state, New Hampshire, opposed the change from "make" to "declare." This decision, precise but not insignificant, confirmed the overarching sense of the convention. Although the president would be granted powers sufficient to make government function more efficiently, only Congress could set lasting policy.

The following day, a Saturday, delegates considered the possibility of an executive council, something akin to the Privy Council under the British system. Charles Pinckney observed that Gouverneur Morris "was not then on the floor," and Morris was known to have decided views on the subject. We do not know why Morris was absent on August 18, but we do know that his peers readily agreed to let the issue ride until he returned. At no other time during the summer of 1787 did the convention suspend discussion because of the absence of a single member.

Morris returned to work on Monday, August 20, and presented a written plan for a council "to assist the President in conducting the public affairs." The chief justice of the Supreme Court would be its president, and its members would include secretaries for domestic affairs, commerce and finance, foreign affairs, war, marine, and state. Other than the chief justice, these council members would hold their offices at the pleasure of the president, who could submit any matter for their consideration but would in no way be bound by their advice. The president, wrote Morris, "shall in all cases exercise his own judgment, and either conform to such opinions or not as he may think proper."

Morris's council, absent the chief justice, closely resembled the modern cabinet, but it differed markedly from the council envisioned by other delegates. For those who remained suspicious of a single executive, the purpose of an executive council was to diffuse power and prevent autocratic rule, and that could happen only if council members were independent of the president. Morris's council, by contrast, was

predicated on the assumption that the president was boss in all matters. His idea was to centralize power, not disperse it. The showdown
between these contradictory notions of an executive council did not
take place at this time. Instead, the matter was sent to a new Committee of Eleven, one representative from each state delegation.[3]

On August 23, with a three-pronged offensive, Morris continued to
attack the authority of the legislative branch. First, he argued against
the appointment of ambassadors and Supreme Court judges by the
Senate. According to Madison's notes, he "considered the body as too
numerous for the purpose [and] as subject to cabal." Morris did not say
who *should* have the power of appointment, but it certainly wouldn't be
the House, more numerous yet. There could be only one other choice,
the president, but Morris did not say that explicitly, nor did he offer a
motion to transfer authority, for such a direct assault would have met
with defeat by an assembly still nervous about the political liability of
a too-powerful single executive. So, after planting the seeds of doubt,
Morris allowed the matter to be "waived."

Immediately, before any other proposition should come to the floor,
Morris offered two motions of a seemingly technical nature. In the
committee's draft, Congress was empowered "to call forth the aid of
the militia, in order to execute the laws of the Union, enforce treaties, suppress insurrections, and repel invasions." Two phrases here—
"execute" and "enforce treaties"—ran counter to his preference for a
strong and independent president. These words should not appear
within a delineation of legislative powers, he reasoned; the president,
not Congress, was to "execute" and "enforce." Morris prevailed easily
in this tighter game, his motions passing with neither argument nor
dissent.

After a feint and a pass on the power of appointments, and then
distancing Congress from executing laws and enforcing treaties, Morris tackled a matter of great import: the treaty-making authority of the
Senate, which would give it the lead in setting foreign policy. Again,
though, his attack was indirect. Morris "did not know that he should
agree" to empowering the Senate with treaty-making authority, but he
let it stand "for the present" and agreed to revert the matter to committee. While he did not have sufficient support for a dramatic change of
power, he did conjure a way to include the president in the process. He
moved that "no treaty should be binding on the U.S. which is not rati-

fied by law," and that meant the president would have to sign on, unless overridden by three-quarters of both the House and the Senate. This seemingly modest alteration appeared winnable, but it was not. Only Pennsylvania, home to both Morris and Wilson, favored the measure.

A pattern was emerging. Although Morris didn't have the votes to transfer significant powers to the president, he could get agreement on small changes while getting the larger issues remitted to committee. By moving the venue, he provided an alternative mechanism for the passage of controversial resolutions. We do not know exactly when this became a conscious strategy, but we do know that in the last two weeks of August, he was more than eager to send issue after issue into committee—and further, the committee report that would eventually emerge bore a striking resemblance to Morris's own views.

By August 24 the convention had worked its way up to Article X, Section 1, of the new draft: "The executive power of the United States shall be vested in a single person. His stile shall be 'The President of the United States of America'; and his title shall be 'His Excellency.' He shall be elected by ballot by the Legislature. He shall hold his office during the term of seven years; but shall not be elected a second time." Here the heavy jockeying began. The proceedings of that day would have immense consequences for the presidency and the nation, so they need to be examined in some detail.

The single executive, his "stile," and his title excited no controversy at this moment, but then came the problem: What, exactly, did "elected by ballot by the Legislature" mean? That seemed to imply both houses of Congress, the Senate and the House of Representatives, but would these bodies vote jointly, or would they each have to approve the president, voting separately?

John Rutledge opened by moving that the word "joint" be inserted before "ballot," and this immediately resurrected the old small-state/large-state controversy that had dominated so much of the early weeks of the convention. Connecticut's Roger Sherman objected that the Senate, which represented states, would lose "the negative intended them in that house"; only separate balloting would maintain that body's integrity. Nathaniel Gorham of Massachusetts, a state with double the population of Connecticut, quickly scolded Sherman for neglecting "the public good," which was "the true object to be kept in view." This triggered a tirade from New Jersey's Jonathan Dayton and David Brearly, who warned that the Senate, in which each state had an equal say, would be overwhelmed in the voting by the much larger House, dominated by large-state representatives. "A *joint* ballot would in fact give the appointment to one House," Dayton complained, and he "could never agree to the clause with such an amendment." Twenty-six years old and the youngest delegate to the convention, Dayton had fought at Brandywine and Germantown when only sixteen, survived wartime captivity, engaged in daring postwar land speculation, and already established a reputation as a hard-hitting politician for issuing statements that resembled ultimatums, such as this one.

That last phrase in Dayton's pronouncement—"could never agree to the clause"—caught the attention of James Wilson and Maryland's Daniel Carroll. The clause Dayton referred to was legislative selection of the president, and his strong opposition signaled to them that support might be weakening for that worn idea. Carroll, who had seconded Wilson's strange elector-by-lot scheme exactly one month earlier, moved "to strike out 'by the Legislature' and insert 'by the people,'" and Wilson now seconded Carroll's motion. This radical alternative, though, had never garnered many votes, and it didn't this time either; only Pennsylvania and Delaware voted in favor of popular election, a proposition that offered no solace to the disgruntled small-state delegates.

So it was back to the matter at hand, how Congress was to select the president. John Langdon and James Madison mounted a two-pronged offensive that was difficult to rebut. First, Langdon announced he was ready to vote against the interests of his own state, New Hampshire, which was smaller than either Connecticut or New Jersey and would presumably lose influence under joint balloting. According to New Hampshire's constitution, he noted, each house voted separately for the state's chief executive, and that system had been "productive of great difficulties." Jealousies resulted when one house rejected a candidate approved by the other, and joint balloting was the only sensible alternative.

Madison followed by noting that small states actually *gained* influence under the joint-balloting plan, which would "give to the largest State, compared with the smallest, an influence as 4 to 1 only, altho the population is as 10 to 1. This surely can not be unreasonable." When the question was called, seven states thought joint balloting was reasonable indeed, while four still objected—New Jersey, Connecticut, Georgia, and Maryland.

Dayton and Brearly, defeated but not vanquished, countered with another proposal: joint balloting but with the congressional delegation for each state casting but a single vote. Without debate, this blatantly small-state proposal picked up the support of tiny Delaware, but it was still defeated, six states to five. There the matter stood: the president would be chosen by a joint ballot of the members of both houses of Congress. It was time to move on—or was it?

Enter once again Gouverneur Morris, not yet ready to concede, who suggested that the president "shall be chosen by Electors to be chosen by the People of the several States." This idea had a familiar ring, and Morris was the only one who bothered to speak in its favor or, more precisely, to speak against the existing plan, selection by Congress. "The legislature will swallow up the whole powers of the constitution," he warned, "but to do this effectually they must possess [select] the Executive." Other delegates could have recited this by rote, Morris and Wilson had said it so many times. Yet Morris was unrelenting, and he forced the issue as never before. "In the strength of the Executive would be found the strength of America," he proclaimed with dramatic flair but to no avail.[4]

The motion failed, but only by a vote of six states to five. Morris had chosen his words carefully, hoping to attract small-state delegates who wanted no part of Wilson's popular election. Electors were to be chosen "by the People *of the several States,*" leaving the path open for one-state, one-vote or to some compromise scheme that would allocate a certain number of electors per state. This almost worked. Three leading carriers of the small-state banner—New Jersey, Connecticut, and Delaware—joined delegates from Pennsylvania and Virginia, the prime proponents of an independent executive, in support of Morris's motion.

A coalition was building, and Morris was tantalizingly close to having his way. If he could convince only one more state delegation to change its mind, presidential selection would be removed from the grip of the legislative branch. Strategically, he separated his defeated motion into two sections. First, did the convention approve of electors "as an abstract question," with no mention of how electors should be chosen? If the answer to that turned out to be yes, delegates could then determine the exact manner of elector selection.

The vote on the first question, the basic idea of electors, turned out a tie, four states in favor, four against, two divided, and the Massachusetts delegation so puzzled by an "abstract" vote it abstained. Technically, by the rules of the convention, the motion "failed the states being equally divided." The issue had been settled "in the negative," as the official journal noted, and that made the second question moot. The convention was ready to move on, and at least for the moment there was nothing more Gouverneur Morris could do. Even so, by obtaining a tie vote on his "abstract" question, this skilled tactician had managed to confuse the matter. That was a victory of sorts, and he would make ingenious use of this one week later, on August 31.

The convention then took up the last two items of Article X, "He shall hold his office during the term of seven years; but shall not be elected a second time," or at least it tried to. Before anything could be said on the matter, Dayton moved to postpone the discussion of these issues, which Morris had previously demonstrated to be integrally linked to the manner of selecting the president. Postponement would give Dayton, Morris, and their allies time to regroup and line up another state or two, and when the length of term and eligibility issues resurfaced, they could possibly change all three decisions at once, as Morris had convinced the convention to do back on July 19. The very word "postponement," though, was anathema to the delegates at this late stage. Dayton's motion "was disagreed to without a count of the States."

Jacob Broom of Delaware, with a more politic approach, moved that term length and eligibility be referred "to a committee of a member from each state." This fared better, achieving a tie vote, but that was not sufficient to pass. Too many weary delegates wanted to dispense with this matter once and for all, and that is precisely what disturbed opponents of legislative selection. Hurriedly, delegates were likely to approve the Committee of Detail's report—a seven-year term and ineligibility, natural corollaries to legislative selection. All three issues would then be settled, and given the delegates' increasing restlessness, they were unlikely to be considered again.

The New Jersey delegation, with no other card to play, requested a postponement "to tomorrow," the longest period of time it could reasonably expect the convention to approve. "Request" is the term used in the official journal, but Madison recorded it differently: the postponement, he wrote, was "at the *insistence* of the deputies of New Jersey." It is reasonable to infer that Dayton, who was taking the lead on this matter, played a heavy hand.

Reluctantly, the convention acquiesced, but "tomorrow" never came. Dayton, Morris, and their allies were in no haste to bring the issues back to the table, for the longer the delay, the more likely the issues would be "committed," or handed over to a committee. They allowed the convention to take up Articles XI through XXII, which took another week. During this time, matters were voted on quickly, with little discussion. If a vote yielded a positive resolution, so much the better, but if it didn't, the issue was sent to yet another Committee of Eleven, to be composed of one delegate from each state. Here, members would deal with "such parts of the Constitution as have been postponed, and such parts of reports as have not been acted on."[5]

Just moments before the state delegations chose their representatives to this committee, the convention tried to finalize Article XXIII of the working draft, which stipulated how the very first election would be conducted. Each state legislature needed to choose its two senators and establish a mechanism for its citizens to elect their congressmen. Then, once Congress convened, it would select the president. This article contained nothing structural. It merely established how Articles IV and V, which provided for selection of members of Congress, and Article X, which provided for legislative selection of the president, would take effect the very first time. It appeared a cut-and-dried matter, with no policy issues at stake.

Yet not so cut-and-dried for Gouverneur Morris, who moved to strike out the clause that directed the first Congress to "choose the President." The matter of choosing any president, including the first one, had not yet been "finally determined," he said. This was incorrect. Selection of the president by the legislature had been settled, and resettled, and resettled again. Only once, more than a month earlier, had it been briefly overturned, and then it was quickly restored.

The previous week, on August 24, delegates had reaffirmed that Congress should choose the president. On that day, the convention had also decided, by a seven-to-four vote, that the selection was to be made by both the House and the Senate, voting jointly. Further, delegates had stipulated that the winner needed to garner votes from an absolute majority of the members present, and in the case of a tie the president of the Senate would cast the determining vote. Precise, well-defined procedures had been incontrovertibly set in place.

All that was a matter of record, entered into the official journal. Two events, however, *could* give the impression the issue had not been "fully determined." First was the tie vote on Morris's "abstract" question of electors. That motion, even if it passed, would not have implemented any change to the existing plan of government. It was presented as a straw poll only so the discussion might continue, and it didn't matter in any case, for by the rules of the convention the motion had failed, but the defeated motion had been a draw, and that produced the confusion that Morris now exploited. He could say in an offhand manner that the matter had not been "finally determined" and thus should be sent to committee.

The other factor that instilled confusion was the August 24 postponement of the length of term and eligibility issues. Although these issues were supposed to be taken up the very next day, this never happened. Thanks to the ingenious conniving of the New Jersey delegation, the Committee of Detail's provisions addressing these matters had not been finalized, so the Committee of Eleven would have to place them on its agenda. Technically, this charge to the committee did not include selection of the presidency, a different though related matter, but by Morris's reasoning, which most of the delegates had come to accept, the three issues needed to be addressed at once. Merely by association, selection of the president could be viewed as an appropriate issue for the committee to take up.

In tandem, Morris and the New Jersey delegation had managed to breathe new life into their opposition to legislative selection. Morris's motion, without debate, prevailed with the dissent of only two delegations. By sleight of hand, selection of the president was placed on the docket for the Committee of Eleven.

Gouverneur Morris must have known he would be appointed as Pennsylvania's representative to the Committee of Eleven. Franklin, who was too ill even to attend on some days, was not fit for committee work. Wilson was still serving on the critical Committee of Detail, which had various assignments of its own. George Clymer had just served on a similar committee composed of one representative from each state. The remaining four delegates from Pennsylvania—Robert Morris, Thomas Mifflin, Thomas Fitzsimons, and Jared Ingersoll—had spoken on the floor, between them, only six times over the course of the convention, a span of more than three months. Gouverneur Morris, by contrast, spoke seven times on that day alone, August 31. Over the previous four days, he had offered up another dozen motions, matching his total for the first four days of August deliberations. If delegates from Pennsylvania wanted a strong voice on this committee, Gouverneur Morris was their obvious choice, and he got the job.

A decade earlier, Morris had served on the committee that drafted New York's first state constitution. There, he succeeded in getting the committee to approve a strong executive office complete with appointive and veto powers, but the committee's report was then overturned by the convention, which created a council of appointments and a council of revisions to water down the governor's powers. Now Morris would once again try to strengthen an executive office within a committee, and this time, with kingly abuses and the hated royal governorships more distant in memory, he might have a better chance of securing approval for a committee report that gave the executive greater authority.

The Committee of Eleven set to work in the Library Room of the State House on Saturday morning, September 1. We have no record of the committee's deliberations, only a few anecdotal recollections. Fifteen years after the fact, Delaware's representative John Dickinson placed himself at the center of the action. Entering a committee session midway, Dickinson wrote to a friend, he delivered a speech denouncing legislative selection of the president. In his telling, Dickinson seems to imply his speech had a strong impact, swaying Gouverneur Morris and others to his position, but that is highly implausible, since Morris needed no convincing. The letter does admit an alternate interpretation, however, that hints at Morris's leadership role within the committee. "Having thus expressed my sentiments," Dickinson concluded, "Governieur Morris immediately said—'Come, Gentlemen, let us sit down again, and converse further on this subject.' We then all sat down, and after some conference, James Maddison took a pen and paper, and sketched out a mode for electing the President agreeable to the present provision. To this we assented and reported accordingly."[6]

Neither Morris, Madison, nor Dickinson was elected to preside over the committee, a position that called for a delegate less overbearing. That role was filled instead by the Honorable David Brearly, chief justice of the New Jersey Supreme Court, who gave the committee an air of objectivity but was a known opponent of legislative selection. In addition to Morris and Brearly, several other committee members had evidenced opposition to legislative selection or had supported an alternate plan. One week earlier Daniel Carroll had joined Wilson in moving for popular elections and then seconded Morris's motion in favor of electors. James Madison, Rufus King, and Pierce Butler had voiced their preference for electors back in July, when Morris staged his major assault on legislative selection. John Dickinson had signaled mixed messages in his two-part solution: first, "the people of each State chuse its best Citizen," and then, "out of the thirteen names thus selected, an Executive Magistrate may be chosen either by the National Legislature, or by electors appointed by it." Hugh Williamson was also on the fence, first opposing special electors, but then working on the details of the elector plan that briefly held sway in late July. Of the remaining three committee members only Roger Sherman was a firm proponent of legislative selection. The other two, Nicholas Gilman and Abraham Baldwin, left no record of their inclinations on this matter.

This committee, considering its composition, was primed to oppose legislative selection, but it needed to come up with an alternative that would not only satisfy a majority of its own members but also hold up on the convention floor. That would not be easy. If an alternate plan ran afoul of a particular interest group, that group could make matters difficult in the floor debates, and delegates seeking the easiest way out would then retreat to legislative selection, as they had done every other time the issue was raised. The committee's "solution," then, must be some sort of compromise.

We do not know how the committee devised its final plan, but by examining the problems they needed to overcome, the prior positions taken by the committee members, the voting records of the states they represented, and the eventual outcome, we can get some sense of how this critical chapter in the creation of the presidency played out behind two sets of closed doors, both the committee's and the convention's.

With popular election of the president off the table, the only available option was some scheme involving intermediate electors. Clearly, these would be chosen in their separate states, but wouldn't electors then be prone to vote for a local favorite son? If so, numerous candidates would garner votes, and unless there were some provision for a runoff between leading contenders, a president could be chosen with but a small fraction of the votes, and these might all come from one state or region.

Further, the number of electors would have to be distributed among the states, and this raised a very familiar problem: Should allocation be by population, or should each state get an equal share? The convention had settled a nearly identical matter once before with its so-called Great Compromise; now the Committee of Eleven would have to confront it again, this time with respect to the presidency.

Finally, how could electors be prevented from engaging in "intrigue" and "cabal," the alleged evil of legislative selection? Why would this duplicate Congress be better suited to its purpose than the existing one?

On Tuesday, September 4, David Brearly reported the committee's bold findings to the convention. No longer would the president be chosen by a joint ballot of Congress, as previously determined; instead, he would be selected by a complicated scheme that added more than three hundred words to the working draft. Here's how the new system worked. Each state was entitled to a number of electors equaling the total of its congressmen and senators, a compromise allocation that replicated the joint balloting by Congress. The manner of selecting electors was left to the state legislatures, which were thereby granted a role in choosing the president. To avoid intrigue and cabal, electors were to meet simultaneously in their separate states. To offset the favorite-son temptation, each elector was to vote for two men, including at least one from another state. The results would then be sent to the Senate, and the president of that body would tabulate the returns. The candidate with the most votes would be president and the runner-up vice president, an office that made its first appearance in the Committee of Eleven's report, three months and a week into the convention's proceedings.

If no candidate appeared on the majority of the electors' ballots, the Senate would choose the president from among the top five vote getters. Although this seemed to contradict the basic premise of electors—to make the executive independent of the legislature—proponents of the new system could argue that all five finalists had been vetted by the electors. The runoff in Congress both solved the problem of a minority president and placated Sherman, an unyielding partisan for the legislative branch, and perhaps Dickinson, whose own scheme allowed Congress to judge among finalists. Allowing the Senate instead of the House to make the final choice was a clear victory for small states, offsetting the advantage of large states in selecting the five leading contenders.[7]

Such was the plan, a composite geared to satisfy many interests.

True, it was untested. Delegates fond of citing historical precedents, often from classical times, could not do so here. Yet at first glance it seemed to address all the projected problems, and that was an achievement in its own right. Further, because the president would no longer be beholden to Congress for his selection, the path was opened for reeligibility, and this permitted shorter terms. Accordingly, the committee's report changed the president's time in office from seven years to four and allowed him to be reelected.

Brearly's presentation appeared to take delegates on the floor by surprise. Bluntly, perhaps angrily, Edmund Randolph and Charles Pinckney "wished for a particular explanation & discussion of the reasons for changing the mode of electing the Executive."

Gouverneur Morris answered immediately with "the reasons of the Committee and his own." His arguments now, identical to those he had made several times before, focused on the problems with the old system: the need for executive independence, the danger of intrigue, the impossibility of reeligibility with legislative selection, and so on, all of which were addressed by the committee's plan for electors. Strikingly absent in Morris's defense of the report, though, was any mention of stage two, the runoff in the Senate. If legislative selection was really such a bad idea, why would they entrust a body of Congress with the decision now?

It was this part of the plan, not the previously controversial elector idea, that raised questions and prompted opposition. Charles Pinckney predicted that in most instances "the dispersion of the votes" among the electors "would leave the appointment with the Senate, and as the President's reappointment will thus depend on the Senate he will be the mere creature of that body." George Mason said he preferred "the Government of Prussia to one which will put all power into the hands of seven or eight men, and fix an Aristocracy worse than absolute monarchy." Any sitting president, because he was known nationally, would be among the top five contestants, and if he could coddle favor with the Senate, he would be reelected time and again. So much for executive independence. So much for rotation in office. The president and the Senate, by teaming up, "will be able to subvert the Constitution."

James Wilson, while joining the opposition, offered two practical suggestions: in order to limit congressional discretion, lower the number of finalists "to a smaller number than five," and to lessen the danger of "cabal," change the venue for a runoff from the Senate to the House.

The House, Wilson explained, was elected by the people every two years and would be "free from the influence & faction to which the permanence of the Senate may subject that branch." These ideas should have appealed to Morris, who, with Wilson, had been pushing all along to protect the president from congressional control and who had probably opposed the Senate runoff within the Committee of Eleven, but Morris was in no position to undermine committee negotiations to which he had been a party, so instead of embracing Wilson's improvements, he offered two uncharacteristically weak defenses. The Senate was better than the House "because fewer could then say to the President, you owe your appointment to us." (Morris himself, had he not been the one to make this argument, would probably have countered that the Senate was *more* likely to engage in intrigue and cabal because of its small numbers.) And in any case, Morris added, too much attention was being paid to the second step of the process because electors in most cases would produce a clear winner.

Morris's arguments failed to convince, and Wilson, among others, continued to challenge senatorial involvement. The new plan, Wilson argued, evidenced "a dangerous tendency to aristocracy; as throwing a dangerous power into the hands of the Senate. They will have in fact, the appointment of the President, and through his dependence on them, the virtual appointment to offices. . . . The President will not be the man of the people as he ought to be, but the minion of the Senate." Wilson's vociferous and continuing denunciation of the plan clearly annoyed his closest colleague. "Mr. Govr. MORRIS expressed his wonder at the observations of Mr. Wilson," Madison wrote in his notes. Morris observed, correctly, that in several ways the committee's plan granted the Senate less power, not more. Within the Committee of Eleven, he had engineered a shift of two highly significant powers—negotiating treaties and appointing ambassadors, Supreme Court justices, and other key officials—from the Senate to the president. (More on these shortly.) Very likely, small-state members of the committee had opposed these moves or at least were reluctant to embrace them, since the Senate, with its equal voting for each state, provided the strongest protection against large-state domination. Also likely, they managed to extract from Morris, as compensation, the Senate runoff, which would give more of a voice to small states. If Morris truly believed that a runoff would rarely be required, he would have thought this a worthwhile trade.[8]

Of the speakers on the convention floor, only Roger Sherman

acknowledged the particular interest of the small states' position in the debate over the Senate runoff. The reason for choosing the Senate over the House was to counteract the large-state advantage in the allocation of electors, he stated openly. Further, when James Wilson suggested that the number of finalists should be fewer than five, Sherman parried that he "would sooner give up the plan." He preferred "seven or thirteen," the more the merrier in order to allow the Senate maximum discretion. Never an advocate of executive independence, Sherman had achieved a backdoor entry to congressional control and was reluctant to give it up. He did make one practical suggestion, and this too demonstrates how small-state interests were driving the debate. He would not be averse to moving the runoff from the Senate to the House if the House voted "by states," one vote for each delegation.

Sherman's new idea did not take hold when he first mentioned it. Large states opposed it, and so did slave states, which enjoyed not merely proportional but disproportional representation in the House because each slave counted as three-fifths of a person and therefore boosted the number of slave-state representatives. Small states and large, slave states and free—hadn't the convention resolved these troublesome differences? Not exactly. The Great Compromise determined the differing compositions of the House and the Senate, but now proponents of each body wrangled over who would have the final say in determining the president, should the electors' voting prove inconclusive.

Only the late hour and the delegates' collective desire to be done with the matter prevented the debate from extending beyond its third day. Finally, Hugh Williamson of North Carolina, a harsh critic of the Senate with its equal-state voting, conceded the issue. The final choice of the president "should be made by the Legislature [the House], voting *by States* and not *per capita*," Williamson stated. With Williamson's support, Sherman's motion to that effect passed easily, with only one state dissenting.

Except for that one amendment, moving the runoff from the Senate to the House, the Committee of Eleven had its way, and it fundamentally altered the president's manner of selection and time in office. The debate on choosing the president consumed so much time and attention that the committee's adoption of a four-year term squeaked through with only token discussion. Another key change in the committee report, reeligibility, was mentioned occasionally, but only as a component of the elector plan. The revised and almost-final draft of the Constitution, which incorporated the Committee of Eleven's suggestions, theoretically allowed an ambitious and enterprising president, reelected every four years, to serve for life. If this attracted little notice among the harried delegates, it would certainly grab the attention of people out of doors, once the convention adjourned.

The Committee of Eleven also proposed two striking expansions of executive power. With the "advice and consent" of the Senate, the president could appoint ambassadors and Supreme Court justices. He could also make treaties, pending approval of two-thirds of the Senate. Both recommendations signaled major reversals. In the Committee of Detail's report of August 6, still the working draft except where amended, powers granted to the Senate alone, exclusive of the House or the president, were spelled out clearly in Article IX, Section 1: "The Senate of the United States shall have power to make treaties, and to appoint Ambassadors, and Judges of the Supreme Court." Now, in an instant, those powers had been transferred to the president, leaving the Senate with only the residual "advice and consent."

Each of these alterations bore Gouverneur Morris's fingerprints. When appointments were discussed on the floor on August 23, he had "argued against the appointment of officers by the Senate." That body, he said, was "too numerous for the purpose," "subject to cabal," and "devoid of responsibility." Although Wilson "was of the same opinion & for like reasons," nobody else came to his support, and the best he could do was get the matter remitted to committee. Since no other member of the Committee of Eleven had voiced opposition to the appointive powers of the Senate, we can safely infer that Morris played a key role in executing the transfer of that authority from the Senate to the president.[9]

Also on August 23, Morris, Madison, and Dickinson had challenged the Senate's exclusive treaty-making authority, with Morris taking the lead. According to Madison's notes, Morris "did not know that he should agree to refer to the making of treaties to the Senate at all." Suspecting he did not have the votes to transfer authority to the president, he dropped the matter "for the present," offering instead an amendment that would require any treaty to be "ratified by a law," meaning that the House, the Senate, and the president would all have to sign on. His amendment failed, but the authority to make treaties, like appointive powers, was referred to the Committee of Detail and finally taken up by the Committee of Eleven, where Morris could finally address a small audience easier to convince.[10]

Although delegates discussed both these dramatic new alterations, they did so more briefly than one might expect. The scant attention is somewhat of a puzzle. Perhaps these changes represented a near consensus, but if so, why hadn't they been suggested and approved before the committee reported them out? More likely, they appeared as reasonable compromises, similar to the two-step procedure the committee implemented for presidential electors. The president would nominate a candidate for office or propose a treaty, which the Senate had to approve. When viewed as safeguards, with each branch checking the other, such measures were less likely to provoke concern and stimulate debate.

Even with modifications that kept the Senate in the mix, these two changes signaled a marked increase in executive powers. The full extent of the shift, though, would not be apparent until the new government was up and running. From the 1790s to today, the president's treaty-making authority has been used to partially offset and to some extent undermine Congress's unique authority to declare war, and his appointive powers have allowed him to shape the direction of the judicial as well as the executive branch of the federal government. We can certainly understand why Morris felt unappreciated when his cohort Wilson, claiming the Committee of Eleven had turned the president into "the minion of the Senate," failed to notice what he had done on behalf of creating a strong executive. A month earlier, Wilson and the five-man Committee of Detail had granted treaty-making and major appointive powers to the Senate; now Morris and the Committee of Eleven were giving the president the lead role. If Wilson failed to take note, we certainly can. Without this move, the office of the president today would be considerably different, and far weaker, than it is.

Time certainly favored Morris and the committee, whose report was in effect a working draft. Many delegates were unwilling, at this late date, to expend energy in overturning proposals within that document. Had such a dramatic leap in presidential powers been suggested in June, July, or August, it would probably have stirred more opposition. By September, the likelihood of major alterations skirting through without full scrutiny was much higher.

The only strong challenge to the committee's recommendation on powers of appointment came from George Mason. Part of the new plan he liked—taking appointive authority away from the Senate—but he didn't understand why the committee ceded that same body the partial power of "advice and consent." That should be the province not of a legislative body but of a separate executive council, which could both aid the president in executing the laws and keep him from abusing his powers. A longtime opponent of a single executive, Mason was still looking for ways to keep "dangerous" powers from being exercised by "the President alone."

Rufus King, opposing Mason, claimed it was simply too late to introduce yet another body into the mix: "The people would be alarmed at an unnecessary creation of a new corps which must increase the expence as well as the influence of the Government." Morris argued more substantively that the president, a single person, was best able to assume "responsibility" for the appointments he made, while the Senate would serve as well as a council to check the president. He then added flatly that an executive council had been proposed but rejected by the Committee of Eleven, as if this alone somehow invalidated Mason's proposal. Despite support from Wilson, the first to propose a single executive, and Franklin, who warned once again not to place "too much confidence in a single person," and Madison, who thought a committee should prepare a detailed draft for the establishment of an executive council, Mason's plan for an independently elected six-man council was rejected, eight states to three.

Once Mason's challenge had been rebuffed, delegates affirmed the Committee of Eleven's recommendation to give the president, with the advice and consent of the Senate, appointive powers. Further, at the urging of Richard Dobbs Spaight, they allowed the president, during a Senate recess, to make appointments on his own "which shall expire at the end of their next session." This last-minute "recess appointment" addendum seemed a natural corollary to the committee's recommendation; since Congress in those days met only sporadically and the Senate would be unable to approve or disapprove the president's nominees, it fell to the president alone to keep the government functioning in its absence. Yet by stating this explicitly, the convention opened the door to a later pro-executive interpretation, which allowed the president to make appointments opposed by the Senate.

The Committee of Eleven's proposal to give the president treaty-making powers provoked additional opposition. Again, though, the basic disagreement focused not on granting the initial power to the president but on the second step, treaty ratification. James Wilson thought that the House of Representatives, in addition to the Senate, should be required to approve the president's treaties, but as usual his protestations on the part of the people's direct representatives were in vain. Another challenge came from Madison, who preferred a low hurdle for treaties of peace. According to the committee recommendation, two-thirds of the Senate would have to approve all treaties, but Madison thought one-half should suffice for "treaties of peace." Without a single speaker for or against, Madison's motion passed "nem con," without dissent.

Immediately, Madison followed with a more striking proposal: two-thirds of the Senate could "make treaties of peace, without the concurrence of the President." Most shocking of all, in retrospect, was this future president's reasoning. "The President would necessarily derive so much power and importance from a state of war that he might be tempted, if authorised, to impede a treaty of peace." If a war-happy president did not want peace, a peace-loving Senate could override him. Gouverneur Morris, quick to respond, assured his fellow delegates that "the power of the president in this case [was] harmless" and that "no peace ought to be made without concurrence of the president, who was the general guardian of the National interests." Morris's president—one man above the political fray—could serve the nation better than those who represented specific interests. In a similar vein, Elbridge Gerry cautioned that the Senate might sell out the nation's "dearest interests," such as "fisheries, territory, etc." By eight states to three, the convention denied the Senate authority to make peace on its own. The president would still have to take the initiative in negotiating a peace treaty.

The following day, September 8, as the first order of business, Rufus King moved to reestablish the two-thirds requirement for Senate ratification of peace treaties. Hugh Williamson, supporting King, noted that one-half of the Senate, if only a bare quorum were present, might be only eight men, possibly from the smallest states. Gouverneur Morris, offering one of the strangest arguments of the convention, came down on the side of Madison and the minimum one-half requirement for treaties of peace. While Madison and others who favored the lower hurdle did so because peace is preferable to war, Morris preferred that option because it would *encourage* the waging of war to pursue national interests. He reasoned that if Congress thought peace would be more difficult to obtain, it would be "unwilling to make war for that reason on account of the Fisheries or the Mississippi, the two great objects of the Union." Facilitating peace would facilitate war, and war, for Morris, had the beneficial effect of making people willing to tolerate a strong, central government. This convoluted argument failed to convince, and Madison's motion was overturned, again eight states to three. Morris's preference for war, though, was in fact reflected in the latest draft, soon to become the final document. To this day, it takes a simple majority of Congress to declare war but a supermajority of the Senate to end one.

By September 8 the two new presidential powers had been confirmed, exactly according to the committee's recommendations. Collectively, they gave more power to the president than they did singularly, for the authority to appoint ambassadors and make treaties signaled executive leadership in the shaping of foreign policy. Following the Committee of Eleven's report, delegates overturned the sense of the convention that had prevailed for over three months. Perhaps, the way the pendulum kept swinging that summer, a few more days might have produced yet one more reversal, and these powers would have reverted back to the Senate or been apportioned in some other combination. The delegates, though, had wearied of these twists and turns, and the convention ended when it did, with presidential powers ascendant.

Even so, the president's clout still paled by contrast with that of Congress. None of his increased powers were intended to affect domestic policy. He possessed no more authority to levy taxes, regulate commerce, borrow and coin money, raise and supply an army, constitute courts, or suppress domestic insurrections than he had when the Committee of Detail submitted its draft a month earlier. The only phrase in the Committee of Eleven's report that could be construed as applying to domestic affairs was his power to nominate, along with ambassadors and Supreme Court justices, "other public ministers," and even here there is no stipulation that these ministers should set basic policy.

The president's augmented powers in the realm of foreign affairs, though striking, were also circumscribed. From the beginning, the "power of war" was off-limits, and that had not changed. The very first response to Randolph's resolution to create a separate office of the executive, back on June 1, had come from Charles Pinckney, a firm proponent of executive power. A "vigorous Executive" was an excellent idea, he declared, but giving the office powers of "peace & war &c." would make it "a monarchy, of the worst kind, to wit an elective one." This was certainly the sense of the convention at that time, echoed by several other delegates. Now, although the "power of peace" (or at least a sizable portion of it) had been handed to the president, the power of war remained precisely where it always had been—with Congress. Unlike discretionary resolutions, which were subject to reversal, this cardinal principle was likely to remain in place no matter how long the convention stayed in session. Not even Gouverneur Morris could devise a plan to challenge Congress's unique prerogative in this matter, and we have no evidence that he tried to.

Any attempt to marshal support for the executive's taking over the power of war would be compounded by lingering suspicions of a standing army. At the convention, attempts by Mason and others to prohibit professional armies fell short. This failure was certain to be noticed out of doors. Imagine how resistance to the final plan would have been magnified if one man alone, the president, were granted the authority to raise and deploy armies as he saw fit. People would insist that America's blood and treasure could not be expended so easily, without discussion, debate, or dissent, and they would probably reject the entire plan.

Without the power of war, the president's authority over foreign policy, although augmented by the Committee of Eleven's alterations, was far from absolute. The convention had leaned in the president's direction as far as it reasonably could, yet he was empowered to "make war" on his own accord in emergencies only, pending approval. That was the way a government must function in a republic.

There was one last challenge to the committee's report. The committee had wanted electors to cast two ballots, but the second ballot created a problem: there was no appropriate office for that man to fill. Undaunted, the Committee of Eleven had conjured a new position, just so electors would have somebody to vote for. Williamson, a committee member, explained to the convention: "Such an officer as vice-President was not wanted. He was introduced only for the sake of a valuable mode of election which required two to be chosen at the same time."

The creation of this new office did address the problem of succession. For the first two months of the convention, nobody had paid any attention to what would happen if a president were killed, incapacitated, or impeached and convicted, for if one president could not serve, Congress would simply choose another. But what if Congress was not then in session? On August 6 the Committee of Detail solved this minor technical problem by specifying that the president of the Senate would fill the office temporarily "until another President of the United States be chosen, or until the disability or the President be removed." That did not sit well with Gouverneur Morris, always wary of Congress's influence over the presidency. As Madison, who shared Morris's concern, pointed out on August 27, "The Senate might retard the appointment of a President in order to carry points whilst the revisionary power [veto] was in the President of their own body." Who, then, *should* succeed a president, if only temporarily? Morris suggested the chief justice, but he found no backers. Madison offered up "the persons composing the Council to the President," which would have made more sense if the president *had* a council, but none yet existed. Williamson then suggested that determining the "provisional successor to the President be postponed," and his motion carried the day.

This of course suited Morris, who was able to solve two problems at once within the Committee of Eleven. Morris had wanted the electors to select two candidates, and fortuitously that second candidate would fill a vacant niche in the new scheme. The elector scheme created a successor to the president who was independent of Congress.

What would the vice president *do*? That was a puzzle. The best the committee could come up with was "ex-officio President of the Senate," with the power to break a tie vote. This assignment angered Mason, who complained that the vice president's role, artificially manufactured by the Committee of Eleven, was "an encroachment on the rights of the Senate," violating the principle of separation of powers. Elbridge Gerry agreed. It was "improper," he said, to give the new office a function within the legislature, because of "the close intimacy that must subsist between the President & vice-president." To which Gouverneur Morris responded wittily: "The vice-president then will be the first heir apparent that ever loved his father."

Morris and the committee prevailed yet again, with only two states voting against the vice president's minimal job description. What we regard today as the second-highest office in the land was a fluke of circumstance, an inadvertent last-minute addition. Had they not felt rushed, delegates might have taken more care and assigned the infant office more definite and appropriate tasks, but they were worn out, and they discussed the matter no further. The vice president was the bastard son of the convention, which knew not how to deal with him.

The convention finished debating the committee's report on September 8, having approved all major changes except the settlement of an unresolved presidential election, which was to be decided by the House rather than the Senate. Electors, not Congress, would choose the president, if a majority settled on one candidate. His term was shortened from seven to four years. Instead of being limited to a single term, he could serve indefinitely, subject to reelection. With the advice and consent of the Senate, he was empowered to negotiate treaties, appoint ambassadors, and choose who would serve on the supreme national judiciary. At no other time in the summer of 1787 did any committee alter prior decisions of the convention in such a sweeping manner. To the Committee of Eleven we owe a good share of the American presidency and the very existence of the vice president.

Also on September 8, the convention appointed a five-man committee to "revise the style" and "arrange the articles which had been agreed to by the House." The committee was to deliver smoother prose, not an altered plan.

Not unexpectedly, Gouverneur Morris was appointed to the new committee. His colleagues were all lucid writers—James Madison, Dr. William Samuel Johnson, Rufus King, and the long-absent Alexander Hamilton, who had returned the week before to play whatever role he could in the final act. Although Johnson, the president of Columbia College, was the senior member and chairman, the committee asked Morris, a supreme stylist, to put his polish on the finished product.[11]

Many commentators have claimed that Morris reached beyond his limited mandate to further his nationalist agenda. The draft he was handed commenced, "We the people of the States of New Hampshire, Massachusetts, Rhode-Island and Providence Plantations," and so on, listing the states north to south, while Morris's version—"We the People of the United States"—left out the individual states, making it clear that this was a direct contract between the people and the national government they were creating. Morris, though, was forced to make this change, for the original made no sense. Rhode Island, which had refused to send delegates, would likely refuse to sign on, as might other states. In that case, the original preamble would become a farcical reminder of the lack of unanimity, and the Constitution would require immediate revision. So a listing of the separate states had to go.

Also in the preamble, Morris expanded the purposes of the new government, and commentators have said this too reflects his preference for a strong central government. The draft he inherited—the people of the states "do ordain, declare, and establish the following Constitution for the Government of ourselves and our posterity"— became in Morris's hand "to form a more perfect Union," and so on, the impressive listing of the Constitution's goals that is with us still. Yet there was nothing new in this. Key phrases such as "common defence" and "general Welfare" were carryovers from the weak Articles of Confederation, as was the idea of securing liberty. Other terms, such as "Justice," "domestic Tranquility," "Blessings," and "Posterity," were used often at the time and not in the least controversial. Ironically, when Morris was doing no more than expressing the general will, later writers have attributed to him an activist role, yet even his biographers have underplayed his dramatic restructuring of the presidency.[12]

The Committee of Style submitted its "final" version on September 12. Although the committee's rewording of the preamble attracted little notice, a few delegates still weren't satisfied with various clauses. Hugh Williamson wanted "to reconsider the clause requiring three fourths of each House to overrule the negative of the President," lowering the hurdle back to its original two-thirds. The higher number, he said, "puts too much in the power of the President." This must have surprised any delegates who recalled that the motion made four weeks past—to change from two-thirds to three-quarters—was made by none other than Hugh Williamson. Back then, Williamson and others had feared the legislature was gaining too much power; now, after the series of recent changes that freed and strengthened the president, he wanted to take a small step in the other direction. Other delegates agreed. In a close battle between fractions, two-thirds beat out three-fourths by six states to four, thereby lessening the presidential veto power by one-twelfth. James Madison, in this particular instance, noted the individual vote within the Virginia delegation: while Mason and Randolph favored the lower threshold, future presidents Washington and Madison preferred to keep presidential power at the higher level.[13]

The attention given to the veto override reveals how seriously many delegates were committed to a proper balance within their new government. While some, like Morris, voted always with the executive, and others, like Sherman, habitually sided with the legislative branch, most viewed themselves as impartial monitors. When one branch seemed to be getting an upper hand, they searched for appropriate adjustments.

In the end, did the convention achieve a proper balance of powers? And just as important: Would the people *think* it had accomplished that goal? Had the delegates created an office that could further efficiency in government and check abuses of the legislature while remaining clear of any monarchical stigma?

The office of the American president was forged by compromise. No delegate, not even Gouverneur Morris, prevailed on every issue. Although he managed in the end to block legislative selection of the president and add some powers to the office, he would have made the president stronger yet, had he alone been the one to decide.

James Wilson won the battle for a single executive, but his push for popular elections never gained traction. Linking the powers of the president with those of the Senate was fraught with danger, he thought, and he was only partially successful in cutting back the Senate's role.

George Mason, Edmund Randolph, Benjamin Franklin, and William Paterson had favored a plural executive at the outset. Outvoted on that score, each did what he could to establish the balance of power that worked for him. Mason had the hardest time with this. He predicted that because of the unholy alliance between the president and the Senate, the new government "would end either in monarchy, or a tyrannical aristocracy." Mason was particularly upset because the convention turned down his suggestion for preventing this, an independent executive council to both advise and check the president.

Roger Sherman was no great fan of executive power, but he ceased complaining about it when it became clear that Congress would still make most major decisions.

On the other hand, the supremacy of Congress worried Charles Pinckney. As late as September 16, the day before the assembly dissolved, Pinckney "objected to the contemptible weakness & dependence of the Executive." Alexander Hamilton no doubt concurred, but he refrained this time from comment.

If each and every delegate had some reservations, did that mean they would oppose the new constitution?

Benjamin Franklin hoped not. Franklin had expressed his displeasure with a single executive and several other measures, but in a masterly and oft-quoted speech on the closing day he promised to lay his reservations aside. "I confess that there are several parts of this constitution which I do not at present approve," he opened, "but I am not sure I shall never approve them." He had lived long, he said, and "the older I grow, the more apt I am to doubt my own judgment, and to pay more respect to the judgment of others." Understanding the necessity of "a general Government" in some form, he would not let his personal reservations get in the way. So Franklin was ready to make his pact:

> Thus I consent, Sir, to this Constitution because I expect no better, and because I am not sure, that it is not the best. The opinions I have had of its errors, I sacrifice to the public good. . . . On the whole, Sir, I can not help expressing a wish that every member of the Convention who may still have objections to it, would with me, on this occasion doubt a little of his own infallibility, and to make manifest our unanimity, put his name to this instrument.

Franklin's appeal was good enough for Gouverneur Morris, who had had his way more often than not and needed no convincing:

> Mr. Govr. MORRIS said that he too had objections, but considering the present plan as the best that was to be attained, he should take it with all its faults. The majority had determined in its favor and by that determination he should abide. The moment this plan goes forth all other considerations will be laid aside, and the great question will be, shall there be a national Government or not?

It was good enough for Alexander Hamilton as well, who had certainly not had his way. "No man's ideas were more remote from the plan than his were known to be," Hamilton admitted, "but is it possible to deliberate between anarchy and convulsion on one side, and the chance of good to be expected from the plan on the other."

Even Dr. Franklin, though, could not convince Edmund Randolph, Elbridge Gerry, and George Mason. These three wanted a second convention, after the people out of doors had seen the plan and offered their input. "It was improper to say to the people, take this or nothing," Mason argued. (Back on August 31, according to Madison, Mason had stated "he would sooner chop off his right hand than put it to the Constitution as it now stands.") Yet the very thought of a brand-new convention, after all the toils of this one, was received as an affront by their fellow delegates. A second convention was rejected out of hand.

The dissent of Randolph, Gerry, and Mason worried others. As Hamilton expressed it, "A few characters of consequence, by opposing or even refusing to sign the Constitution, might do infinite mischief." That's why Franklin proposed a way to project the appearance of unanimity, even though none existed. After the document as a whole was approved by a vote of the state delegations, each delegate, even the dissenters, could sign as a "witness" to "the unanimous consent of the States."

This ploy was not actually Franklin's, however. According to Madison, the "ambiguous form" was "drawn up" by Gouverneur Morris and then "put into the hands of Doctor Franklin that it might have the better chance of success." To the end, Morris played the master strategist, devising both the scheme and the devious manner of presentation, but this time his subterfuge failed. Even Charles Pinckney, Morris's staunch ally on behalf of an independent executive, would not abide it. "We are not likely to gain many converts by the ambiguity of the proposed form of signing," he said. Instead, Pinckney "thought it best to be candid and let the form speak the substance."

So it would be. Pinckney, Morris, Franklin, Wilson, Hamilton, Madison, Sherman, and thirty-two others affixed their names to the proposed form of government, with its newly created office of the president. Mason, Gerry, and even Randolph, who had introduced the first draft, did not. Randolph explained that his refusal to sign did not imply he would oppose the plan in the end. He wanted only to remain "free to be governed by his duty" to the people. After apologizing personally to Dr. Franklin, he promised not to "oppose the Constitution without doors."

Gerry and Mason made no such pledge. Gerry listed eleven specific complaints with the document and predicted it would promote a civil war in his home state of Massachusetts. Mason vowed to oppose the new plan when it came to a vote in Virginia. Back on June 4, as he argued against a single executive, Mason had warned, "The genius of the people must be consulted," and now at last that would happen.

PART III

Field Tests

CHAPTER SIX

Selling the Plan

George Mason stewed. His last-minute attempt to add a Bill of Rights had failed to garner the support of a single state delegation, his call for an executive council had fallen on deaf ears, and his final warning against "the danger of standing armies in time of peace" had been summarily dismissed. He was greatly concerned for the fate of the nation and the cause of liberty, and nobody seemed to be listening. So on the back of his copy of the Committee of Style's printed draft, he "drew up some general objections, which I intended to offer, by way of protest," as he reported to Thomas Jefferson, in France at the time, but he was "discouraged" from reading his objections on the floor "by the precipitate, & intemperate, not to say indecent manner, in which the business was conducted, during the last week of the convention, after the patrons of this new plan found they had a decided majority in their favour."[1]

Mason's first and primary objection was the absence of a "Declaration of Rights." Since the state declarations did not apply to the new national government, he argued, the people's liberties were "no longer secured." Beyond that, Mason listed a dozen other reasons to oppose the Constitution, and several of these touched on the powers allotted to the Senate and the president.

The Senate and the president, in combination, had the power to make treaties and appoint "ambassadors and all public officers" with absolutely no input from the people's only true representatives in the House. Treaties had the force of law, but they were not made like other laws, which required House consent. Further, since the Senate tried impeachments, the president was beholden to it. The Senate, unlike the House, would be "continually sitting," and members would serve lengthy terms. Senators could "accomplish what usurpations they please upon the rights and liberties of the people." It didn't have to be that way, if only the convention had granted Mason his independent executive council.

The stage was set for cabal, Mason continued. If some designing men tried to seize power and were consequently convicted of treason, the president had the full and unchecked authority to pardon them, should they be his friends or allies. Mason also complained of the "unnecessary office of the Vice-President, who for want of other employment is made president of the Senate, thereby dangerously blending the executive and legislative branches." The Senate-and-president combination was dangerous enough in any case, and the vice presidency seemed to bond them even tighter.[2]

Mason had presented these objections during the convention and they were rejected, so now he searched for alternate venues. Gouverneur Morris, when his views did not prevail, had also taken them elsewhere, but Morris had narrowed the field, not broadened it. Morris needed to convince only five of ten committee members to go his way, while Mason had to address the entire nation—a tall order. If he succeeded in raising the alarm, the people themselves would then call for a second convention, and that venue would be more conducive to providing safeguards for liberty and guarantees against governmental abuse.

Mason started his mission the moment the convention ended, perhaps even a day or two before. He made copies of his objections and gave them to local political operatives in Philadelphia whom he suspected would be likely allies. He also gave a copy to Elbridge Gerry, a fellow non-signer, to circulate in Massachusetts, and Gerry, on his way home, showed it to like-minded political figures in New York, a state currently ruled by dedicated foes of a centralized government. Most significantly, he sent a copy to Richard Henry Lee, who was representing Virginia in Congress, currently meeting in New York. At least on paper, Congress still exercised whatever authority resided in the Confederation; it was his best, most immediate hope for overruling the group in Philadelphia.

Then Mason headed south to his home plantation, Gunston Hall, only five miles downstream from Mount Vernon on the right bank of the Potomac. Along the way, near Baltimore, his carriage tipped over, causing him much loss of blood and severe head and neck pains.[3]

George Washington, traveling separately from Mason, also suffered a mishap while heading back to the Potomac. On Wednesday, September 19, at the Head of Elk, he came across a creek swollen by rain. Unable to ford at the usual spot, he risked crossing on "an old, rotten & long disused bridge," as he wrote in his journal. His lead horse fell fifteen feet into the river, almost dragging his baggage-laden carriage with it. While Mason's injury attracted no attention, Washington's near fall became the story of the hour. Two newspaper accounts of the incident were reprinted a total of seventy-one times over the next two months, in every state except North Carolina. According to the first, "His Excellency had alighted in order to walk over the bridge, which fortunate circumstance probably saved a life so dear to his country." (The term "alighted" was misleading, perhaps deliberately so. Washington had been riding in his carriage, not upon the horse.) The second article celebrated the "providential preservation of the valuable life of this great and good man . . . for the great and important purpose of establishing, by his name and future influence, a government that will render safe and permanent the liberties of America." This is what Mason and other opponents of the proposed Constitution were up against. They could not contest the office of a chief executive without seeming to oppose Washington himself, who more than likely would become the first president under the new plan.[4]

When Mason and Washington arrived home, they found their corn crops wanting. While in Philadelphia, they had been informed this might be so, but the shortage was even worse than they thought. Neighboring North Carolina, however, produced an abundant harvest that year, and Mason had made some contacts there through his fellow delegates. Washington knew this, and on October 7 he wrote to his neighbor: if Mason wanted to purchase North Carolina corn, "I would gladly join you." Later that day, Mason responded: "If I can be of any service to you in making such a contract as you approve, it will give me a great deal of pleasure." All very practical and cordial. This was life as usual for such close neighbors, and it continued despite their political differences.[5]

Washington was not shocked by Mason's brash opposition to the proposed Constitution, but he was clearly upset. Mason had "rendered himself obnoxious in Philadelphia by the pains he took to disseminate his objections," he wrote to Madison. ("Obnoxious," in those days, connoted insistent or insufferable, not loathsome or repugnant.) "To alarm the people, seems to be the ground work of his plan." Mason would have agreed with this last statement; his list of objections would eventually find its way into twenty-five different newspapers, from Maine to South Carolina.[6]

As Mason pushed resistance, Washington promoted adoption. He did not step aside and let others do the work of advocacy, as is often reported. He wrote to other supporters, he tried to convince fence-sitters, he strategized, he arranged for publication of pro-Constitution materials, and he exerted his personal influence. Immediately upon his return to Mount Vernon, he sent copies of the proposed Constitution to three former governors of Virginia, Patrick Henry, Benjamin Harrison, and Thomas Nelson. "I accompany it with no observations," he wrote at the outset, and while it is true he made no reference to the specific contents of the plan, he did comment on its importance: "I wish the Constitution which is offered had been made more perfect, but I sincerely believe it is the best that could be obtained at this time; and, as a Constitutional door is opened for amendment hereafter, the adoption of it under the present circumstances of the Union is in my opinion desirable." Had the convention failed to draft new rules, he closed, "anarchy would soon have ensued—the seeds being richly sown in every soil."[7]

More letters followed. To Henry Knox, his former general whom Congress had appointed secretary of war, Washington touted the virtues of the Constitution while warning Knox to expect "our Govr [Edmund Randolph] & Colo. Mason" to do all in their power "to alarm the people." To David Stuart, Mason's fellow representative from Fairfax County in the House of Delegates, he passed along James Wilson's detailed rebuttal of Mason's objections. Perhaps Stuart could arrange for the "re-publication" of Wilson's argument, he suggested—not that Mason really needed any rebutting, he noted, since "every mind must recoil" at his ideas.[8]

When Hamilton and Madison, separately, sent him the first "Publius" essays, later published as *The Federalist,* Washington forwarded them, at Madison's request, to a contact in Richmond, the state capital, for republication there. "Altho' I am acquainted with some of the writers who are concerned in this work," Washington noted, "I am not at liberty to disclose their names, nor would I have it known that they are sent by *me* to *you* for promulgation."[9]

While Washington's political activism appeared to run counter to his public persona, his commitment to nationalism was hardly new. When he retired as commander in chief back in 1783, in a letter he termed his "legacy," Washington had presented his own "system of policy," a broad outline for a stronger central government. There should be "an indissoluble union of states under one federal head," he had said. "There should be lodged somewhere a supreme power to regulate and govern the general concerns of the confederated republic, without which the union cannot long endure." By "supreme power" he meant neither God nor an individual executive but a national government, a "supreme authority" over and above the separate states. Now his wish for a national government was almost fulfilled. Only one step remained: ratification of the convention's proposed Constitution.[10]

The new plan would not be approved, though, unless Americans relinquished "their local prejudices and policies," to use the words of his legacy letter. They needed "to make those mutual concessions which are requisite to the general prosperity, and in some instances, to sacrifice their individual advantages to the interest of the community." Opponents of the plan were not doing that, Washington believed. Although Mason and others used high-toned arguments, they were motivated by local interests and jealousies. Mason's more famous arguments demanded a Bill of Rights and an executive council, but Washington believed his true reason for opposing the Constitution was that it ran counter to Virginia's interests. In his objections, Mason insisted that "commercial and navigation laws" should require a two-thirds vote so "the five Southern states, whose produce & circumstances are totally different from that of the eight Northern & Eastern states," would not be "ruined." This was the sort of language that absolutely infuriated George Washington. He too was a Virginian, but the "separate interests" of the states, even his own, needed to be reined in. "That there are some . . . who wish to see these states divided into several confederacies is pretty evident," he wrote to David Stuart. "But as nothing in my conception is more to be depreciated than a disunion, or these separate confederacies, my voice, as far as it will extend, will be offered in favor of [union]."[11]

Washington had no good words to say about those "who are no

friends to general government—perhaps I might go further, & add, who would have no great objection to the introduction of anarchy & confusion." Such adversaries were "more active & violent" than were friends of the Constitution, and their appeals were "addressed to the passions of the people, and obviously calculated to rouse their fears." Washington's demonizing the opposition served a purpose. By viewing them as selfish and inherently disruptive, he skirted any real issues they might pose. The structure of the Constitution was not at issue, merely the fact of its existence. All substantive critiques—including serious questions about the powers, manner of selection, and term in office of the president—could therefore be ignored. If these presented problems, they could be fixed later.[12]

Washington's commitment to a stronger union, combined with his dim view of the opposition, fueled his own passions, and according to eyewitness reports his renewed sense of purpose was good for his health and spirit. "He is in perfect good health, & looks almost as well as he did twenty years ago. I never saw him so keen for any thing in my life, as he is for the adoption of the new form of government," wrote Alexander Donald, who stayed for two days at Mount Vernon in October.[13]

At least initially, Washington did not wish to go public with his advocacy. His private secretary, Tobias Lear, knew this, so when Lear published a refutation of Mason's objections in the *Virginia Journal,* he did so under the name of Brutus, and he made a point of not telling his employer what he was doing. On December 27, however, an excerpt from one of Washington's many letters supporting the Constitution was published in *The Virginia Herald.* There was "no alternative" between the "adoption" of the Constitution and "anarchy," he wrote, as he had written several other times in the previous three months, but this time his dire warning was read by the public. Over the next three months, forty-nine newspapers from Georgia to New Hampshire reprinted the former commander in chief's passionate support of the new plan. Washington was a bit taken aback, but not dismayed. He complained to Charles Carter, the recipient of the letter that became public, but not so sternly as one might expect:

> Altho' I have no disinclination to the promulgation of my sentiments on the proposed Constitution (not having concealed them on any occasion), yet I must nevertheless confess, that it

gives me pain to see the hasty and indigested production of a private letter handed to the public. . . . Could I have supposed that the contents of a private letter (marked with evident haste) would have composed a news paper paragraph, I certainly should have taken some pains to dress the sentiments . . . in less exceptionable language, and would have assigned some reasons in support of my opinion.[14]

"Reasons," though, were not the issue. The newspapers reprinted the letter not because of the argument it made but because of who made the argument. Washington's endorsement had a far greater impact than the most cogent of essays, and supporters of the Constitution exploited it brazenly. "Is it possible," asked one writer in *The Independent Gazetteer*, "that the deliverer of our country would have recommended an unsafe form of government for that liberty, for which he had for eight long years contended with such unexampled firmness, consistency and magnanimity?" Another proponent suggested "that the Federalists should be distinguished hereafter by the name of Washingtonians, and the Anti-Federalists by the name of 'Shayites.'"[15]

Claims of Washington's importance in shaping the new government sometimes overshadowed the evidence. A writer in *The Massachusetts Gazette* reported with confidence a tale from the convention: Washington had held the floor "two hours at a time, in speaking upon some parts of the proposed system," and "he advocated every part of the plan with all those rhetorical powers which he possesses in eminent degree." According to Madison's notes, Washington spoke substantively exactly once, and then but briefly on the final day of the convention.[16]

Washington's impact was no secret. William Grayson, a Virginia Anti-Federalist, listed an impressive array of leading figures on his side that included not only Mason and Richard Henry Lee but also three former governors, "most of the judges of the General Court," and several others. All of these, though, were offset by one key Federalist, General Washington, "who is a host within himself." Washington's support made the structural arguments of his opponents moot. When they issued dire warnings about power-hungry presidents taking advantage of the new system, Washington, a flesh-and-blood counterexample, made them look foolish. Nobody could imagine that George Washington, who had voluntarily relinquished his authority, would ever succumb to foreign intrigue or cling to power or team up with factions or lead an army against his own people. Richard Henry Lee tried to muster his own heroes—Moses and Montesquieu—to counter Washington, but this retort seemed a mark of desperation.[17]

At the Federal Convention, Washington had said little but exerted great influence merely by his presence; delegates might not have settled on a single executive so readily had they not looked to him as a model. Perhaps, too, they would not have ceded to Gouverneur Morris's relentless push to free the office from congressional selection. Almost certainly, delegates would have been more reluctant to allow indefinite terms, opening the possibility of a president for life. That was pushing the limits of what people out of doors would accept, and without Washington delegates would probably have reined themselves in and not risked a backlash. Now that the debate had moved out of doors, Washington's support was skewing the battle over ratification. There can be no doubt that the new office would have received closer public scrutiny had Americans not felt so comfortable with making the nation's deliverer, General George Washington, its first occupant.

All eyes were on Richmond in June 1788. In the nine months since the Federal Convention had submitted its plan for public approval, eight states had ratified the Constitution, and if Virginia followed suit, the new rules would become the law of the land, and the four holdouts would most likely fall into line. On the other hand, if Virginia rejected the Constitution, neighboring North Carolina, where Anti-Federalist sentiments ran strong, would probably follow its lead. If those two states then formed their own confederacy, as some Anti-Federalists threatened and all Federalists feared, South Carolina, Georgia, and likely Maryland would find more in common with their slave-society compatriots than with the old United States and withdraw their prior votes for ratification, and the fast-growing territories west of the Appalachians, Kentucky and Tennessee, would undoubtedly side with the southern confederacy as well. One nation would become two. Further, once Virginia rejected the Constitution, its leading resident, George Washington, would become ineligible for the presidency of the United States.

Virginia's epic battle over the Constitution took place in an unlikely venue. Back in October 1787, when the state legislature called for a ratification convention, people hoped it would meet in the brand-new state capitol, which Thomas Jefferson modeled after the ancient Roman temple Maison Carrée. That would have been a grand opening for the noble home of Virginia's republican government, but come June, the building was still under construction, so the convention met instead in a large wooden structure known locally as Mr. Quesnay's Academy. The French chevalier Quesnay de Beaurepaire, who wanted to establish a European-style cultural center in Virginia, intended the building to house theatrical productions, and here indeed was the best show in town. The actors, the greatest statesmen in Virginia and many would say in the nation, played both to each other and to members of the public who crowded into the balcony gallery.[18]

This venue suited the legendary Patrick Henry perfectly. Henry had been a major force in Virginia politics since bursting onto the stage during the Stamp Act resistance almost a quarter century earlier. He had drummed up support for the war, served two extended terms as governor, and excited audiences as no other revolutionary could. At a time when political oratory was treated as something of a sport, Henry was universally regarded as a superstar. Now, with thundering voice and dramatic gestures, the state's most influential Anti-Federalist would make the most of his talents. In characteristic style, he would pose rhetorical question after rhetorical question, each one proving his point beyond all doubt. "Your passions are no longer your own when he addresses them," said George Mason, his ally on this occasion.[19]

On June 5, the third day of debates, Patrick Henry took the floor early and held it until the meeting adjourned. Although the convention had agreed to address the proposed Constitution point by point and the topic on the table was the composition of the House of Representatives, Henry veered far from that subject. The Constitution "has an awful squinting," he declared. "It squints towards monarchy. And does not this raise indignation in the breast of every true American?" (This "squinting" image became a popular refrain among Anti-Federalist polemicists.) Henry continued:

> Your president may easily become a King. . . . If your American chief be a man of ambition and abilities, how easy is it for him to render himself absolute! . . . If we make a King, we may prescribe the rules by which he shall rule his people, and interpose

such checks as shall prevent him from infringing them. But the President, in the field, at the head of his army, can prescribe the terms on which he shall reign master. . . . Can he not at the head of his army beat down every opposition? Away with your President, we shall have a King. The army will salute him Monarch; your militia will leave you and assist in making him King, and fight against you. And what have you to oppose this force? What will then become of you and your rights? Will not absolute despotism ensue?[20]

David Robertson, the Federalist-leaning lawyer who used shorthand to record the debates as he listened from the gallery, broke off at this point, unable to keep pace with Henry's invective. "Here Mr. Henry strongly and pathetically expatiated on the probability of the President's enslaving America, and the horrid consequences that must result," he jotted down.[21]

Did Henry really believe his apocalyptic prophecy? Was he absolutely horrified by the executive office the framers of the Constitution tried to impose on the American people? His assault on the presidency needs to be placed in the context of his other tirades at Virginia's ratifying convention. Almost as dangerous as the president were "two sets of tax-gatherers—the State and the Federal Sheriffs." State tax collectors, "those unfeeling bloodsuckers," had been bad enough, and federal collectors, more remote from the people, would of course be much worse:

> The Federal Sheriff may commit what oppression, make what distresses he pleases, and ruin you with impunity: For how are you to tie his hands? Have you any sufficient decided means of preventing him from sucking your blood by speculations, commissions and fees? Thus thousands of your people will be most shamefully robbed.[22]

Congress, too, received its share of Henry's blows. "We ought to be exceeding cautious in giving up this life—this soul—of money—this power of taxation to Congress," he warned. "Must I give my soul—my lungs, to Congress? . . . What powerful check is there here to prevent the most extravagant and profligate squandering of the public money?"[23]

For Henry, Congress's power to regulate commerce under the new plan was particularly worrisome. One of the hottest political topics in the nation was John Jay's tentative agreement with Spanish ministers. Jay was ready to bargain away American rights to shipping on the Mississippi in return for favorable trade concessions that would benefit eastern merchants, but according to the Articles of Confederation he would need the votes of nine of the thirteen state delegations in Congress to cement the deal. Five southern states with access to the West doomed the potential treaty, but under the new Constitution a simple majority in Congress would suffice. The North thus joined the president, federal tax collectors, and Congress on Henry's list of villains. If the Constitution were ratified, northern representatives would "give away this river," and that was just the beginning of northern tyranny. On June 24, as the convention reached its climax, Henry warned his fellow delegates and the onlookers in the gallery that it was only a matter of time before northern congressmen would "liberate every one of your slaves." The proposed Constitution gave them "the power in clear unequivocal terms . . . to pronounce all slaves free," and they "will clearly and certainly exercise it."[24]

We have no way of determining whether Patrick Henry was more worried about the president, tax collectors, Congress, or the North. Once he decided to oppose the Constitution, he utilized his immense powers of persuasion to their best advantage. The president is even worse than a king? If that instilled doubt, he'd use it. Tax collectors will bleed you dry? Try that one too. Congress will take away your slaves? That should work in this venue.

Henry's blanket indictments of the proposed Constitution were not unusual. For some Anti-Federalists, the new office of the presidency may have triggered resistance to the plan, but for others federal taxation, the loss of state and local control, the prospect of a standing army, or the lack of guarantees for basic liberties might have raised more serious concerns. Whatever their individual reasons, those who decided against the Constitution tried to defeat it by using any and all arguments they could muster, so they naturally raised alarms about the powers of the presidency. Since the Articles of Confederation had lacked an executive branch, all these powers were entirely new and potentially suspect. Item by item, each enumerated power became the object of complaint.

The president's role as commander in chief was a ready target. A

Virginia writer, under the name Impartial Examiner, labeled the president "generalissimo." Mercy Otis Warren, writing as A Columbian Patriot, called him a "despot" who could "draw out his dragoons" to suppress those who opposed him. Benjamin Workman, a mathematics instructor at the University of Pennsylvania who assumed the name Philadelphiensis, wrote that an American "king with a standing army at his disposal ought to cause the blood of a free citizen to boil with indignation." He predicted that under the president's leadership, the government would become "*despotic* and *oppressive,* and the people will become *abject slaves*." Elections would be worthless, he said. The government would soon be composed "only of an *emperor and a few lordlings,* surrounded by thousands of blood-suckers and cringing sycophants."[25]

The presidential pardon, Anti-Federalists argued, was discretionary and unrestrained. Logically, they were on strong ground here. The framers had wanted to check the authority of abusive courts, but in doing so, they gave the president a power that could not be overruled by any governmental body under any circumstance. "The President ought not to have the power of pardoning, because he may frequently pardon crimes which were advised by himself," Mason argued at the Virginia ratifying convention. "It may happen, at some future day, that he will establish a monarchy, and destroy the republic. If he has the power of granting pardons before indictment, or conviction, may he not stop inquiry and prevent detection? The case of treason ought, at least, to be excepted."[26]

Anti-Federalists attacked the various ways the executive could interfere with the legislative branch, thereby undermining the separation of powers, which Federalists claimed to hold so dear. The vice president, second-in-command to the chief executive, presided over the Senate, a legislative body, for no apparent reason. The president had the power to convene or adjourn the two houses of the legislature. (Although he could convene Congress only on "extraordinary occasions" and adjourn it only temporarily when the two houses disagreed on the timing for adjournment, Anti-Federalists likened the president's power to that of the British Crown, which had dissolved colonial legislatures at will.) Worse yet, the president could interfere with legislative functioning by vetoing a bill at his discretion. True, his "negative" could be overridden by two-thirds of each house of Congress, but Anti-

Federalists preferred to downplay that provision. The writer using the name Impartial Examiner acknowledged the two-thirds override but quickly suggested it would give the president "in the legislative scale of government a weight almost equal to that of two thirds of the whole Congress." Then, to ramp up the argument, the writer created and attacked a phantom absolute veto:

> If the system proposed had been calculated to extend his authority a little further, he would preponderate against all—he alone would possess the sovereignty of America. For if the whole executive authority and an absolute *negative* on the legislature should become united in one person, . . . he will be elevated to the height of supremacy. . . . [H]e cannot be the object of any laws; he will be above all law. . . . How near will the president approach to this consummate degree of power![27]

While most attacks on the presidency portrayed the office as being too powerful, one, ironically, cast it as being too weak. Since the Senate had "a negative upon the President" in powers of appointment and treaty making, it could tie his hands and destroy the "independence and purity" of the executive. He would become the tool of "the ruling junta" in the Senate, and members of that unholy body, elected for repeatable six-year terms, would likely serve for life. The Senate could thus "dictate" to the president, and because it also enjoyed greater powers than the House, it would essentially "govern alone." An author calling himself Federal Farmer held that "by giving the senate, directly or indirectly, an undue influence over the representatives, and the improper means of fettering, embarrassing, or controuling the president or executive, we give the government, at the very outset, a fatal and pernicious tendency to that middle undesirable point—aristocracy."[28]

The "aristocracy" charge was bold and biting; like "monarchy," it carried a negative connotation that Anti-Federalists readily put to political purpose. Philadelphiensis predicted that the president, if he "not be a man of an enterprising spirit," would become "a *minion* of the aristocratics" in the Senate. A writer calling himself John Humble, using raw satire, tapped into the egalitarianism that lay behind the national hatred of aristocracy: "Now we the *low born*, that is, all the people of the United States except 600 or thereabouts, *well born*, do by this humble address, declare, and most solemnly engage, that we will allow and admit the said 600 *well born,* immediately to establish and confirm this most noble, most excellent and truly divine constitution." This kind of primitive class consciousness made the Senate, the new government's vestigial aristocratic body, a particularly soft target for the Constitution's critics.[29]

At the close of the Federal Convention, a disgruntled George Mason had warned, "The dangerous power and structure of the government . . . would end either in monarchy, or a tyrannical aristocracy; which, he was in doubt, but one or another he was sure." After the convention Anti-Federalist polemicists followed Mason's lead, tagging the Constitution with both labels even if they appeared to contradict each other. Was the Senate or the president the main problem? It didn't matter which, so long as the Constitution would be derailed.[30]

Mason himself, along with several other Anti-Federalists, offered a cogent argument that challenged the powers of the presidency and the Senate simultaneously. The president, he claimed, was not the minion of the aristocratic Senate, nor was the Senate under the wing of a monarchical president. Instead, the Constitution would allow the Senate and the president to work in tandem to circumvent the people's representatives in the House and take charge of the government. Mason presented this argument forcefully to the Virginia convention:

> The Constitution has married the President and the Senate— has made them man and wife. I believe the consequence that generally results from marriage, will happen here. They will be continually supporting and aiding each other. They will always consider their interests as united. We know the advantage the few have over the many. They can with facility act in concert and on an uniform system. They may join scheme and plot against the people without any chance of detection. The Senate and the President will form a combination that cannot be prevented by the Representatives. The Executive and legislative powers thus connected, will destroy all balance.[31]

Even impeachment, the final defense against tyranny, would not suffice to check a president who was in collusion with the Senate. Since the Senate tried cases of impeachment, the president would be "tried by his counsellors," Mason said. "The guilty try themselves."

. . .

How to assess these various arguments against the presidency presents something of a puzzle. Which features were truly repugnant to Anti-Federalists? If large numbers of citizens at the time severely objected to the president's role as commander in chief, the presidential pardon or presidential veto, the vice president's role as presiding officer in the Senate, the sharing of power between the president and the Senate, or any other specific provision of the Constitution with respect to the executive office, then that provision does not enjoy the blessings of a consensus of the founding generation. Legally, this does not affect its standing, but historically and perhaps ethically that provision would be tainted. If such were the case, we have been living under a rule that a significant proportion of the people we respect as our founders thought was flawed.

While the true feelings of Anti-Federalists cannot be established by taking every attempt to derail the Constitution at face value, they can be surmised by examining the actual amendments to the Constitution that these people offered during the ratification debates. Two days after the Virginia convention formally ratified the Constitution on June 25, 1788, it proposed 40 amendments and sent them on to the other states for their consideration. Virginia was not the only state to do so. The South Carolina convention proposed 4 amendments, Massachusetts 9, New Hampshire 12, North Carolina 46, Rhode Island 21 plus 18 "principles" it wanted to add to the Constitution, and New York 32 amendments plus 24 principles. In addition, a majority committee from Maryland suggested 13 amendments, a minority committee from the same state another 15, and a minority report from Pennsylvania 15. Altogether, delegates to nine of the state ratification conventions suggested 249 additions or changes to the Constitution. These proposals offer a clearer indication of popular sentiments than do the political arguments that appeared in the press or were offered at the ratifying conventions. They were intended not to sway public opinion but to refine the actual workings of the new government. Like the Constitution itself, each addition or change was vetted and approved by a deliberative body, and these bodies represented broader constituencies than did the Federal Convention.[32]

Many of the proposals were duplicated, and about half concerned the kinds of protections that eventually wound up in the Bill of Rights, but there were also several dozen distinct suggestions for improving elements within the body of the Constitution. Some of these were offered by several states, suggesting widespread discontent. Seven state conventions and the Pennsylvania dissenters, for instance, wanted to prohibit Congress from imposing taxes until it had first requisitioned the states and the states had failed to come through. Six states sought to prevent Congress from granting monopolies or giving any "exclusive advantages of commerce" to a single company. These economic concerns weighed heavily on people.

A few amendments concerned the presidency. These can be placed in two groups, the first dealing with the president and military power, the second with a president's terms in office. New York and Maryland wanted to prohibit the president from commanding an army in the field. New Hampshire, Virginia, New York, North Carolina, Rhode Island, and the Maryland minority wanted to require a supermajority in Congress to establish a standing army in peacetime. Virginia, New York, North Carolina, and the Pennsylvania and Maryland minorities wanted to limit federal control of the state militia, which, once nationalized, would be under the control of the president. Taken together, these amendments suggest widespread apprehension over the possible abuse of military power. Delegates to the Federal Convention had understood this and tried to address it by placing the military under civilian control, but at least in the minds of some their move backfired. Although the president was a civilian leader, placing him at the head of an army and allowing him to assume field command involved risks that called for further safeguards.

The other concern on people's minds was the lack of rotation in office, as people said at the time, or term limits, as we say today. The president could potentially stay in office for life, and this seems to have been cause for great alarm. Anti-Federalist writers raised the subject repeatedly, and four states took definite action to limit the president's tenure. Virginia's proposed amendment read, "No person shall be capable of being President of the United States for more than eight years in any term of sixteen years," and North Carolina used the exact same wording. New York stated, "That no person be eligible to the office of president of the United States a third time," while Rhode Island asserted that the president and all members of Congress "should at fixed periods be reduced to a private station, return into the mass of the people, and the vacancies be supplied by certain and regular elections." The subject had arisen many times during the Federal Convention, and not until the dramatic turnaround on September 4, less than two weeks before adjournment, was the president allowed to remain in office for more than a single term. Before that, delegates had repeatedly voted against repeatable terms for the president.[33]

These amendments suggest that people were more worried about a president abusing his authority on a grand scale—staying in office indefinitely or, worse yet, using an army to keep himself there—than about his limited veto, his relation with Congress, his treaty-making power, his authority to make appointments, his ability to pardon criminals, his salary, or any particular aspect of his office other than his role as commander in chief. Although all of these powers faced resistance, they did not lead to a rash of amendments to change the scope of executive authority. (There was one exception: New York wanted to require congressional assent to presidential pardons, but no other state followed suit.) We can safely infer that if a particular concern did not warrant any proposed amendments, it probably did not, by itself, cause widespread opposition to the Constitution.

A case in point: the fate of George Mason's proposal for an executive council. To reduce the influence of the Senate and preserve the separation of powers, Mason wanted to strip that body of its "advice and consent" participation in making appointments and treaties, executive functions that were improperly placed in the legislative branch and should be assigned to a more appropriate body. The Federal Convention had turned a cold shoulder to this idea, but Mason continued to push it at Virginia's ratification convention. There, he chaired a caucus of Anti-Federalists who compiled a list of amendments, and to this group he proposed the creation of a separate council "to assist in the administration of government." The council would join with the president in "making treaties" and "appointing ambassadors, other public ministers and or counsels, judges of the Supreme Courts, and all other officers of the United States, whose appointments are not otherwise provided by the Constitution." It would also select its own leader, who would succeed the president. With this bold stroke, Mason proposed to circumvent two troublesome features of the Constitution: the vice president's role as president of a legislative body and the convoluted method of choosing a vice president through the elector system. Mason's amendment, though, would have required dramatic revisions in several places within the Constitution. Even his Anti-Federalist allies reasoned that this would never happen, and they failed to report his amendment out of committee.[34]

Apparently, delegates to the Federal Convention had succeeded in creating a presidential office that triggered only two red flags that might endanger ratification. Yet if people worried about presidential abuse on a grand scale, why did they not seek an amendment to alter the method of presidential selection? The electoral system was new and untested, and some thought it could undermine the entire new plan of government. William Grayson, a former officer in the Continental army and future U.S. senator, explained at the Virginia convention that if only two of the ninety-one electors voted for a particular candidate, yet nobody else appeared on the majority of the electors' ballots, that candidate could still be one of the five leading contenders. Then, when the sixty-five members of the House of Representatives voted by state delegation on these finalists, this candidate could be elected president with as few as fifteen votes from small-state delegates. A distinct minority in Congress could thereby conspire to select a president who would do its bidding. The United States would have "a government of a faction," not of the people.[35]

The elector system was "rather founded on accident, than any principle of government," in Grayson's words, but it was an accident with a purpose. A last-minute entry at the Federal Convention, it was intended to bypass congressional selection on the one hand and popular election on the other. As Madison stated, the best way to keep people at arm's length from their government was to create "successive filtrations" in the electoral process, and the jumble created by Gouverneur Morris and the Committee of Eleven did precisely that. People elected their state legislators; these men determined the choice of electors in "such manner" as they wished (they could either do it themselves, hold statewide elections, hold district elections, leave the task to county conventions, or whatever); the electors then voted for the president and the vice president; finally, if there was no clear majority, members of the House of Representatives made the final selection from among the finalists selected by electors. Anti-Federalists picked up on the "filtration" scheme and pounced on it. A New York writer calling himself Cato wrote, "It is a maxim in republics, that the representative of the people should be of their immediate choice; but by the manner in which the president is chosen he arrives to this office at the fourth or fifth hand." Republicus, from Kentucky, commented wryly, "An extraordinary refinement this, on the plain simple business of election; and of which the grand convention have certainly the honour of being the first inventors."[36]

The presidential elector system proved difficult to defend. Madison admitted it was a "compromise," and rather than touting its virtues, he mustered no more than a nothing-is-any-better apology. "It is observable," he told the Virginia convention, "that none of the honorable members objecting to this, have pointed out the right mode of election. It was found difficult in the [Federal] Convention, and will be found so by any gentleman who will take the liberty of delineating a mode of electing the president." Madison had a point. Although the elector system lacked any coherent rationale, it was difficult at the time to imagine an acceptable alternative to congressional selection of the president. Popular elections for governors were still regarded as novel, and they were not practiced south of New York. Further, how could popular elections be implemented on a nationwide scale? Who would be allowed to vote—and who could even address the suffrage issue? State legislatures, with their very different qualifications for the franchise? The federal Congress, already suspect for usurping state powers? If the president were actually chosen by popular election—one citizen, one vote—people from small states would fly into a rage. So would southern slave owners, unless they received an extra three-fifths of a vote for each of their slaves. Any new method of selecting the president would have to address the same tangle of problems that puzzled delegates to the Federal Convention. The task was daunting (although not necessarily impossible), and we have no record that anybody at the state conventions tried seriously to work out the details of an answer. Hence, no amendment was offered, and the elector system, strange and rambling as it was, survived as a fallback. Once Morris and the Committee of Eleven concocted the idea, the delegates to the Federal Convention accepted it because they could think of none better, the ratification conventions did likewise, and we are stuck with it today, warts and all.[37]

At the Federal Convention, the most insistent proponent of popular elections had been James Wilson, that unlikely populist who had once fired into a crowd of protesters from his home and subsequently huddled in an attic to escape the people's wrath. Wilson had also been the first to suggest a system of electors, but that was clearly his second choice. Every time the subject came up, he touted the virtues of popular elections for all offices. That was the only way to honor both the letter and the spirit of popular sovereignty that buttressed the new government, he argued. After the convention, however, Wilson changed his stance. Perhaps by way of apology, he tried to explain why the delegates had not opted for popular election of the president. "It was the opinion of a great majority in Convention, that the thing was impracticable" on a nationwide scale, he said. Left unsaid: the "great majority" did not include Wilson, who was repeatedly voted down.[38]

Wilson changed his position on other matters as well. At the convention, he had suggested that the people themselves, not state legislators, should choose their senators; this would make public officials more accountable, he held. He also wanted to give the House some say in ratifying treaties, rather than leave that power exclusively with the Senate. He argued passionately against the "blending" of senatorial and presidential powers, and to counter this, he had supported Mason's call for an executive council. He was worried that under the new configuration, "the President will not be the man of the people as he ought to be, but the minion of the Senate." The Senate had "a dangerous tendency to aristocracy," he said, so he tried repeatedly to tone down its powers.

After the convention, though, Wilson tried his best to sell the plan, even though it included many features he had opposed. No longer worried about the finer points, he became a crusading Federalist. In a major address to some four thousand people gathered at Philadelphia's State House Yard shortly after the Federal Convention submitted its work to the public, Wilson countered George Mason's objections point by point. Suddenly Wilson opposed Mason's council. There was no need for one because the Senate posed no danger, he now said. To counter Mason's prediction that "this government will commence in a moderate aristocracy" and then produce either "a corrupt aristocracy" or a "monarchy," Wilson countered, "Perhaps there never was a charge made with less reasons than that which predicts the institution of a baneful aristocracy in the federal senate"—a charge he himself had made just four weeks earlier.[39]

James Madison, like Wilson, had taken positions at the Federal

Convention that he would not promote later. Madison had been slow to arrive at his views of the presidency. Back in April, before the convention, he had confessed to Washington that he had yet to "form my opinion" about how a national executive "ought to be constituted," nor did he have specific notions about "the authorities with which it ought to be cloathed." Throughout the Federal Convention, the man often called the Father of the Constitution searched for the answer, or rather answers, for in Madison's mind the devil was in the details. While some entertained grand visions for the presidency and others feared those grand visions, Madison sought only to perfect a delicate balance of authority. He neither promoted nor denounced presidential powers with blanket statements; he only wanted to fine-tune them.[40]

Yet Madison's fine-tuning did not coincide with the will of the convention. The threshold for overriding a presidential veto should be three-fourths instead of two-thirds, he said. Fearing senatorial influence on the president, he opposed trying impeachments in the Senate. With Mason and Wilson, he was one of the few who supported a separate executive council. He thought the power to pardon people convicted of treason was "peculiarly improper for the president"; what if the president himself was somehow linked to the case? He thought that a treaty of peace should require only a simple majority of the Senate, not a two-thirds supermajority, and that the Senate should have the authority to conclude a peace treaty without presidential approval, since a president might have too much at stake in the continuation of a war.[41]

Madison lost out on all these matters, so to support ratification, he would have to argue in favor of measures he had once opposed. The Senate did not have too much influence over the president, he would have to say. There was no need for an executive council. No president would ever prolong a war needlessly. People did not have to worry about a president pardoning his friends or co-conspirators, and if ever a president did step out of bounds, the Senate was a suitable body to try his impeachment. Would Madison now be able to argue these points convincingly? Further, could he answer the large and sweeping questions about the presidency, which he might not have fully resolved to his own satisfaction? Perhaps it was best that he allow his partner in persuasion, Alexander Hamilton, to take the lead in explaining the presidency during the ratification debates.

Madison and Hamilton, of course, were the primary authors of the famous Federalist Papers, eighty-five separate essays first published in newspapers and then gathered into two volumes titled *The Federalist*. Hamilton had conceived the idea with his fellow New Yorker John Jay, and they had asked Gouverneur Morris to join them in writing a series of in-depth articles addressing each major component of the proposed Constitution. Morris declined, having retreated from the political scene to pursue his business interests with Robert Morris, but Madison agreed to be the third partner. Then Jay fell ill and was able to contribute only minimally, and that left Madison and Hamilton to take on the bulk of the project.[42]

When these two divided up the various aspects of the Constitution, they decided Hamilton would be the one to tout the virtues of the presidency. "The constitution of the executive department of the proposed government claims next our attention," Hamilton wrote at the outset of *The Federalist* 67, and for the next eleven essays he tried to reassure a suspicious public that they had little to fear from a single chief executive. Issue by issue he addressed recess appointments, the elector system of selection, the four-year term and reeligibility, the absence of a council, the need for a single executive, the presidential veto and presidential pardon, the role of commander in chief, the treaty-making and appointment powers, and so on.

In *The Federalist* 68, Hamilton defended the unique manner of selecting the president, which placed even this full-throated promoter of the Constitution a bit on the defensive. "If the manner of it be not perfect, it is at least excellent," he stated at the outset. In order to extol the virtues of the plan, he revealed that the framers had insisted that the people participate in selecting their president. Since "it was desirable that *the sense of the people* should operate in the choice of the person to whom so important a trust was to be confided," they "referred it in the first instance to an *immediate act of the people*," who would select their "agents in the election." The emphases are mine, but the repetition is his. Over and over Hamilton put the people at the center of the formula. He did speak of electors, but he hid them as best he could behind an assumed populist argument. "The executive should be independent for his continuance in office on all but *the people themselves*," he stated, although in fact it was the electors, not the people, who would choose. From there it was only one small step to factual misrepresentation, and Hamilton did not hesitate to take it. "*The people of each state shall choose a number of persons as electors,*" he wrote flatly. (This was no incidental error; in *The Federalist* 77, he wrote again that the president was selected "by persons *immediately* chosen by the *people*.") According to the actual Constitution, though, the manner of appointment of electors was entirely up to the *legislature* of each state, not the people, and in fact many state legislatures in the early Republic would simply choose electors themselves, leaving "the people" entirely out of the process.

Hamilton was a most unlikely proponent of people power. In the notes he prepared for his monumental speech to the Federal Convention on June 18, he had proposed a strong executive "capable of resisting the popular current" and "the unreasonableness of the people." A prime function of the office was to keep the people in check, he had said back then, and he chastised his fellow delegates for giving up too much ground to democracy: "Gentlemen say we need to be rescued from the democracy. But what the means proposed? A democratic assembly is to be checked by a democratic senate, and both these by a democratic chief magistrate." Now, as he tried to sell the plan to the people, he heralded their alleged participation in the selection of a president, even to the point of distorting the document he was defending.[43]

Before continuing with his itemized list, Hamilton addressed the deep-seated fear that the American president would be a king in sheep's clothing. To do this, in *The Federalist* 69, he first created a caricatured portrait of the British monarchy that Revolutionary-era Americans had embraced in their national narrative. The British king, in Hamilton's depiction, was an absolute tyrant, unchecked in any way by Parliament. Compared with such a monarch, the American president looked benign. Over and over, Hamilton noted that the president possessed no more structural powers than the governor of New York, a not-so-subtle swipe at his political antagonist Governor George Clinton. Of course Hamilton knew better than this, but by pretending that the British Revolution of 1688 had never happened and that British Whigs had absolutely failed in their attempt to create a mixed system, Hamilton turned people's exaggerated fears to his own advantage.

The supreme irony here is that during the Federal Convention, behind closed doors on June 18, Hamilton had claimed "that the British Government was the best in the world; and that he doubted much whether any thing short of it would do in America." Now he boasted there was a "total dissimilitude" between the American president and the "King of Great-Britain, who is an hereditary monarch"; then, in pushing for a strong executive, he had declared the president "ought to be hereditary, and to have so much power, that it will not be his interest to risk much to acquire more." Now he stated, "The qualified negative of the president differs widely from this absolute negative of the British sovereign"; back then, he wanted to give the chief executive an absolute "*negative* upon all laws about to be passed." Now he assured the public that the president "will have only occasional command" of state militias; at the convention, he wanted "the Militia of all the states to be under the sole and exclusive direction" of the United States and its commander in chief, not occasionally, but always.

Why the turnaround? Hamilton was telling people what they wanted to hear. This hardly diminishes the importance of his arguments in *The Federalist*, but magnifies them. We cannot look to Hamilton's essays for insights into the mind of a man whose ideas were deemed unacceptable at the Federal Convention, but when we view them as political documents, they teach us a great deal. Hamilton understood his opposition, and by observing the ways he tried to win it over, we can better understand his audience. Hamilton had learned from his misstep at the convention. This time, he would stay strictly within the mainstream, and his attempt to do so helps us decipher what that mainstream was.

In crafting the Constitution, delegates to the Federal Convention had referred often to what they called "the genius of the people." Edmund Randolph (June 1), George Mason (June 4, 7, and 20), James Wilson (June 7 and 19), Elbridge Gerry (June 12), Charles Pinckney (June 25), and Oliver Ellsworth (August 18) used that term. Afterward, in *The Federalist* (12, 22, 39, and 55), Hamilton and Madison also gave nods to the genius of the people. Many doubted the people's abilities to judge wisely, but Federalists and Anti-Federalists alike realized they would have to address what we call today public opinion. In the ratification debates, each side wanted to influence public opinion, but to do that, they first had to understand it. They needed to know what and how people thought, and that is precisely why we can use Mason's objections, Henry's speeches, Wilson's address at the State House

Yard, and *The Federalist* to help us understand the audiences they were intended to address.

First and foremost, the American public demanded a republican form of government with no vestiges of monarchical or aristocratic prerogatives. Anti-Federalists played on this often, while even Federalists like Hamilton, John Adams, and John Dickinson, who admired Britain's mixed monarchy, had to toe the line. In the notes to his June 18 speech at the Federal Convention, Hamilton had written, "It is said a republican government does not admit a vigorous execution. It [republican government] is therefore bad; for the goodness of a government consists in a vigorous execution." Now, in the opening to *The Federalist* 70, he proclaimed boldly that the idea that "a vigorous executive is inconsistent with the genius of republican government" was "destitute of foundation." That false notion was "not without its advocates," he noted disdainfully, even though he had been one of them. Hamilton would have been immediately rejected by his potential audience had he *not* proclaimed his support for republican principles and argued that the proposed Constitution implemented them.

At first glance, it would appear the nation's embrace of republican principles favored Anti-Federalists. Republican government meant limited government, and this played into the hands of Patrick Henry and others who warned that the new form would be too large, too strong, and potentially too intrusive. "Liberty and property," the rallying cry of the prewar protest movement, was deeply ingrained in America's political culture. If citizens were to make a new contract with their government, they wanted to prevent that government from taking what they already had. So when Federalists argued for a stronger government, and in particular for a strong and independent executive arm, they needed to reassure the public that the government could still be held close by and accountable. The people would control the president, they had to declare. Hence Hamilton's dramatic change of tone from the convention to the ratification debates and his deliberate misrepresentation of the electoral process.

Federalists, too, used republican principles to their advantage. One way to limit the abuse of governmental power was to separate the branches of government and allow them to check each other. Both sides cited Montesquieu on this. While Anti-Federalists argued that the separation of powers was blurred in the proposed Constitution, Federalists claimed that the newly created office of the president could counteract "legislative tyranny." Under the Articles of Confederation, Congress *was* the government, and even at the state level legislatures dominated other branches. With a weak or nonexistent executive, there was no parity. People had therefore grown accustomed to blaming Congress or state legislatures for any complaints about government, and Federalists found these bodies were easy targets. "Legislative authority" tended to "absorb every other," Hamilton wrote in *The Federalist* 71. State assemblies "seem sometimes to fancy that they are the people themselves, and betray strong symptoms of impatience and disgust at the least sign of opposition from any other quarter." Worse yet, legislative bodies were prone to "the spirit of faction," as Hamilton observed in *The Federalist* 73. When a faction took over the legislature, and then the legislature ruled unchecked, the few could control the many—but not under the new plan, Hamilton declared. An independent president would be "a salutary check upon the legislative body, calculated to guard the community against the effects of faction."

Anti-Federalists, like Federalists, railed against "faction." The Senate was dangerous because it was so small, insular, and enduring. Senators, who were not elected by the people, would serve long terms with no accountability. Isolated within their chamber, they could scheme and connive; in the end, a tiny group would prevail and wield immense power. The House, too, was prone to faction. As we have seen, William Grayson revealed how a few congressmen from small states could manipulate the elector system to choose the president and create "a government of a faction." Today, we decry partisanship and Washington insiders; in the founding era, people likewise derided the spirit of faction or the spirit of party. Congress bashing, a favorite political sport today, has deep roots dating from the founding era. Then, as now, it was practiced across the political spectrum, uniting Americans in an odd assault on their own government.

Here at last was a point of agreement. If the Constitution did in fact become the law of the land, the president, who was responsible to the nation as a whole, might be able to counterbalance the tendency for factions to rule. Federalists promised this, and Anti-Federalists could at least take solace in it. If a president could avoid becoming the tool of Congress, he might just be able to keep factions at bay. That was certainly the thinking of the two men who pushed hardest at the Federal

Convention to establish the executive's independence from the legislature. Gouverneur Morris insisted the president should be "the general guardian of the National interests," while James Wilson wanted him "to stand the mediator" between factions. Citizens of all persuasions could unite around that ideal.[44]

In the end, not enough Americans feared the presidency with sufficient zeal to prevent ratification. Some tried to place limits on a president's time in office, and a few tried to guard against his military muscle, but no changes were made. The presidency survived intact, exactly as it emerged from the Federal Convention. Yet for the Constitution's opponents, all was not lost. During the ratification debates, Anti-Federalists complained that George Washington, above reproach and therefore unchallengeable, had lined up against them; after ratification, though, Washington suddenly turned into an ally of sorts. He appeared fair, honorable, and not vindictive. Their problems with the presidential office had stemmed not from its likely first occupant but from powers that might be abused later. So when Washington agreed to serve, Anti-Federalists believed they might receive at least a temporary reprieve. The first president would line up squarely against party and faction. He would not let one group, in this case his Federalist friends, dominate another, even if they had been his opponents.

This was the hope, at any rate. It was not an unreasonable one. Washington did have the good of the nation at heart, no doubt about that. He understood that the American people, currently divided, needed to be healed and united, and he even threw his support behind a Bill of Rights, which many of his fellow Federalists staunchly resisted. That was certainly a start, but overcoming differences would not come easily. Issues would inevitably emerge, and with them factions and parties. The notion that one man, exercising transcendent leadership, could somehow put the brakes on divisiveness would soon be put to the test.

CHAPTER SEVEN

The Launch

On the first day of 1789, George Washington wrote to William Pierce, a fellow delegate to the Federal Convention, who was soliciting an appointment as collector for the port of Savannah. Washington "sincerely & fervently" hoped not "to have any agency in the disposal of federal appointments"—meaning, of course, he did not wish to be chosen for the office of president. "Should it (contrary to my wishes) fall upon me, I shall certainly be disposed to decline the acceptance, if it may, by any means, be done consistently with the dictates of duty." Yet the very next day, Washington informed James Madison he had something private he wished to send him, so private that he could not entrust it to "an uncertain conveyance." This turned out to be a seventy-three-page rambling draft of an inaugural address he would deliver to Congress, should he become president. At first glance, the two letters seem contradictory and perhaps even hypocritical, but in fact they were both honest and heartfelt, if not exactly forthright. Washington did not seek the job and seemed genuinely to wish that "some other person" be elected who could "fully execute all the duties full as satisfactory as myself"; on the other hand, he knew very well that nobody else would be able to unite a divided nation, and uniting the nation was first and foremost among a president's responsibilities. This was a momentous and pivotal moment. If he shirked his duty now, "some very disagreeable consequences" might ensue. "For the good of my country," and to receive the respect of his countrymen, which he had always desired and some say craved, he really had no choice.[1]

Washington never did deliver that particular address, which in the next century was torn to pieces by Jared Sparks, the noted collector and editor of Washington's writings, and handed out bit by bit to autograph seekers. Enough shreds have been recovered to give a sense of the work, in which the first president endeavored to exculpate himself from the apparent sin of assuming the office. It would undoubtedly have been the most apologetic inaugural address in history ("From the bottom of my soul, I know, that my motives on no former moment were more innocent than in the present instance") and perhaps the most philosophical ("If a promised good should terminate in an unexpected evil, it would not be a solitary example of disappointment in this mutable state of existence").

The actual speech Washington delivered to Congress on April 30, after his inevitable election and reluctant acquiescence, was much shorter but no less unassuming. He professed his own "deficiencies" in "civil administration," appealed to "that Almighty Being who rules over the Universe," and renounced "every pecuniary consideration" for his service. After reminding congressmen that the president was empowered by the Constitution to recommend "such measures as he shall judge necessary and expedient," he offered a few words of avuncular advice: embrace "no local prejudices, or attachments; no separate views, or party animosities," and act according to "the pure and immutable principles of private morality." That was the extent of the direction offered by the first president of the United States—almost. Cleverly, he declined to weigh in explicitly on the most disputed topic of the hour— whether to amend the Constitution—but his manner of doing so left no doubt where he stood. While he assumed Congress would "carefully avoid every alteration which might endanger the benefits of an united and effective Government," he likewise assumed it would display "a reverence for the characteristic rights of freemen, and a regard for the public harmony" and figure out how such rights and harmony should be "safely and advantageously promoted." No representative or senator in Federal Hall, the newly renovated home for Congress, could mistake the message: protect the structure of the Constitution, but avoid further discord by ceding to Anti-Federalist demands for a Bill of Rights.[2]

This is how Washington hoped to lead, gently and by example. He would take the government and the people by the hand and show them the high moral ground. Together, under his tutelage, the people and their representatives would eschew selfish interests and work toward the good of the whole. "Party animosities" and "local prejudices" constituted the greatest impediment to effective governance, and the overarching goal of the president must be to keep these at bay.

After Washington delivered his address, the new president and members of Congress repaired to St. Paul's Chapel to attend "divine service." The Senate then returned to its chamber and appointed a three-man committee to draft a response to "his most gracious speech," as Vice President John Adams, presiding over the Senate, called it. Pennsylvania's prickly Anti-Federalist William Maclay, though, took offense at the honorary words "his most gracious." They were "the same that are usually placed before the speech of his Britannic Majesty," he noted; their use by the Senate would "give offense" to the people, who had just endured "a hard struggle for our liberty against kingly authority." In his journal, which contains the most detailed extant account of the first Senate, Maclay recounted the sharp debate that ensued between himself and Adams, who saw no reason to object to a practice simply because it had been used by "that Government under which we had lived so long and happily formerly." Herein lay the source of much tension, which the Federal Convention and the ratification debates had not finally resolved. Would the office of the presidency be entirely removed from monarchical connotations, or was there some merit in the pomp and circumstance that commanded elevated respect and anchored and unified the people of Great Britain?[3]

Maclay won that initial symbolic skirmish, and "his most gracious" was stricken from the record, but another such battle, larger and more significant, soon followed. Several senators, supported with zest by the body's president, John Adams, reasoned that granting the president some lofty title would "add greatly to the weight and authority of the Government both at home and abroad." Various suggestions were offered: "Excellency" (a title already applied to state governors and to General Washington, when he was commander in chief during the war), "Elective Highness," and finally "His Highness the President of the United States of America, and Protector of Their Liberties," a convoluted title embracing both monarchical and republican connotations.

Maclay, of course, adamantly rejected any such "high-sounding, pomp-ous appellation," while Adams argued that calling the chief executive officer simply "President" was demeaning because "there were presi-dents of fire companies and of a cricket club." For the better part of several days, May 8 and 9 and again on May 14 and 15, senators sparred, with Adams emerging victorious this time around. Yet "His Highness" was exactly the sort of haughty tone that Anti-Federalists had feared from the upper house of Congress, and with an early application of the Constitution's checks and balances the House refused to go along with any title beyond "President of the United States of America." Although the lofty title failed to make it all the way through Congress, the very idea of it exacerbated unhealed wounds. David Stuart, who regularly kept Washington apprised of the political mood in Virginia, informed the president, "Nothing could equal the ferment and disqui-etude, occasioned by the proposition respecting titles. As it is believed to have originated from Mr. Adams & [Richard Henry] Lee, they are not only unpopular to an extreme, but highly odious. Neither I am convinced, will ever get a vote from this State again." Further, Senate approval of "His Highness" was construed by Virginia Anti-Federalists as "verification of their prophecies about the tendency of government. Mr. Henry's description of it, that it squinted toward monarchy, is in every mouth, and has established him in the general opinion, as a true Prophet."[4]

However powerful the office of the president might become, Washington had no official duties during his early months in office. The primary function of the chief executive was to execute the laws, but Congress had yet to pass any legislation. The president was also supposed to appoint judges, but Congress hadn't created any courts, so there were no judgeships to fill and of course no federal criminals to pardon. The president was empowered to "require the Opinion, in writing, of the principal Officer in each of the executive Departments," but there were no such departments and hence no such officers. Theo-retically, Washington could negotiate a treaty, but he would have to do so without any executive infrastructure and "with the Advice and Con-sent of the Senate," whatever that might entail. There were only two powers he could exercise on his own: he could receive ambassadors if some should arrive at his doorstep, and as commander in chief he could issue orders to the 682 federal troops scattered in six western outposts and the arsenals at West Point and Springfield. This was the extent of his discretionary authority.[5]

While there was little of substance to command his attention, Washington busied himself with establishing presidential protocol "in all matters of business & etiquette." Fully appreciating the symbolic importance of his office, he tried to discover the proper balance between "too free an intercourse and too much familiarity" on the one hand and "an ostentatious show" of monarchical detachment on the other. How, and how often, should he make himself accessible to the public, to members of Congress, or to personal friends? Should he participate in "great entertainments" on national holidays, and if so, which ones? Would it be appropriate to tour the country during recesses of Congress? "Many things which appear of little importance in themselves and at the beginning, may have great and durable consequences from their having been established at the commencement of a new general Government," he believed. Whatever he did would establish a precedent; collectively, these precedents would set the tone of the presidential office and help define the relationship between the people and their government. Washington's first job as president, then, was to establish what it meant to be a president. He solicited advice from James Madison, Alexander Hamilton, John Adams, John Jay, and Robert R. Livingston, and in the end he developed "a discriminating medium," as he called it, that suited him well. Yes, he would meet the public, but only at specified times and in appropriate venues. He would be the people's friend, but he would also "preserve the dignity & respect . . . due to the first Magistrate."[6]

While Washington established presidential protocol and considered applications for posts that did not yet exist, Congress alone conducted the pressing business of government. First on its agenda was raising money for operations, without which all else would be futile. For over two months it debated a list of import duties, each of which angered some particular constituency. Also, to placate Anti-Federalists, some congressmen wanted to develop a Bill of Rights; if Congress failed to introduce any amendments to the new Constitution, state conventions would likely do so instead, and these might attempt to tinker with the body of the document. Further, it fell to Congress to establish the remainder of the federal edifice. Neither the executive branch (save for the president) nor the judicial branch would even exist until the legislative branch created it. As David Humphreys and Washington stated in their first draft of the inaugural address, Congress was "the first wheel of the government—a wheel which communicates motion to all the rest."[7]

In the process of establishing the various executive departments, Congress hotly debated the balance of power between the legislative and the executive branches, a prominent issue at the Federal Convention and the subject of some controversy during the ratification debates. At issue was the "Advice and Consent" phrase in the second paragraph of Article II, Section 2 of the Constitution. The president was empowered to "nominate" major public officials—these included ambassadors, Supreme Court justices, and "other public Ministers and Consuls," commonly understood to include the heads of executive departments, but these would not become official appointments until approved by the Senate. This compromise, pushed by the Committee of Eleven near the end of the Federal Convention, failed to resolve a major question: Who, if anyone, held the power of *removal*? Whoever possessed authority to dismiss an executive officer could effectively control that person's actions, yet the framers, in a rush to complete their work, had entirely overlooked the issue.

On June 16, a Tuesday, the House of Representatives took up a committee's draft for the creation of the Department of Foreign Affairs, to be headed by a secretary of foreign affairs who would be "removable from office by the President of the United States." This phrase, which followed a list of the secretary's duties, excited far more interest than the duties themselves, and Alexander White of Virginia moved to strike it out. White and several others explained why. "If the Senate are associated with the President in the appointment, they ought also to be associated in the dismission from office," they reasoned, and Congress therefore had "no right to deprive the Senate of their constitutional prerogative." This was not only constitutional law but also sound policy. Senators, with their long terms, were intended to provide stability; they would prevent a president from arbitrarily removing officers who were adequately performing their jobs. "A change of the Chief Magistrate, therefore, would not occasion so violent or so general a revolution in the officers of the Government, as might be expected if he were the sole disposer of offices."

Some speakers also argued that the Constitution *did* provide for the dismissal of federal officers: "The President, Vice President, and all civil Officers of the United States, shall be removed from Office on Impeachment for, and Conviction of, Treason, Bribery, or other high Crimes and Misdemeanors." Although this seemed to compete with the notion that the Senate and the president, without the House, would share the power of removal, at least it kept the power out of the hands of the president alone. At first glance, the impeachment argument appeared sound, for "all civil Officers" would certainly include the secretary of foreign affairs and other heads of departments that Congress was about to create, but in fact it carried little weight. The standards for impeachment were strict, while it was easily argued that officers should sometimes be removed for less heinous offenses. Inability to perform a job adequately should be sufficient grounds for removal, although not impeachment. So the question remained: Who, exactly, would remove the heads of executive departments, the president alone or the president with the advice and consent of the Senate?[8]

James Madison offered a cogent defense of presidential removal power. First, he noted that where the Constitution was "silent," as it was in this case, "an exposition of the constitution may come with as much propriety from the Legislature, as any other department of the Government." Then he offered his own "exposition," based on the first sentence of Article II of the Constitution, "The executive Power shall be vested in a President." Each branch was to remain distinct unless otherwise stipulated, and although the Constitution did allow some instances of shared power, whenever these were not explicitly stated, executive functions, including removal of executive officers, must revert to the executive department, headed by the president. Like his opponents, Madison argued his approach was not only constitutionally sound but also good policy. The president was "appointed at present by the suffrages of three millions of people," and that number would soon increase as the population expanded. "With all the infirmities incident to a popular election, corrected by the particular mode of conducting it, as directed under the present system, I think we may fairly calculate that the instances will be very rare in which an unworthy man will receive that mark of the public confidence which is required to designate the President of the United States." The president, in other words, was to be trusted to exercise the power of removal judiciously because he would be a trustworthy person, certified by the people through what he euphemistically called the "particular mode" of presidential selection by electors. Here was a sweeping endorsement of all presidential powers, based on the assumption that the president alone represented *all* the people. Madison would soon come to question this line of reasoning in other matters, but for now he stuck to a rather circular logic: powers could safely be granted to the president because the Constitution had done such a marvelous job in ensuring he would be a good man.

Madison used another line of reasoning as well. If the president required the concurrence of the Senate before removing an executive officer, that officer could ensure his tenure in office simply by courting the approval of the majority of senators. The secretary of foreign affairs and other important officials would thus come under the sway of legislators instead of the chief executive, and executive accountability would be lost. Department heads could endure in office indefinitely, while the president had to stand for reelection every four years. The entire notion of a single chief executive would thus be undermined, or, in Madison's dramatic words, "the power of the President" would be reduced "to a mere vapor."[9]

The dispute continued. With the original document "silent" on the matter, each representative had a chance to say his piece, and most did. For members of the House who had attended the Federal Convention, arguing over the proper balance of power among the branches must have felt familiar, and for those who had not participated in framing the Constitution, here was their chance. One after another weighed in, and as they did, speakers on both sides vied with each other for who could best convey the overwhelming sense of gravitas. "The decision that is at this time made, will become the permanent exposition of the constitution; and on a permanent exposition of the constitution will depend the genius and character of the whole Government," Madison said. "I own to you, Mr. Chairman, that I feel great anxiety upon this question . . . because I am called upon to give a decision in a case that may affect the fundamental principles of the Government under which we act, and liberty itself." Not to be outdone, Georgia's James Jackson declared, "The liberties of my country may be suspended on the decision of this question," but top honors probably went to Richard Bland Lee, cousin to Richard Henry Lee. "The day on which this question shall be decided will be a memorable day, not only in the history of our own times, but in the history of mankind," Lee predicted. "On a proper or improper decision, will be involved the future happiness or misery of the people of America."[10]

Notwithstanding the hyperbole and seemingly pervasive sense of self-importance, this was in fact an issue of lasting significance. If Congress decided one way, department heads would be under the direct command of the president, and there would in fact be a single chief executive; if it decided the other way, executive department heads would wind up either answering to the Senate or playing the Senate against the president, effectively creating fiefdoms within their respective fields of authority. Whether or not any of these scenarios would spell an end to liberty or result in the happiness or misery of the American people, resolution of the removal debate would fundamentally shape the distribution of authority in the newly created government. Pending the outcome, there would or would not be an institution resembling what we now call the president's cabinet.

On a matter deemed this critical, no representative dared call the question to end discussion until midway through the third day of debates, and even then, when some tried, Thomas Sumter from South Carolina "begged gentlemen not to be so precipitate" and then warned them sternly, "If they considered the importance of the question, and the consequences of the decision, they would reflect more deliberately before they gave their votes." Whether reflections and deliberations continued, the rhetoric certainly did, and nobody tried to stop it for another day and a half, even though there is no indication that a single member wavered the slightest from his prior position. Finally, late on Friday afternoon, after four full days of debates (captured in 125 pages of the *Annals of Congress*), the motion to strike "to be removable from office by the President of the United States" failed by a vote of 34 to 20. No other phrase, clause, or sentence commanded such attention or excited such passion during the First Federal Congress; even the Bill of Rights, the lack of which had almost doomed the Constitution, failed to occupy Congress as fully as the great removal debate.[11]

And that debate was not yet over. After passing the House, the president's power to remove the secretary of foreign affairs (and by implication other department heads) was taken up by the Senate, where it faced tougher resistance. Senators, unlike representatives, had a stake in the matter: they would gain immeasurable influence over the governmental apparatus if they insisted on a share of removal power. Throughout history, few governmental bodies had opted for less power instead of more, but would the fledgling U.S. Senate do so now? Only a strong dose of disinterested republican virtue, a firm ideological commitment to the need for greater executive authority, or an anticipation of increased favors from the executive would cause senators to vote against their apparent self-interest.

The Senate debate commenced on July 14 and lasted three days, but unfortunately, because the Senate met behind closed doors, the only record of their debates is William Maclay's one-sided journal, in which he gives himself center stage. "It is a maxim in legislation as well as reason," Maclay told his colleagues, "that it requires the same power to repeal as to enact. The depriving power should be the same as the appointing power." This was the opposition's bare-bones argument. To represent the opposing view, Maclay in his journal summarized a speech by Connecticut's Oliver Ellsworth: "I buy a square acre of land. I buy the trees, water, and everything belonging to it. The executive power belongs to the President. The removing of officers is a tree on this acre. The power of removing is, therefore, his. It is in him. It is nowhere else." In Maclay's account, Vice President Adams played a major role, not by making speeches, but by cajoling wavering senators. "Everybody believed that John Adams was the great converter," Maclay wrote, and Adams did more than convert. The final vote was ten in favor and ten opposed, so Adams, exercising for the first time his constitutional authority to break a tie, settled the matter in favor of the president's exclusive removal power. This caused Virginia's Anti-Federalist William Grayson to lament, "The matter predicted by Mr. Henry is now coming to pass: consolidation is the object of the new Government."[12]

For want of a single vote in the Senate, the presidency might have been fundamentally altered. Imagine the secretary of state and other cabinet officials responsible equally to the Senate and to the president. Although it is difficult to second-guess history, at the very least this would have led the Senate to become more involved in executive matters. Possibly, too, department heads would not have changed with each administration, and this continuity across administrations would naturally have diminished a president's control over policy issues. That, in turn, might have lessened the politicization of executive matters, or conversely it might have heightened politicization by involving the Senate. All this is conjectural, but this we know: the president's cabinet, if it existed at all, would not be the same as it is today.[13]

The removal debate was truly a continuation of the Federal Convention. One-third of the men who had framed the Constitution took part in this unexpected sequel. Half of the Senate's twenty members were convention veterans, along with eight representatives in the House. Of these eighteen men, twelve thought the president should have exclusive removal powers and six did not. Disagreement of this order was hardly new—most issues at the convention had been contested as well—but the notion that the Constitution had neglected to address an issue with such significant implications was unnerving. Yes, framers and other supporters of the Constitution had readily admitted that the document was not perfect and would probably have to be amended to suit future needs, but they thought they had provided clear enough instructions to start the government rolling, and they had not.[14]

Key to the problem was the Constitution's vague term "Advice and Consent," with no further exposition of what that might mean—how and when advice might be given, how and when consent was to be determined, a more precise stipulation of the extent of the powers the president and the Senate were to share, and some basic guidelines for their implementation. In retrospect, if not at the time, it is not surprising that the lack of clarity would lead to unresolved issues that required clarification.

Less than a month after the removal debate, the "Advice and Consent" clause was again put to the challenge. President Washington and his temporary secretary of war, Henry Knox, a holdover from the confederation government until Congress established a new Department of War, wanted to stabilize relations with Indian nations on the southern borderlands. Spain, which controlled the Mississippi River and was offering arms and trade to southern Indians, now presented a significant impediment to American expansion, so the neutralization of the Creeks, Cherokees, Chickasaws, and Choctaws was a top priority of the new American government. This was difficult, though, because white Americans were steadily encroaching on Indian lands from the east. Negotiations were in order. Treaties needed to be made and upheld, but according to the Constitution the president could only "make Treaties . . . by and with the Advice and Consent of the Senate." Today, we assume that the president first concludes a treaty and then brings it to the Senate for "consent." At the time, though, Washington and anybody else who took the Constitution at face value reasoned that "by and with the Advice . . . of the Senate" required him to seek senatorial input before or during treaty negotiations, not just afterward.

That is why President Washington and Secretary Knox, on the morning of August 22, 1789, a Saturday, entered the Senate chamber to seek that body's advice. Indian commissioners were scheduled to meet with Creek leaders on September 15, and before that meeting they needed instructions from those who set policy, the president and the Senate. To this end, Washington composed a letter explaining the recent history of white-Indian relations in the region, followed by an extensive list of specific questions he wished senators to consider. The problem, it seems, was that Creeks had supposedly ceded land in three treaties concluded with Georgia in 1783, 1785, and 1786; whites had then moved onto those lands, but Creek leaders now denied "the validity of the said treaties." How should the commissioners proceed if they concluded the treaties had been "formed with an inadequate or unauthorized representation of the Creek Nation" or were signed "under circumstances of constraint or unfairness of any sort"? Should they insist on a new treaty, and if so, what concessions should they offer in return for land that was already being claimed by white Georgians? Washington posed a dozen such questions concerning the Creeks and three more that addressed ongoing relations with Cherokees, Chickasaws, and Choctaws.[15]

Again, we have only one full-throated account of what happened inside the Senate chamber that day, composed of course by William Maclay, whose journal so often mocked the official proceedings. Maclay never came down sternly on Washington, but he refused to accord the president the deference offered by others. He had described the president's inaugural address in cartoonish terms—"agitated and embarrassed more than ever he was by the leveled cannon or pointed musket," Washington had supposedly trembled, fidgeted with his fingers, and gestured with an awkward flourish, leaving "an ungainly impression"—and now too Maclay sought to reveal the comic elements in an allegedly staid and somber venue. This time Washington chose not to read his letter but handed it instead to Adams, who read it in his capacity as president of the Senate. According to Maclay, Adams "hurried over the paper" in such a manner that nobody could hear: "Carriages were driving past, and such a noise, I could tell it was something about 'Indians,' but was not master of one sentence of it." Robert Morris asked Adams to read the letter again, and then, immediately, Adams repeated the first item and "put the question: 'Do you advise and consent, etc.?'" When nobody rose to speak, Maclay, the Senate's designated gadfly, stepped up. If he had not done so, he worried, "we should have these advises and consents ravished, in a degree, from us."

"The business is new to the Senate," Maclay said. "It is of importance. It is our duty to inform ourselves as well as possible on the subject. I therefore call for the reading of the treaties and other documents alluded to in the paper before us." Maclay thought Washington evinced "an aspect of stern displeasure" at his attempt to slow down the process, but the president's feelings notwithstanding, the senator prevailed, and he and his colleagues began to consider the items point by point. There were so many documents to be read and points to be considered, however, that the Senate decided to send the matter to a committee and take it up at its next session on Monday, two days hence. According to Maclay, that proved too much for Washington. "This defeats every purpose of my coming here," he supposedly said. He then "cooled by degrees," but he departed soon thereafter with "a discontented air."

Washington's appearance on the Senate floor was a flop by anybody's standards. Maclay thought it inappropriate for the president "to tread on the necks of the Senate":

> I saw no chance of a fair investigation of subjects while the President of the United States sat there, with his Secretary of War, to support his opinions and overawe the timid and neutral part of the Senate. . . . He wishes us to see with the eyes and hear with the ears of his Secretary only. The Secretary to advance the premise, the President to draw the conclusions, and to bear down our deliberations with his personal authority and presence. Form alone will be left to us. This will not do with Americans.[16]

Undoubtedly, Washington was just as displeased with the encounter. He was no stranger to seeking advice, but not in a venue such as this. On countless occasions during the Revolution the commander in chief had convened his war council; never did he take that body's advice lightly, and often he allowed it to overrule him. Then, however, he was dealing with colleagues who shared both the information he had at his disposal and a certain level of professional expertise relevant to the items under consideration, whereas now members of the Senate were ill informed and not particularly conversant in the matters placed before them. Collectively, they saw themselves as a deliberative body; individually, each valued philosophical correctness and speechifying, sometimes at the expense of taking action. Was this really the right body to issue advice? And even if it were, what was to be gained by the president sitting through the arduous process?

The August 22 convergence of the executive and the legislative branches raised a serious question about the constitutional role of the Senate: Did it, or did it not, perform the function of an executive council? George Mason, at the Federal Convention and during the ratification debates, had lamented the absence of a separate and independent executive council, and here was a reason why. "Advice and Consent" might be a handy phrase, but this meeting revealed that offering advice and granting consent are two very different activities. If Washington sought only consent, he would have negotiated treaties first and then brought them to the Senate for ratification, as is done today, but the president asked for advice, as the Constitution stipulated, and to give advice, the Senate needed time to study the matter and engage in meaningful deliberations, which could not happen during one brief encounter. In this instance the Senate, with Washington again in attendance, resumed considerations two days later and responded to his questions, affirming his intentions on most but not all of the items, but the incident set a poor precedent. Would senators suspend their normal operations and take a rush course in diplomacy each and every time the executive department wanted to enter into negotiations with an Indian or European nation? How could they be kept apprised of the intricacies of international councils that might well occur on the other side of the Atlantic? Most critically, was this really the proper role of the upper house of the *legislature*?

The notion that the Senate would do the job of an executive council proved unworkable the first time it was put to the test. That body could serve as a check on the president's power to negotiate treaties, but it was not particularly suited to offer counsel. Fortuitously, by affirming the president's right to remove department heads, Congress had just facilitated the creation of a separate body of advisers who *would* offer counsel: the president's "Cabinet Council," as it was called in the early Republic. Although the word "cabinet" did not enter common usage for another four years, the outcome of the removal debate confirmed that the president would be able to work closely with his department heads, who would function as his inferiors. Washington would make full use of these officers. Setting precedent in this as in all other matters, he would consult them frequently, using the expertise of each in his particular field while also seeking their collective advice on a host of issues. In today's parlance, they would be his team, his administration.

First, though, the Congress needed to finish creating the various executive departments, Washington had to choose the men he wished to head them, and the Senate then had to confirm his nominations. This all happened at the tail end of Congress's first session. For secretary of state the president chose his fellow Virginian Thomas Jefferson, the former governor of Virginia and experienced minister to France whom Washington had worked with in the Virginia House of Burgesses before the war. Henry Knox, who had served as Washington's chief of artillery during the Revolution and succeeded him as commander in chief at war's end, continued in his role as secretary of war. Washington offered the job of secretary of the Treasury first to the one and only "Financier," Robert Morris, the nation's most experienced administrator who had led the country out of bankruptcy at the close of the war; when Morris declined, he tapped the prodigy Alexander Hamilton, the general's former aide-de-camp who had served under Morris during the Financier's "reign" and who would pursue Morris's nationalistic economic agenda. The last major position, attorney general, went to Edmund Randolph, who had been Virginia's attorney general for a decade before he became its governor; although Randolph had not signed the Constitution, his support for ratification had been critical at the Virginia convention the following year. (Absent from the list was James Madison, certainly one of Washington's closest advisers, who was invaluable to the president as an emissary in the House of Representatives.) Although highly consequential, Washington's selections provoked no immediate controversy, and senatorial confirmations proceeded smoothly. Even Hamilton, who had aroused some controversy during the ratification debates for his allegedly monarchical views and whose policies would soon prove so divisive, breezed through the Senate without opposition.

By September 29, when Congress adjourned its first session, two branches of the new government had performed the jobs expected of them. Washington had set the tone, established protocols and precedents, and appointed the team that would anchor his administration. Congress, faced with a heavier agenda, had set import duties, sent a Bill of Rights to the states for ratification, settled the delicate constitutional issue of removal, established executive departments and a federal judicial system that included district courts to maintain local integrity, and confirmed Washington's appointments to his cabinet and to the Supreme Court. The judiciary still existed on paper only, but the legislative and executive branches of government were up and running. Two weeks later Washington reported to Gouverneur Morris, who was tending to business in London and Paris, "It may not be unpleasing to you to hear in one word that the national government is organized, and as far as my information goes, to the satisfaction of all parties— That opposition to it is either no more, or hides its head." This was Washington's dream: a nation coming together around shared principles. To achieve such a result was the very reason he had accepted the presidency.[17]

Six days after Congress's adjournment, Washington noted in his diary: "Had conversation with Colo. Hamilton on the propriety of my making a tour through the Eastern states during the recess of Congress to acquire knowledge of the face of the Country the growth and agriculture there of and the temper and disposition of the inhabitants towards the new government." Hamilton "thought it a very desirable plan and advised it accordingly," as did Knox the following day. Left unsaid, but certainly understood: the tour would undoubtedly *promote* a positive "temper and disposition" of New Englanders "towards the new government." Knowing he would enhance national unity by his very presence, Washington traveled more than five hundred miles on dirt and stone-studded roads, viewed the countryside, and visited sixty cities and towns in Connecticut, Massachusetts, and New Hampshire from mid-October to mid-November. In each one, proud Americans celebrated the new president and by implication the new government. It was a triumphal tour. While celebrants thought they were honoring their great leader, that leader treated their celebration as one more affirmation that the Constitution was working.[18]

Although Washington gave the debut of the new government a glowing review, the unveiling of the American presidency was not an unqualified success. As evidenced by the removal and treaty issues, the Constitution left some questions unanswered, and these would not be the only ones. Other issues were likely to surface, and as they did, they would be debated by Congress, the judiciary, and the public. The document the framers created was not some algorithm that could be dutifully followed to achieve optimum results. Instead, by necessity, it would have to be treated as an incomplete and therefore evolving guide that pointed in a general direction but left more room than some might prefer for interpretation—and, like it or not, discretion.

CHAPTER EIGHT

Washington and the Challenge to Transcendent Leadership

At the Federal Convention, Gouverneur Morris, pushing to shape an independent presidency, had suggested a subtle but highly significant change in wording. As of August 24, the working draft stated that the president "*shall*, from time to time, give information to the legislature, of the state of the Union," and "*may* recommend to their consideration such measures as he shall deem necessary, and expedient." Why only "may"? It should be the chief executive's "*duty*" to make recommendations to Congress, Morris argued. To "prevent umbrage or cavil" when a president tried to initiate legislation, Morris moved to strike out the word "may," and he had his way without debate. The impact of this small change was monumental. At Morris's request, Article II, Section 3 of the U.S. Constitution states unequivocally that the president *shall* take a lead role in shaping public policy.

Dutifully, in pursuance to the constitutional demands on his office, President Washington prepared a brief and carefully worded message to the second session of the First Federal Congress, which convened early in January 1790. In the nation's first State of the Union address, Washington outlined with broad strokes the path he wished Congress to take. Save for Morris's attention to detail more than two years earlier, Washington would have had to tread lightly, fearful of being accused of meddling. As it was, the president could speak his mind, respectfully but forcefully.

Washington "read his speech well," noted the acerbic William Maclay, usually a harsh critic. His suit was jet-black, suggestive to Maclay of mourning clothes and befitting the solemn occasion. To the president's right stood the Senate and its president, John Adams; to his left were members of the House and their Speaker, Frederick Muhlenberg, a Lutheran pastor from Pennsylvania, along with the department heads, Knox, Jefferson, Hamilton, and Randolph. At this early stage, with federal judges yet to be sworn in and an administrative machinery yet to take hold, this small audience—fewer than one hundred men—constituted the full extent of the federal government.[1]

Washington's speech was short, scarcely three printed pages, and "hastily" delivered within ten minutes. After an uplifting introduction—"I embrace with great satisfaction the opportunity, which now presents itself, of congratulating you on the present favourable prospects of our public affairs"—the president succinctly cataloged a dozen items he wished Congress to consider in its "consultations for the public good." Topping the list, predictably, were military matters. "Providing for the common defence will merit particular regard," he told the legislative branch of the federal government. To effect this, he called on Congress to provide "comfortable support of the officers and soldiers," establish a uniform plan of military discipline, station troops in the West, and promote the domestic manufacture of military supplies. He asked, too, for funds to support a team of foreign ambassadors and emissaries. His domestic agenda included a "uniform rule of naturalization"; uniform currency, weights, and measures; "due attention" to a post office and post roads; and "the advancement of agriculture, commerce and manufacture, by all proper means." He dwelled the longest on the need to promote "science and literature." Since knowledge, he said, "is in every country the surest basis of public happiness" and the best "security of a free Constitution," education served "every valuable end of government." Citizens needed to learn how to "distinguish between oppression and the necessary exercise of lawful authority" and to "discriminate the spirit of liberty from that of licentiousness, cherishing the first, avoiding the last." Washington did not specify an exact program—the public good might be "best promoted by affording aids to seminaries of learning already established, by the institution of a national university, or by any other expedients"—but he left no doubt that in his mind, the "necessary and proper" clause of the Constitution covered governmental support of education.[2]

Then, for his final recommendation, Washington directed his words exclusively to the "Gentlemen of the House of Representatives." He noted "with peculiar pleasure" that the House, just before adjourning in September, had directed Secretary of the Treasury Alexander Hamilton to prepare a plan "for the support of the public credit." The president had nothing specific to say on the matter, but he wished to emphasize the subject's importance, and he entreated the House, which was empowered by the Constitution to take the lead in all money bills, to involve "the other branch of the Legislature" in its considerations. It was "superfluous," he said, to raise a matter in which "the character and permanent interests of the United States are so obviously and so deeply concerned," but raise it he did. How could he not? Without credit, the new government would cease to function.

Washington's address, no doubt intentionally, served as the perfect setup for Hamilton, who finalized his report the very next day. Five days after that, on January 14, Hamilton submitted his findings and suggestions directly to Congress—*not* to the president. From our present perspective, the order of communications and chain of command appear curious, but Congress had commissioned the report and Congress would receive it. We have no indication that Washington was directly, or even indirectly, involved. The president had selected Hamilton because of his studied expertise in finances, a field in which Washington possessed no special knowledge. Implicit in the nomination was an expectation that Hamilton could figure a way to get the struggling nation on its feet, and once Hamilton was on the job, Washington stepped aside. He would make his wishes known on military matters to Secretary Knox and on diplomatic matters to Secretary Jefferson, but on financial matters he gave his secretary of the Treasury free rein.

Hamilton's plan was multifaceted, with each component playing an integral role in the overall scheme. First, as Congress requested, the secretary tabulated the extent of public debt, which by the standards of the day was huge: $54 million owed by the federal government, and another $25 million owed by state governments. Next, he argued forcefully that federal debt obligations must be honored in full; nothing short of that would inspire confidence among future lenders. Bonds would be retired only gradually, but in the meantime they would yield a respectable interest, to be paid out quarterly. Once people developed confidence in these moneymaking notes, the notes could trade at a stable rate on the open market, thereby increasing the nation's liquid capital. Further, the federal government would assume all state debts. This would lessen the burden of direct taxation imposed by state governments, and it would also give the moneyed class a vested interest in the security and well-being of the national government. That, indeed, was the final object. In the future, if the United States needed money, investors would trust the government sufficiently to lend it more. The public credit would be secured.[3]

How would all this be funded? The federal government, unlike state governments, was empowered to pass import duties, which were less intrusive than direct taxation on people or property. To the duties already in place, Hamilton proposed to add what we call today "sin taxes" on coffee, tea, and distilled liquor. These were "pernicious luxuries," he pronounced, which were "consumed in so great abundance" that they produced "national extravagance and impoverishment." Liquor, he claimed, was the worst of all. "The consumption of ardent spirits particularly, no doubt very much on account of their cheapness, is carried to an extreme, which is truly to be regretted, as well in regard to the health and the morals, as to the economy of the community." Taxing distilled spirits would simultaneously fund the national debt and improve the nation's morals. This idea was hardly new. Back in 1750, four years before submitting his noted Albany Plan, Benjamin Franklin had advocated funding a pan-colonial council by taxing "strong liquors" and licensing public houses; now Hamilton once again launched an assault on the American appetite for liquor while using the funds it could generate for the public good.[4]

The Treasury secretary, unlike the president, did not address Congress in person. That would have been bad form, an apparent attempt to intrude in legislative deliberations—but this was for form only because the report, although solicited, *was* intended to influence legislation. Hamilton spelled out a clear program, complete with highly detailed drafts of two revenue-producing bills involving "spirits distilled within the United States" and "certain inland duties on foreign wines." Then, appearances be damned, Hamilton aggressively lobbied for his program. "Mr. Hamilton is very uneasy, as far as I can learn, about his funding system," Maclay recorded in his diary on February 1. The House was about to consider his suggestions, and according to Maclay the Treasury secretary first lobbied the Speaker and then "spent most of his time in running from place to place among the members." A week later, just after debate had commenced, Maclay wrote, "Hamilton, literally speaking, is moving heaven and earth in favor of his system." He deployed a minister to support it before congressmen "as if he had been in the pulpit" and mobilized the Society of the Cincinnati, his fellow officers from the Revolutionary War, to push for it out of doors. Hamilton, an officer in the executive branch of government, had become an active advocate for specific legislation.[5]

Was this what the framers had intended? True, thanks to Gouverneur Morris, the *president* was required to *recommend* measures to Congress, but did that entitle *another* executive officer, operating without direction or even input from the president, to *push* for specific legislation? Maclay questioned the propriety of Hamilton's advocacy. The Constitution had eschewed the parliamentary system, in which ministers combined executive and legislative roles, but now the Treasury secretary, "in the style of a British minister," had "sent down his bid."[6]

Maclay and many others also opposed the substance of Hamilton's plan, which clearly favored some groups of citizens over others. During the Revolutionary War, Congress had paid soldiers and farmers with bills of credit, not hard cash, but many recipients, needing real money for current expenses, relinquished their notes to speculators for a small fraction of their face value. Now, if Hamilton had his way, those speculators would be rewarded with windfall profits. A note yielding 6 percent interest on the face value, but purchased for twenty cents on the dollar, would produce a 30 percent annual interest on the investment, and when the note was finally paid off, it would yield a 500 percent profit. James Madison, among others, thought this highly unfair. He suggested tracking down the original owners and giving them a share of the profits, a policy dubbed "discrimination."

Although Madison's discrimination scheme, arguably unworkable in the absence of reliable records, was defeated in Congress by a convincing thirty-six-to-thirteen vote, out of doors it was widely popular, particularly among those who would have to assume the brunt of the tax burden to pay off wealthy speculators. Just west of the Appalachian Mountains, particularly in Pennsylvania, farmers turned their corn and wheat crops into market whiskey. Hamilton's taxes threatened their livelihoods, and to compound the injury, his plan placed the revenues from these taxes in a specific fund used only to pay off wealthy note holders. In the minds of these westerners, Hamilton had schemed to transfer money directly from ordinary, hardworking citizens into the hands of a moneyed eastern elite.

Hamilton's plan caused another regional division as well. Four southern states (Virginia, Maryland, North Carolina, and Georgia) had already retired most of their war debts, while several northern states, in particular Massachusetts, had not, and states that had already paid off were understandably reluctant to bail out the others. In the House, federal assumption of state debts initially failed by two votes, but in a brokered deal that brought the national capital to the Potomac, it finally squeaked through.

President Washington took no public stance on these legislative matters. Congress had commissioned the report from Hamilton, and it was up to Congress to implement his suggestions—or not. If he was concerned about the divisive impact of Hamilton's measures, he kept that to himself as well. Any intrusions on his part might raise questions as to his objectivity and transcendent leadership.

Yet when Hamilton submitted a second report on the public credit to Congress at the close of 1790, Washington engaged in the argument. At issue was Hamilton's new proposal for a national bank, capitalized and directed primarily by private investors but receiving up to 20 percent of its capitalization from the federal government. Banknotes issued from this formidable private-public partnership would function as liquid capital, more solid than the paper currency issued by the confederation government, which had lost virtually all its value. Functionally, the bank seemed like a good way to get the nation's economy rolling while not endangering public credit, but Washington had his doubts. Where, exactly, did the U.S. Constitution authorize such an arrangement?

The first clause of Article I, Section 8 empowered Congress to lay taxes and pay debts, while the second clause permitted it to borrow money; together, these covered all aspects of the initial phase of Hamilton's plan. Even so, there was no mention in the Constitution of chartering banks, which had been a province of the states, and certainly no word of granting one group of private investors special standing in federal law. Troubled, Washington asked Attorney General Edmund Randolph for a legal opinion. As the House was debating the bill, Randolph and Washington discussed the matter twice, and the president asked for a considered, written opinion by the government's official legal expert. Randolph came back with a decisive answer: Congress did not possess a constitutional authority to incorporate the Bank of the United States. There was no specific clause empowering it to do so, and the final clause of Article I, Section 8, which allowed it to "make all Laws which shall be necessary and proper for carrying into Execution the foregoing Powers," was subject to dangerous abuse. Randolph closed his response with a rhetorical question: "Let it be propounded as an eternal question to those, who build new powers on this clause, whether the latitude of construction which they arrogate, will not terminate in an unlimited power in Congress?"[7]

The bill to incorporate the bank passed the House on February 14 by a thirty-nine-to-twenty vote, just shy of the two-thirds supermajority that body would need to override a presidential veto, should Washington decide to oppose it. Having held office for almost two years, Washington had not vetoed any bills, and to do so would certainly ignite a political storm, but with his attorney general firmly opposed to the bank on legal grounds, the president certainly had to consider issuing the nation's first "negative," as they said at the time. According to the Constitution, he had exactly ten days to make up his mind.

After receiving Randolph's opinion, Washington asked Secretary of State Jefferson to weigh in, and on February 15 Jefferson, like Randolph, issued a strong statement opposing any act of incorporation. He understood the practical reasons for preferring banknotes to paper money, but that did not justify bypassing the Constitution. "Perhaps indeed bank bills may be a more *convenient* vehicle than treasury orders, but a little *difference* in the degree of *convenience,* cannot constitute the necessity which the constitution makes the ground for assuming any non-enumerated power."[8]

The following day, just over a week before his decision-making deadline, Washington forwarded Randolph's and Jefferson's arguments to Hamilton and asked for a response "so that I may be fully possessed of the argument *for* and *against* the measure before I express any opinion of my own." The president was acting exactly as the framers intended. He had stayed out of congressional deliberations, but now that the matter was placed before him for his signature, he maturely considered whether it was in accordance with the Constitution. Even George Mason, who had regretted the absence of an executive council, could have taken heart by Washington's use of his closest advisers, had he been privy to the inner workings of the administration.[9]

Hamilton did not respond immediately, and in the meantime

Washington asked Madison, who had led the opposition in Congress, to draft a veto message "to be ready in case his judgment should finally decide agst the Bill for incorporating a National Bank, the Bill being there before him." If Washington had made such a determination, and if he had followed Madison's draft, here is how he would have explained his decision: "I object to the Bill because it is an essential principle of the Government that powers not delegated by the Constitution cannot be rightfully exercised; because the power proposed by the bill to be received is not expressly delegated; and because I cannot satisfy myself that it results from any express power by fair and safe rules of implication."[10]

Washington never did deliver that message. Two days before the deadline, Hamilton gave the president a sweeping rebuttal to the opponents' arguments. "Every power vested in a government," he proclaimed, "includes . . . a right to employ all the *means* requisite, and *fairly applicable* to the attainment of the *ends* of such power, and which are not precluded by restrictions and exceptions specified in the Constitution, or not immoral, or not contrary to the ends of political society." This was exactly the all-encompassing interpretation Randolph warned against, but Hamilton argued that Randolph, Jefferson, and Madison, in their narrow interpretation of "necessary and proper," would "beget endless uncertainty and embarrassment" and cripple the legitimate functioning of government. Were "light houses, beacons, buoys & public piers" absolutely necessary to governmental operations? No, a country could exist without them—and it would have to if his opponents had their way, because the construction of these public works was not included in the eighteen powers relegated to Congress. Yet wouldn't it be foolhardy to deem a government-supported lighthouse unconstitutional?[11]

After delivering his hard-hitting reply, Hamilton hammered home his points in person, all morning and until two in the afternoon the day before the president needed to make his final decision. Not surprisingly, when that decision came, it was in Hamilton's favor. Washington was a true believer in a strong central government. He had advocated it for years, and he had come out of retirement to facilitate it. To veto the bank would have undercut his work on several counts. Politically, it would have alienated his Federalist allies. Since this would be his first veto, and since both houses of Congress had passed the measure by wide majorities, Washington's "negative" would be presented as a

usurpation of his powers, even though it was safely within his constitutional prerogatives. More important, to base his veto on a limited
interpretation of the "necessary and proper" powers of Congress would
have hampered government precisely at a time when it needed to be
strengthened. A practical man, a military man, Washington was not
prepared to retreat this far. The government must move forward.[12]

Moving forward with Hamilton's bank, though, did have its costs.
As with the earlier aspects of the Treasury secretary's plan, opposition out of doors was stronger than opposition within Congress. The
national bank was widely regarded as a federal encroachment on state
authority and a power grab by moneyed interests. Farmers who objected
to paying taxes for the aggrandizement of speculators doubled their
opposition to the federal government, allegedly now in the hands of
bankers. Main Street's demonization of Wall Street had its roots in the
tussles over Alexander Hamilton's financial plan, measures that President Washington did not initiate but did eventually approve.

By 1794, local defiance of the federal government's economic policies had developed in Kentucky, Maryland, Virginia, the Carolinas, and
Georgia, while resistance in Pennsylvania was turning into a full-scale
rebellion. Angry farmers closed roads to impede the travel of tax men,
threatened collectors with humiliation and bodily harm, organized
committees of correspondence, and erected liberty poles, all reminiscent of Revolutionary days. As opposition mounted and spread, some
dissidents even threatened secession. Hamilton called the protests the
Whiskey Rebellion, a name that has stuck to this day, and he tried
to convince Washington to crush it with military force, regardless of
the outrage such an action might engender. "I have long since learned
to hold popular opinion of no value," Hamilton freely admitted.
At first Washington resisted Hamilton's counsel. "To array citizen
against citizen," he wrote, was a step "too delicate, too closely inter-
woven with many affecting circumstances, to be lightly adopted." In
the end, though, Washington acquiesced and called out troops. Riding
at the head of 12,950 militiamen called up from four states, the president of the United States, as authorized by the Constitution, headed
west across Pennsylvania to "suppress" an "insurrection."[13]

This was not how Washington had imagined his role. He had
wanted to avoid discord and had done his best to do so. He had favored
a Bill of Rights solely to satisfy opponents of the Constitution. He

had treated opposition leaders respectfully, even inviting the irascible William Maclay to dinner. The very day Hamilton completed his first financial report, Washington had boasted to Catharine Macaulay Graham, the highly touted British historian, that the American government was "the last great experiment, for promoting human happiness, by reasonable compact, in civil society." It was to be "a government of accommodation as well as a government of laws," guided not only by "firmness" but also by "prudence" and "conciliation."[14]

The implementation of Hamilton's financial plan, though, polarized Americans to such an extent that Washington opted for firmness over accommodation or conciliation. Despite his vow to remain above partisan politics, he could no longer appreciate the plausible viewpoints of his opposition, as a truly disinterested leader must do. According to Washington, western protesters were stirred to act not by their own reasonable grievances but by the "Democratic Societies" of his political adversaries, "the same set of men endeavoring to destroy all confidence in the Administration." These people hoped "to disquiet the public mind" and "draw a line between the people and the government," and that's why they convinced gullible farmers "that their liberties were assailed." When explaining his repression of the insurgency to Congress, the president closed by "imploring the Supreme Ruler of nations" to counter "the machinations of the wicked" and bring them to their senses. By appealing to God to change the minds of political foes, Washington unwittingly demonstrated that his attempt to transcend partisanship was coming up short.[15]

Citizens of the early Republic divided over foreign policy issues as well as domestic matters, and these divisions raised questions about the nature and limits of executive authority. Who had the power to shape foreign policy—Congress, the president, or some combination? Since the Constitution had not addressed this question directly, political actors during the turbulent 1790s tried to fashion answers that suited their ideological slants and/or their immediate political ends.

The background: Britain was at war once again with France, hardly an unusual occurrence for the eighteenth century, but this time there were extenuating circumstances that affected the allegiance of many Americans. One-third of a century earlier, when Anglo-Americans drove France from North America, allegiances were never in question, but this time, while some continued to favor Britain, the former mother country with whom Americans still shared a language, a culture, and close commercial ties, others favored France, which had come to the aid of the newly independent nation during the Revolutionary War and which was in the midst of its own revolutionary fight for liberty. Anglophiles refused to repudiate the British tradition they had inherited, while Francophiles refused to repudiate the 1778 treaty alliance with France, signed at the darkest hour and still legally binding. Francophiles accused their opponents of being monarchists who still honored the British king; Anglophiles treated their opponents as dangerous Jacobins, bent on destroying the fabric of civil society.

Fault lines overlapped the schisms that had developed over domestic policy. The mercantile class tended to favor Britain, America's most frequent trading partner, while those favoring France, noting that pro-British merchants were the very same men who were getting rich from Hamilton's financial program, called them "*mushrooms* of the funding systems." Those favoring Britain, including Hamilton himself, claimed the opposition was composed of warmed-over Anti-Federalists "busy in undermining the Constitution and government of the U. States . . . by striving to destroy the confidence of the people in its administration." According to Hamilton, the same "secret clubs" that opposed his funding plan were "dispatched to distant parts of the United States" to stir up "partisans of the disorganizing corps" and mobilize sympathy for France.[16]

Characteristically, Washington tried to steer a middle course, but once again he found the middle road could readily vanish. On April 22, 1793, he issued an executive proclamation pledging the United States to "pursue a conduct friendly and impartial toward the belligerent powers." To this end he wrote, "I . . . exhort and warn the citizens of the United States carefully to avoid all acts and proceedings whatsoever, which may in any manner tend to contravene such disposition." Further, he promised to prosecute anyone who aided or abetted the hostile actions of either power or who in any way "violate[d] the law of nations with respect to the powers of war."[17]

Where in the Constitution did the president acquire the power to issue such a proclamation?

Nowhere, said James Madison. Pointing to powers granted to Congress under Article I, Section 8, he observed, "The right to decide the question whether the duty and interest of the U.S. require war or peace . . . seem to be . . . vested in the Legislature." Congress alone had the power to "declare war" and "define and punish . . . offenses against the law of nations."[18]

Not so, said Alexander Hamilton, always a firm advocate of executive authority, who used the proclamation as an occasion for putting forth his own interpretation of the Constitution. Although the proclamation had nothing to do with the duties of the secretary of the Treasury, he wrote a series of letters to the pro-administration *Gazette of the United States*, using the pen name Pacificus to suggest the president's proclamation would keep the nation from war. "The Legislative Department is not the *organ* of intercourse between the U. States and foreign nations," he declared. "It is charged neither with *making* nor *interpreting* treaties." The judiciary litigated "specific cases," but it played no role in setting policy. That left the executive as the sole "organ of intercourse between the nation and foreign nations." Britain, France, Spain, and the rest each had a head of state, after all. The United States needed one man to stand up to these foreign monarchs and represent American interests to the world.

Hamilton continued his argument. Article II of the Constitution—"The executive Power shall be vested in a President"—was a general grant of power. While this grant was modified in a few specific instances, such as the Senate's authority to ratify treaties and Congress's power to declare war, "with these exceptions the EXECUTIVE POWER of the Union is completely lodged in the President." Congress had already conceded as much during the great "removal debate" of 1789, he noted.[19]

Secretary of State Jefferson was furious. Hamilton had thrown himself into a matter outside his field of authority, he had advocated a position with which Jefferson disagreed, he had claimed for himself the exclusive authority to interpret the Constitution, and, worst of all, he had used the occasion of Washington's proclamation to promote executive powers that were antirepublican and dangerously expansive. As a fellow member of Washington's "cabinet" (that word was just coming into use), Jefferson felt constrained from answering Hamilton directly, but he believed passionately that someone should. So he wrote to Madison, enclosing two of Hamilton's articles:

You will see in these Colo. H's 2d. & 3d. Pacificus. Nobody answers him, & his doctrine will therefore be taken for confessed. For god's sake, my dear Sir, take up your pen, select the most striking heresies, and cut him to peices in the face of the public. There is nobody else who can & will enter the lists with him. Never in my opinion, was so calamitous an appointment made, as that of the present minister of F. here. Hotheaded, all imagination, no judgment, passionate, disrespectful & even indecent towards the P. in his written as well as verbal communications, . . . urging the most unreasonable & groundless propositions, & in the most dictatorial style &c. &c. &c.[20]

With some reluctance, Madison agreed to rebut Hamilton. Adopting the pen name Helvidius (Helvidius Priscus was a Roman statesman allied with Brutus and Cassius), Madison penned six letters for the press that countered Pacificus point by point and shrank the executive back down to a size the author deemed more appropriate for a republican government. He detailed each of the powers granted to the executive by the Constitution and argued that none of them enabled the president, by himself, to issue a proclamation that determined matters of war and peace. The closest approximation to such a power was his authority to negotiate treaties, but this was a power he shared with the Senate, and logically it could not be construed as "executive." To "execute" presupposed the prior existence of a law, or in this case a treaty, and in a republican government laws and treaties, which were binding on citizens and therefore required legal sanction, could not be deemed legitimate unless approved by the legislature. That's why treaties needed Senate ratification. "Although the executive may be a convenient organ of preliminary communications with foreign governments, on the subjects of treaty or war, and the proper agent for carrying into execution the final determinations," the president alone could not be the "essential agency which gives validity to such determinations." True, the British monarch had such authority, but that only fed Madison's most hard-hitting point: Hamilton had retreated from republicanism and wanted to base the U.S. executive on the concept of "*royal prerogatives* in the *British government.*" Madison had heard Hamilton state this in so many words at the Federal Convention, and now, although his adversary shied from terminology that would undercut his cause, he was still trying to nudge the new American government toward a British model.[21]

Five years earlier, Hamilton and Madison had collaborated on *The Federalist*, often treated as the definitive explication of the views of the framers. In that work, Madison had not addressed the president's treaty-making power, but Hamilton, in *The Federalist* 75, did expound on the matter, and his views there were diametrically opposed to those he now expressed:

> Though several writers on the subject of government place that power [making treaties] in the class of executive authorities, yet this is evidently an arbitrary disposition; for if we attend care-fully to its operation, it will be found to partake more of the legislative than of the executive character, though it does not seem strictly to fall within the definition of either of them. The essence of the legislative authority is to enact laws, or, in other words, to prescribe rules for the regulation of the society; while the execution of the laws, and the employment of the common strength, either for this purpose or for the common defense, seem to comprise all the functions of the executive magistrate. The power of making treaties is, plainly, neither the one nor the other.

The power to make treaties, he concluded, "seems therefore to form a distinct department," partly executive and partly legislative. The executive was "the most fit agent" to negotiate a treaty, "while the vast impor-tance of the trust, and the operation of treaties as laws, plead strongly for the participation of the whole or a portion of the legislative body in the office of making them." This applied not only to making treaties but also to all "foreign negotiations." A president, who served for a lim-ited time and would then have to return to the private sector, could be influenced by avarice or ambition, he admitted. It was therefore *utterly unsafe and improper . . . to commit interests of so delicate and momentous a kind, as those which concern its intercourse with the rest of the world, to the sole disposal of a magistrate created and circumstanced as would be a Presi-dent of the United States*" (emphasis added).

This was not far from the argument Helvidius was presenting in 1793, and Madison even closed his first essay by quoting Hamilton's *Federalist* 75 verbatim. That argument, unlike Hamilton's later Pacifi-cus argument, "was made at a time when no application to *persons* or *measures*" could lead to "bias," Madison stated. In a sense, Madison had it backward. Now, when Hamilton expressed unqualified support for executive power, he was revealing his true views, as he had outlined in his daylong speech at the Federal Convention; in the *Federalist,* by contrast, he had been playing to an audience, giving his readers the words he thought they should hear in order to support ratification, even though those words contradicted his deeply held preference for the primacy of executive power.[22]

That Madison and Hamilton could hold such differing interpretations of the Constitution should come as no surprise. In fact, there was no easy answer to the conundrum of who, in a republican form of government, should control the nation's relations with "the rest of the world." Delegates had found that out at the Federal Convention. From the outset, when Wilson first proposed a single executive, they resisted giving him the powers of "peace & war &c.," to use Charles Pinckney's language, as summarized by Madison in his notes. When the Committee of Detail allocated powers early in August, it allowed the president to "receive ambassadors," but that was the extent of executive involvement in foreign policy. It entrusted the Senate with the power to "make treaties" and "appoint ambassadors," and it gave the shared power to "make war" to the Senate and the House. According to that draft, the Senate would likely take the lead in shaping foreign policy.[23]

Not until Gouverneur Morris and the Committee of Eleven reported to the convention floor on September 4 did the president acquire the power to make treaties and appoint foreign officers, and even then he would need Senate approval on both counts. If James Wilson had had his way, treaties negotiated by the president would have required ratification by the House as well. Other laws needed approval from both houses of Congress, and "as treaties are to have the operation of laws," he argued, "they ought to have the sanction of laws also." Wilson's motion for House ratification, though based on sound logic, failed by a vote of ten states to one. Delegates believed that since House members stood for election every two years, that body lacked the permanency necessary to establish a stable foreign policy, and even Wilson admitted that the House, because it was the larger branch of Congress, might compromise the "secrecy" appropriate to international negotiations.[24]

That left the House of Representatives, the only body directly elected by the people, with a limited role in shaping foreign policy: it could declare and fund war, but these were its only specified powers.

This was something of an embarrassment for a republican government, but when Pierce Butler and Elbridge Gerry moved "to give the Legislature power of peace, as they were to have that of war," their motion failed to garner the support of a single state delegation. The motion was not even discussed.[25]

Who, then, *did* hold the "power of peace"? The president, with the concurrence of two-thirds of the Senate, could negotiate a treaty to end a war, but that was only the most literal aspect of the "power of peace." More broadly, who had the responsibility of keeping the nation *out* of war? This large and fundamental question was never fully explored at the Federal Convention. Even after two critical powers—making treaties and appointing ambassadors—were switched by the Committee of Eleven from one branch to another, delegates failed to address the issue of who would formulate an *overall* foreign policy, one that encompassed the possibilities of both war and peace. This allowed Hamilton, writing as Pacificus six years later, to proclaim, by his own interpretation, that while Congress had the "right to make war," it was the duty of the president "to preserve peace till war is declared." While that sounded like a tidy solution, it begged the larger question: Who was really in charge, anyway? Did the president command foreign policy during times of peace, while Congress assumed it during wartime? If so, then authority shifted in an instant, the moment war was declared, and this made little sense. In truth, the complex web of authority allowed no easy answers.[26]

The Constitution did not allocate the direction of foreign policy to one branch or the other, and because it didn't, future government officials would be left to work out the details, case by case, argument by argument, crisis by crisis. Both the president and Congress, at different times, could and did take the lead in claiming special powers. In 1793, Washington decided, simply by doing so, that the president could issue what amounted to a proclamation of neutrality, but the following year Congress decided, also by doing so, that *it* could issue a proclamation of neutrality. For better or worse, the framers' failure to address the general issue of foreign policy has resulted in a more evolutionary assignment of governmental powers than the presence of a written constitution would seem to imply.

Ironically, attempts to avoid the hostilities between Britain and France led to increased political hostilities here in America. Late in 1793 and early in 1794, acting on official orders, British ships seized almost 250 American ships and reportedly mistreated many of the captured seamen. Britain justified these seizures by claiming, correctly, that the United States was trading with France through the West Indies, but that justification did nothing to quell the popular outrage in America. Inhabitants of eastern seaports seethed at the British seizures, while some westerners, seeking access to and control over the Mississippi River, threatened to violate Washington's neutrality order by joining a French expeditionary force to take the Mississippi region from Spain. Anti-British sentiment reached a fever pitch when newspapers reported that Lord Dorchester (formerly Guy Carleton), the governor-general of Canada, had told an assembly of Native Americans that Britain would be their ally if they waged war against the United States. Responding to popular pressure, Congress had to take some action to counter what Americans perceived as British aggression on both land and sea. Acting contrary to Washington's proclamation, which enjoined Americans to remain "friendly and impartial" to both Britain and France, the House passed overwhelmingly a nonimportation bill designed to punish Britain by inhibiting its commerce. Step-by-step, the nation seemed to be moving toward war.

Just before that bill arrived at the Senate, Hamilton and a caucus of Federalist senators proposed to Washington that he dispatch a special mission to London to address American grievances. The president agreed, and using his constitutional power of appointment, he tapped John Jay, chief justice of the Supreme Court, to head the mission, but Jay was a political liability. Back in 1786 he had tried to bargain away American access to the Mississippi in return for favorable trade arrangements and stabilized boundaries with Spain, but his proposed treaty met with great resistance in the South and the West and was rejected by Congress. Now, when his nomination came before the Senate on April 19, 1794, opponents moved that it be shelved on constitutional grounds: "To permit Judges of the Supreme Court to hold at the same time any other office or employment, emanating from and holden at the pleasure of the Executive, is contrary to the spirit of the Constitution, and, as tending to expose them to the influence of the Executive, is mischievous and impolitic," they argued. While that case would seem compelling to us today, Federalists in the Senate defeated the measure and confirmed the nomination.[27]

Jay's appointment changed the political landscape, at least for the time being. Federalists argued persuasively that any measure intended to stifle British commerce would undermine Jay's ability to reach an accord, and the nonimportation bill crumbled in the Senate without serious debate.

On the diplomatic front, Washington's decision to send an envoy to Britain might well have prevented (or at least delayed) a war, but he paid a political price. Due to Jay's unpopularity, whatever treaty he negotiated would be suspect from the start, and when Jay did return home with a paper in hand, wanting only ratification by the Senate, that paper raised a nationwide political storm.

On the surface, the treaty appeared to have accomplished some goals. Britain agreed to withdraw its posts south of the Canadian border and submit border disputes to arbitration. Further, Britain promised to repay American merchants for recently seized ships and merchandise, but there was a price. The treaty established a process to arbitrate the claims of British merchants for unpaid debts, which Americans worried would allow Loyalists to be compensated for property confiscated during the war. There was an intangible price as well. Citizens of neither the United States nor Britain would be permitted to join the services of a nation at war with the other, nor could one nation harbor, supply, or trade with privateers from an enemy nation. So much for attempts by private American citizens to aid the French cause.

The central thrust of the treaty, though, was to normalize trade relations between the two nations, excellent news for pro-British merchants in the United States. The nuts and bolts of the twenty-eight provisions ensured that importers and exporters on both sides would not suffer from any disagreements between the two governments. Trade restrictions were eased or lifted. Merchants, even privateers, were guaranteed safe haven in each other's ports, and no goods could be confiscated without due process. Article 10 stipulated that in the event of war between Britain and the United States, no money deposited in any bank could be sequestered, "it being unjust and impolitick that debts and engagements contracted and made by individuals having confidence in each other, and in their respective governments, should ever be destroyed or impaired by national authority, on account of national differences and discontents." Article 26 struck a similar chord: "If at any time a rupture should take place (which God forbid) between His Majesty and the United States, the merchants and others of each of the two nations, residing in the dominions of the other, shall have the privilege of remaining and continuing their trade so long as they behave peaceably and commit no offence against the laws."[28]

The favors and securities offered to merchants pleased one group of Americans but angered others, who argued that the treaty violated the spirit of neutrality by favoring Britain over France. It prohibited the United States from honoring the 1778 "perpetual" alliance with France, they noted. Further, while it ensured that merchants would be paid for seized ships, it failed to return the actual seamen, nor did it promise that seamen would not be taken and impressed into British service in the future. Finally, one additional group focused on what the treaty did *not* accomplish: slave owners were upset that Jay, who opposed slavery, failed to obtain payment for the enslaved men and women who had escaped or been carried away during the Revolutionary War.

Opponents of the treaty started to mobilize even before the precise terms were known, and as they did, they raised several procedural and constitutional issues:

- How could the chief executive command the services of the chief judicial officer in a matter that overlapped legislative jurisdiction? This seemed a clear contradiction of the Constitution's separation of powers.

- The Constitution required not only the consent of the Senate but also its advice, yet the Senate was never queried. True, that body confirmed Jay's nomination, but it played no role in determining his instructions or negotiating the treaty.

- The treaty was submitted to the Senate for ratification even before its contents were known to the public. Anti-Federalists had always been worried that the president-Senate nexus would cut citizens out of the loop, and here was a case in point.

- Several articles of the treaty regulated commerce, which, according to Section I, Article 8, should be the purview of Congress. This meant the House, as well as the Senate, should be included in the ratification process.

It is difficult to determine whether these complaints contributed significantly to the treaty's unpopularity or were simply used as arguing points to justify a position taken on other grounds, but in either case constitutional issues were raised, and treaty opponents in the nation's largest state acted on them. The Virginia legislature proposed four constitutional amendments it wished its representatives and senators to present in Congress. The first stipulated that any treaty "containing any stipulation upon the subject of the powers vested in Congress by the eighth section of the first article" of the Constitution—including, of course, the regulation of commerce—must gain the approval of *both* houses of Congress before taking effect. The next two weakened the influence of senators, one by lessening their terms from six to three years, the other by taking away their power to try impeachments, thereby preventing any collusion between the Senate and the president. Finally, the Virginia legislature demanded that federal judges be forbidden to hold "any other office or appointment whatever." These were the sorts of amendments that had been proposed during the ratification debates, and they met the same fate. No state legislature other than Virginia's was willing to challenge the very structure of the fledgling Constitution so directly at this time.[29]

Still, even after Jay's Treaty was ratified by the Senate and signed by the president, opponents continued to fight against it. The arbitration commissions established by the treaty required funding, so the agreement could not take effect until the House appropriated some money. That meant the House needed first to approve the *purpose* of the appropriations, and with this in mind it began to address the merits of Jay's Treaty. What did it intend? How was it negotiated? Seeking answers, it requisitioned the instructions given to Jay and other relevant documents from President Washington. Claiming what we now call executive privilege, Washington immediately and forcefully refused to deliver any papers.

Two arms of government were at an impasse, and the Supreme Court, which today we would expect to decide the matter, had not yet asserted its authority to step in. Possession being nine-tenths of the law, Washington held on to the documents. Still, the House continued to debate whether to fund the treaty, and the outcome was not predetermined. The key vote in the Committee of the Whole resulted in a dead heat, 49 to 49; Chairman Frederick Muhlenberg, who had formerly been allied with the treaty's opponents, then broke the tie and voted for funding. A few days later Muhlenberg was stabbed by his brother, a fierce foe of the treaty.[30]

The Federalist victory over Jay's Treaty completed a clean sweep for Washington and the powers of the presidency. First, Congress conceded that the president could remove executive officers on his own accord, without congressional approval. Then one of Washington's key appointees, Secretary of the Treasury Hamilton, took the lead in domestic legislation, and when Congress approved Hamilton's measures, which included strengthening the central government by the assumption of state debts, the nation's credit was salvaged—a key item on the president's agenda. When westerners resisted central authority and even flirted with secession, Washington quelled the disturbances with a show of military force. With his proclamation of 1793 he established a lead role for the presidency in shaping foreign policy; then, using his constitutional power of appointment, he dispatched an envoy to Britain to normalize commercial relations and keep war at bay. The resultant treaty was confirmed by a two-thirds vote of the Senate, exactly as specified in the Constitution. When House members tried to assert authority that Washington believed was not covered by the Constitution—demanding executive documents and withholding funds from a legal treaty—they failed. Every contested power was decided in the president's favor. In the waning days of the Federal Convention, at Gouverneur Morris's instigation, the executive office had begun to expand, and that trajectory continued on the ground during the first eight years of the early Republic. By the time Washington left office, it seemed clear that the president was no longer Congress's junior partner.

Yet politically, Washington failed to accomplish one of his overarching goals: unite the nation. Although the Bill of Rights had gone a long way toward healing old wounds, Hamilton's financial plan and the disputes over foreign policy opened new ones. By the mid-1790s, patriotic Americans of opposing persuasions were celebrating the Fourth of July with parallel parades and competitive street theater, complete with burning effigies. As the political field polarized, rhetoric became more extreme, and in the closing years of Washington's second term the president himself became an object of scorn. Some critics even called for his impeachment.[31]

Accustomed to nearly universal acclaim, Washington viewed criticism as attacks on government itself. Political foes were not simply wrong or mistaken but malevolent destroyers of the nation, some even bent on leading it into foreign (French) hands. Such thoughts, and the statements and policies they produced, belied his avowed intention to unify.

Meanwhile, Jefferson and other opponents of Hamilton's financial plan and Jay's Treaty were beginning to see themselves as a defined political force with coherent policies, a "party." While Washington continued to use the term "party" with the traditionally negative connotation, Jefferson, who had come to oppose anything and everything Federalist, was starting to embrace it. "Were parties here divided merely by a greediness for office, as in England, to take a part with either [party] would be unworthy of a reasonable or moral man," he wrote on the last day of 1795. "But where the principle of difference is as substantial and as strongly pronounced as between republicans & the Monocrats of our country, I hold it as honorable to take a firm & decided part, and as immoral to pursue a middle line, as between the parties of honest men, & rogues, into which every country is divided." Note the appellations: "republicans" and "Monocrats." Unlike the old Anti-Federalists, who were named by their opponents, Jefferson and this group managed to commandeer a positive label that endured.[32]

So there they were, two parties, Republicans and Federalists (to give each party a name of its own choosing). Political scientists argue whether these were proto-parties, with defined sets of political beliefs and strategies but lacking organization, or true parties, but the argument is academic. Political life in America was already polarized, notwithstanding Washington's desire to keep it from becoming so, and institutions would soon evolve to represent this. In fact, Washington's decision not to seek a third term facilitated and accelerated the process.

Washington had wanted to return to private life at the close of his first term, but divisions stemming from Hamilton's financial plan threatened unity, and leaders from both sides leaned on him to continue. This time he could not be dissuaded. Although political differences were more pronounced than ever, personal criticism had certainly exacted a toll, and he was tiring. To justify his retirement, Washington convinced himself that the nation was now on more solid footing and could get by without him. Federal authority had been affirmed by the suppression of the Pennsylvania rebellion. Attachment to France and war with Britain had been avoided. An important treaty had been negotiated and ratified according to constitutional procedures. Presidential precedents and powers had been established. It was time for a new leader to take over.

Even so, the retiring chief executive worried for the nation's future and wanted to offer some parting words of advice. Four years earlier, when he thought he would retire, he had asked Madison to draft a farewell address, but now Madison was firmly in the opposition camp, and he leaned on Hamilton instead. Personally this made sense. Washington and Hamilton had been in a trusting, professional relationship for two decades. They both believed in a strong central government and "vigorous" executive leadership, and even though Hamilton had recently resigned as secretary of the Treasury, he had shaped the policies of Washington's administration, not only on the domestic front, but with respect to international diplomacy as well. Politically the two were wedded, and they passed drafts of the address back and forth until Washington settled upon a final version.[33]

Even so, Hamilton was a strange ally for a president who viewed himself as a unifier. Shortly after leaving his cabinet post, during the height of the controversy over Jay's Treaty, he had attended a so-called town meeting in the open space by New York's Federal Hall and tried to command the attention of some five thousand people. Promptly at noon, when the event was supposed to commence, he took the podium and "attempted to harangue the people." He was shouted down. Later he tried again, but as he addressed the crowd, "very few sentences could be heard, on account of hissings, coughings, and hootings." That's how a Republican newspaper described the incident; a Federalist observer added, "Stones were thrown at Mr. Hamilton, one of which grazed his head." Rebuffed by the anti-treaty crowd, Hamilton engaged in personal altercations and wound up challenging two different antagonists to duels. This was the man President Washington chose to write his Farewell Address, his last opportunity as a public official to bring the nation together.[34]

Was the address that Hamilton and Washington jointly wrote and Washington released to the press in September 1796 an inspirational appeal for unity or a defense of Federalist policies? Logically, it could not be both. Or could it? Washington hoped his address would accomplish two tasks at once. He started by championing the "unity of government," urging "respect for its authority, compliance with its laws, [and] acquiescence in its measures," and declaring the Constitution "sacredly obligatory upon all." Yet unity, he warned, was threatened by "internal and external enemies" of legitimate government who acted "often covertly and insidiously" to tear the nation apart. Particularly dangerous were extralegal organizations that challenged existing authority:

> All combinations and associations, under whatever plausible character, with the real design to direct, control, counteract, or awe the regular deliberation and action of the constituted authorities, are ... of fatal tendency. They serve to organize faction, to give it an artificial and extraordinary force; to put, in the place of the delegated will of the nation the will of a party, often a small but artful and enterprising minority of the community.

Washington's contemporaries understood that by "combinations and associations" he meant the Democratic-Republican Societies and similar political clubs that dissented from the policies of his administration. These groups promoted "the spirit of party" with all its "baneful effects," and this sort of factionalism, the outgoing president declared, "serves always to distract the public councils and enfeeble the public administration. It agitates the community with ill-founded jealousies and false alarms, kindles the animosity of one part against another, foments occasionally riot and insurrection." All blame for disorder and disunity thus fell upon the Federalists' political foes.[35]

Did that mean Washington failed to acknowledge the legitimacy of dissent? Not exactly. In fact, he had always sought divergent viewpoints before making decisions. On numerous occasions during the Revolutionary War he had allowed his Council of War to talk him out of undertaking brash attacks. Before authorizing a national bank and before placing his signature on Jay's Treaty, he had solicited advice from advocates and opponents alike. When Jefferson fell out with Hamilton and threatened to resign his cabinet post, Washington had tried to persuade him to stay on, hoping to preserve diverse counsel. In all such instances Washington had acted as a leader among leaders, an exemplar of republican governance who listened to all sides of an argument before determining the optimum course.

Yet for Washington organized politics out of doors, practiced by private citizens who had been neither elected nor appointed to any office, was a different matter altogether. Today, we see extra-governmental venues for public debate as natural and perhaps even necessary components of political life, but Washington and others who held to a model of wise and disinterested leadership believed that groups with political agendas interfered with legitimate government, and in his Farewell Address, with Hamilton's help, the first president of the United States warned the nation of the dangers they presented.

His warnings were of little avail. To Republicans, Washington's farewell was more a call to battle than a unifying message. They did not feel like enemies of the Union, as Washington and Hamilton made them appear. They opposed policies of the Federalist-dominated government, actions that in their view undermined the core principles upon which the nation was founded. While many (but not all) had opposed the Constitution during ratification debates, they had agreed to abide by it and submitted proposals for alterations they thought would make the new rules more consistent with republican values. They organized in "combinations" because without organization, changes would be difficult to effect.

Republicans took particular offense at the president's extensive justification of his foreign policy. Following Hamilton's draft in the final substantive section of his address, Washington devoted some twelve hundred words to explaining why the United States should "stay clear of permanent alliances with any portion of the foreign world." This section of the address has resonated with isolationists in subsequent times, who, with Washington, have asked: "Why, by interweaving our destiny with that of any part of Europe, entangle our peace and prosperity in the toils of European ambition, rivalship, interest, humor or caprice?" This call for neutrality, though, was not so well received by his political opponents at the time, who saw quite clearly that "permanent alliances" referred to one specific alliance that was supposed to be permanent, the 1778 treaty with France that Washington, with Jay's Treaty, had broken. For Republicans, Washington's alleged neutrality actually reflected Federalist policy, pro-British and anti-French, and this was more an invitation to battle than a peace offering. Even Fisher Ames, a die-hard Massachusetts Federalist, read Washington's farewell that way. "It will serve as a signal, like dropping a hat, for the party racers to start," he wrote upon reading the address.[36]

In short, while we read the Farewell Address today as Washingto-
nian, the final appeal of a beloved father to avoid quarreling at home and
entanglements abroad, Republican adversaries read it as Hamiltonian,
a justification of Federalist policies and a call to continue them. Yet
Hamilton was out of office, and soon Washington would be too. Now
at last the dissenting Republicans had a chance to redirect the nation
along lines they deemed more suitable, but to do so, they believed they
would need to capture the presidency.

Bracing for this Republican assault, Federalists doubled down on
the presidency as well, and without Washington to lead the defense,
they appeared as desperate as their opposition. The nation, already torn,
would nearly fracture as the two emerging parties competed for the
post Washington had solidified. In the framers' minds, and in Washington's as well, the presidency was supposed to counteract partisan
politics; now the prospect of capturing that expanding office encouraged Americans in both camps to become more partisan than ever.

CHAPTER NINE

System Failure: Partisan Politics and the Election of 1800

On January 25, 1789—ten days before electors were to assemble in their respective state capitals to cast their votes for the first president and vice president under the new Constitution—Alexander Hamilton had written nervously to his colleague from the Federal Convention James Wilson: "Every body is aware of that defect in the constitution which renders it possible that the man intended for Vice President may in fact turn up President." Washington would be almost everyone's choice for the top spot, but each elector was to vote for *two* men, without distinguishing between president and vice president. This created a potential problem that Hamilton foresaw and wished to prevent. Might John Adams, who provided regional balance and whom Washington had informally endorsed, actually receive *more* votes than Washington himself? "Every body sees that unanimity in Adams as Vice President and a few votes insidiously held from Washington might substitute the former for the latter," Hamilton warned. "And every body must perceive that there is something to fear from the machinations of Anti-foederal malignity."[1]

"What in this situation is wise?" he asked, and then he posited an answer. Federalists should arrange for sympathetic electors to "throw away a few votes" for Adams to ensure he would not overtake Washington. They couldn't throw away too many for fear an Anti-Federalist might capture the number two spot, but in the ten days before electors were to cast their votes, they should get just the right number of electors—"7 or 8," Hamilton suggested—to vote for someone other than Adams so Washington would be president and Adams vice president.

Although Hamilton's fears in this case were not well-founded (Adams received only 36 votes compared with Washington's 69), they caused him to make a remarkable admission: the Constitution, which he had done so much to promote, could be gamed, and to prevent his foes from doing so, he would game it preemptively. To do this, though, he tried to influence presidential electors behind closed doors. In the parlance of the times, he engaged in "intrigue."

This was not what the framers of the Constitution had intended. When the Committee of Eleven reported its elector scheme on September 4, Gouverneur Morris rose immediately to "give the reasons of the Committee and his own," as Madison wrote. "The 1st was the danger of intrigue & faction" if the president were selected by Congress. "As the Electors would vote at the same time throughout the U.S. and at so great a distance from each other, the great evil of cabal was avoided," he explained. Under such conditions, it would be "impossible" for any cabal to "corrupt" the electors.[2]

Hamilton, in *The Federalist* 68, had elaborated on this theme. "Nothing was more to be desired than that every practicable obstacle should be opposed to cabal, intrigue, and corruption," he stated. "The convention have guarded against all danger of this sort with the most provident and judicious attention." Voting separately and independently, "under circumstances favorable to deliberation," electors would "enter upon the task free from any sinister bias." Each would exercise his best judgment, free from any influence.

That men as practical and tough-minded as Morris and Hamilton could believe they had devised a system that "guarded against all danger" from influence is difficult to explain. Clearly, the system invited intrigue. It practically summoned men with political motivations to take advantage of the lack of distinction between votes for president and votes for vice president, as Hamilton feared Anti-Federalists would do and he did do at the very first opportunity. Also, because electors were chosen long before they cast their votes, they were open prey for those who wanted to affect their decisions. Further, because men who chose electors (that could be either state legislators or the voting public) cared more about who would *be* president than who would *vote* for president, they might well demand some sort of promise or pledge from a would-be elector before giving him their votes. With all these opportunities, why *wouldn't* men with common interests join together (that is, form cabals) and plot privately (engage in intrigue) to influence the choice of president?

Voting through electors was only the first of a two-step process. If a group with common interests believed it could muster a majority in the House of Representatives, it could lobby electors to vote for diverse candidates so there would be no clear majority; then the election would be settled in the House, where that group would prevail. Conversely, if a group were poorly represented in the House, they could lean on electors who preferred other candidates to cast second votes for theirs; if just over half the electors agreed on a vice president, and preferences for president varied, the alleged vice president would become president without congressional involvement. Finally, whenever an election was thrown into the House, backers of the top five candidates would be foolish *not* to engage in intrigue, trying to attract support in return for promises or favors. This was exactly the scenario Gouverneur Morris and others had tried to prevent by instituting electors, but there it was, a major component of the system.

So again, how did members of the Committee of Eleven, who devised the method of presidential selection, and those on the convention floor who approved it, and Federalists who gave it rave reviews, miss all this? Partly, as mentioned, by the time the plan came to the floor, delegates were too tired to ask the hard questions. But that is not the full reason, for the central question—whether the plan was really intrigue-proof—could have been answered in the negative with hardly a second thought.

At least three other contributing explanations come to mind. First, the framers wished too hard. After struggling for three months to create an independent presidency and coming up empty, delegates to the convention simply willed that an unacceptable answer be acceptable. Putting on blinders had become their only option. From a human perspective, this is understandable; the framers were giving birth to a new form of government, and like any parents they entertained the highest hopes for their offspring. Envisioning the best, they embraced an idealistic fantasy of republican virtue and attributed nothing but the purest of motives to presidential electors. Since the notion was new and untested, there was no evidence to contradict their strange hypothesis: electors could be immunized from influence because they served only for a moment. Somehow, the electors' temporary status would remove them from all political context.

Electors would also meet simultaneously at thirteen different locations, and this "detached and divided situation" (Hamilton's words) allegedly removed them further yet from political heat. Gouverneur Morris, in his persuasive speech at the Federal Convention on July 19, proclaimed that a nationwide election "throughout so great an extent of country could not be influenced, by those little combinations and those momentary lies which often decide popular elections within a narrow sphere." This wishful argument suggests another reason for their miscalculations: because they associated cabal and intrigue with the goings-on in European national cities like London and Paris, they assumed that decentralizing the election process would prevent small groups from meeting in secret and exerting undue influence. This narrow definition of cabal and intrigue led them to underestimate the extent and depth of the influence wielded by small, private groups in political life at any level or location. Intrigue could not be prevented by simple geographic manipulation. Almost any delegate to the Federal Convention, had he looked over the list of political figures with whom he corresponded, could have determined as much. Hamilton, for instance, discussed his plan to influence electors with friends in at least six of the eleven states voting in the first federal election. Was that not intrigue, simply because communications were by mail? Was this group, which hoped to determine who would be the president and the vice president of the United States, not a faction or even a cabal? Participants did not view themselves in that manner, partly because they were not whispering in the halls of some European court, and partly because intrigue ran counter to republican ideology and they could not bear to view their own activities as contradicting what had become a national credo.[3]

Finally, men who devised and approved the electoral system failed to fully comprehend many factors that could foster intrigue and cabal. They believed that "greediness for office," to use Jefferson's term, led to European-style political divisions, which were characterized in the American mind by intrigue and cabal, but this definition was too limited; even in Europe, motivations were more varied than that limited model would suggest. They understood, too, that local and regional interests in the United States would lead men to divide into factions, engage in intrigue to influence governmental policies, and in worst-case scenarios form cabals that tried to seize power, whether by legitimate means or otherwise; indeed, that's why they sought a method of electing the president that would not fall prey to this tendency. As Madison famously wrote in *The Federalist* 10, since "the causes of faction cannot be removed, . . . relief is only to be sought in the means of controlling its *effects*," and among those anti-faction safeguards was the decentralization of electors. The framers, though, failed to grasp the depth of feeling and commitment that would emerge as competing groups grappled for the soul of a nation that was still being defined, nor did they foresee that cross-regional alliances among emerging factions would tie constituencies together into national parties. Further, they did not predict that in the new order public concern over governmental matters would highlight these naturally occurring divisions, thereby adding to the dangers posed by partisan politics. In sum, although we might forgive them this oversight, they did not predict that multiple factions would lead in the end to a two-party system, and that in order for either of these two parties to capture the highest office in the land, political agents would *necessarily* try to influence the selection of presidential electors, and after electors were chosen, each party would seek to secure commitments to vote for particular candidates. In the end, polarized parties would defeat the basic premise of electors, which was to remove the choice of the president from "any sinister bias."

The framers' illusion did not last long. In a pamphlet penned during the ratification debates, the ardent Federalist Noah Webster had boasted, "The president of the United States is elective, and what is a capital improvement on the best governments, the mode of choosing him excludes the danger of faction and corruption." In 1800, however, next to these words in a personal copy of his own pamphlet, he jotted down, "This proves how little dependence can be placed on theory. Twelve years experience, or four elections, demonstrates the contrary."[4]

The earliest real test of the elector system did not come until 1796, the first contested presidential election. Without Washington in the mix, there was no longer an iconic figure to mask the system's imperfections. In a competitive election, could the complex formula detailed in the Constitution yield a chief executive who would not only have the support of a majority of presidential electors or state delegations in the House of Representatives but also command the respect of a broad majority of American citizens?

In the spring of 1796, several months before Washington's formal resignation, Federalists and Republicans alike began to discuss among themselves strategies for securing the presidency. First and foremost, each group reasoned it should unite around a candidate or, because of the peculiarity of the system, two candidates. Unless they did so, a preferred choice would be unlikely to muster votes from more than half the electors. Decision making and organization were prerequisites for success.

Republicans settled quickly on the former secretary of state Thomas Jefferson, certainly the highest-ranking figure among them. They paid scant attention to the vice presidency; the Constitution had vested little authority in that office, and besides, there was no other candidate with significant national appeal. Their main job, as they saw it, was to ensure that John Adams, Washington's heir apparent, did not automatically ascend to the highest office. Adams's pro-British leanings, which allegedly included an infatuation with British-style monarchy, made him extremely unpopular with Republicans.

Federalists, conversely, viewed their central task as keeping Jefferson from becoming president. In the words of Oliver Wolcott Jr., who had taken over as Treasury secretary when Hamilton stepped down in 1795, "The election of Mr. Jefferson, I consider as fatal to our independence." If Jefferson became president, he would "innovate upon and fritter away the Constitution." Was John Adams, however, really the best candidate to beat Jefferson? He had little support in the South, so his fellow Federalists naturally worried he could not muster the necessary votes among electors. Strategically, they cast about for a southerner of their persuasion, someone who could bring at least a few electors their way. Some thought Patrick Henry might consent to run. He had immense regional appeal, and he had warmed to the Constitution and the Federalists since opposing them during the ratification debates. Hamilton and others, though, did not trust Henry's politics, and besides, Henry showed no interest. Federalist insiders also discussed running Thomas Pinckney, a Federalist from South Carolina who had just negotiated a widely popular treaty with Spain that secured rights to the Mississippi River. On May 4, 1796—more than four months before Washington informed the nation he would not seek a third term—Hamilton wrote to Rufus King, a Federalist strategist from Massachusetts: "I rather wish to be rid of P.H., that we may be at full liberty to take up Pinckney. . . . Mr. P—— ought to be our man." If Pinckney became president, he would owe his office to Hamilton and his friends, while Adams would have earned it in his own right. In the words of Hamilton's confidant Robert Troup, "We [will] have Mr. Pinckney completely in our power."[5]

In the first stage of politicking, Federalists did not have to confront the Adams-or-Pinckney issue; they needed only to ensure that people of their persuasion were chosen as electors. In eight of the sixteen states (Kentucky, Tennessee, and Vermont had been admitted to the union), electors were selected by the legislatures, where political lines had already been drawn. Of the eight states with popular elections, only two, Pennsylvania and Maryland, were seriously "in play," as we say today. Knowing this, partisans on both sides organized by forming tickets of electors who would essentially be pledged to vote for their party's candidates. Voting by ticket was not new, but this was the first time the practice was used for a presidential election. In a remarkable display of party unity, the fifteen Republican candidates for electors in Pennsylvania received nearly the identical numbers of votes in areas flooded by their printed tickets, and so did the fifteen Federalist candidates in areas they covered. In the end, statewide, fourteen of the fifteen candidates on the Republican ticket prevailed. Unless Adams could somehow pick up a few stray votes in the South, it looked as if Jefferson would prevail.[6]

It was time to activate the Pinckney strategy. Immediately following the Pennsylvania election, Oliver Wolcott wrote to Hamilton: "The Federal ticket is lost here. There are still hopes that Mr. Adams will be elected, but nothing more. I hope Mr. P. [Pinckney] will be supported as the next best thing which can be done. Pray write to our Eastern friends." (New England, New York, and New Jersey were often referred to in those times as the eastern states rather than the northern states.) Hamilton needed little prodding. He had already been promoting Pinckney, and now he redoubled his efforts by writing "some additional letters to the Eastward enforcing what I had before written." One of these letters, written to "———" and apparently duplicated several times, survives. "All personal and partial considerations must be discarded, and every thing must give way to the great object of excluding Jefferson," he wrote. Although most Federalists now agreed that both Adams and Pinckney would be on the ticket, he suspected that some New Englanders, partial to Adams, would "withhold votes from Pinckney," fearing "he may outrun Mr. Adams." This was precisely the strategy he had advocated in the first presidential election, when he suggested electors "throw away" a few votes for Adams, but now he feared the consequences. If Adams did not have enough votes to defeat Jefferson, Pinckney still might, but only if New Englanders supported the full party ticket. "Pinckney has the chance of some votes southward and westward, which Adams has not. This will render our prospect in the main point, the exclusion of Jefferson, far better."

How would Adams and those close to him relate to the well-reasoned scheme of Hamilton, Wolcott, and their cohorts? Knowing this was a touchy matter, Hamilton closed his letter: "I never was more firm in an opinion than in the one I now express, yet in acting upon it there must be much caution and reserve."[7]

As it turned out, Adams managed just enough electoral votes in the South (four from Maryland and one each from Virginia and North Carolina) to prevail; he needed seventy to win and received seventy-one. Had all Federalists held firm to the party ticket, Pinckney would have tied Adams and the final choice between them would have been made by the House of Representatives. Had all but one or two Federalists voted the party line, Pinckney would have received enough votes to become vice president. Hamilton's letters, though, did not have the impact he had hoped for, and several New England electors "threw away" their votes for Pinckney for fear of his overtaking Adams. Jefferson, meanwhile, mustered sixty-eight votes. Even though not one of those came from any state north and east of the Delaware River, Jefferson had been elected vice president.

A president from one party and his possible successor from the opposition? Although that might appear strange to us, many Americans at the time were quick to embrace this fortuitous outcome. If ever there was hope for transcending the partisan divide, this was it. Perhaps the framers had it right after all.

Adams, for his part, embraced Jefferson as vice president. Although the two had fallen out politically, Adams recalled the critical days in Congress during the lead-up to independence, when they had worked "together in high friendship." Even during their rupture in the early 1790s, Adams had mixed his criticism with guarded respect. When Jefferson resigned his post in Washington's cabinet in 1793, Adams commented to his wife, Abigail, "I have so long been in the habit of thinking well of his abilities and general good dispositions, that I cannot but feel some regret at this event: but his want of candour, his obstinate prejudices, . . . and his low notions about many things have so nearly reconciled me to it, that I will not weep." Now he was willing to forget the bad and focus on the good, assuming that Jefferson's "good sense and general good disposition" would allow them to renew their "ancient friendship."[8]

Jefferson was equally accommodating. From his home in Monticello, he wrote to Adams directly just before the final results were known: "The public & the papers have been much occupied lately in placing us in a point of opposition to each other. I trust with confidence that less of it has been felt by ourselves personally." He then predicted Adams would prevail in the election because he himself had no support in the North and Hamilton's attempt to elect Pinckney would fall short. ("Indeed it is impossible that you may be cheated of your succession by a trick worthy the subtlety of your arch-friend of New York," he commented.) He wished Adams's administration "may be filled with glory," and he concluded amiably, "'Tho' in the course of our own voyage thro' life, various little incidents have happened or been contrived to separate us," he still retained "for you the solid esteem of the moments when we were working for our independence, and sentiments of respect & affectionate attachment." Meanwhile, Jefferson instructed Madison, his ally in the House of Representatives, "to solicit on my behalf that Mr. Adams may be preferred" in case the election would be decided there. "He has always been my senior, from the commencement of my public life, and the expression of the public being equal, this circumstance ought to give him the preference."[9]

The goodwill was contagious. Benjamin Franklin Bache's strident Republican newspaper, *Aurora,* momentarily changed its tone: "ADAMS and JEFFERSON, lately rivals, and competitors for the most distinguished station which a free people can confer, appear in the amiable light of friends. . . . Surely this harmony presages the most happy consequences to our country." The conciliatory tone was echoed on the other side by the staunch Federalist Rufus King: "The change of the Executive here has been wrought with a facility and a calm which has astonished even those of us who always augured well of the government and the general good sense of our citizens. The machine has worked without a creak."[10]

Aiding the reconciliation between Adams and Jefferson was their shared antipathy to Hamilton, who had plotted against both of them. Writing to Madison about "Hamilton's insurrection," Jefferson held that Adams was "the only sure barrier against Hamilton's getting in," while Adams complained to his wife, Abigail: "There is an active spirit in the Union, who will fill it with his politics wherever he is. He must be attended to, and not suffered to do too much." On one level, the split within Federalist ranks would seem to work against Adams as he tried to unite the nation behind him, but in a sense it played in his favor, freeing him from any possible need to maintain party loyalty. Positioned between polar opposites—Jeffersonian Republicans and Hamiltonian Federalists—Adams could pursue his own course, which is precisely what he wished to do in any case.[11]

Adams had always been a proponent of independence on all levels: independence from Great Britain, independence of one branch of government from another, and independence of each individual to make his own decisions. ("I must think myself independent, as long as I live. The feeling is essential to my existence," he wrote to his son John Quincy Adams in later years.) According to the political philosophy he had long advocated, independence was absolutely essential to the proper functioning of the presidential office. In a republic, governmental authority should be divided among branches with equal power. Within the legislative branch, an upper house would represent aristocratic interests and a lower house democratic interests. Since these frequently conflict, an independent executive, which Adams impoliticly referred to as monarchical, would hold and manage the scale, keeping the competing interests well balanced. The reason he had wanted to call the president "His Highness" or "His Elective Highness" was to dignify the office and elevate it above all others, so contending factions would submit to its arbitration. To arbitrate fairly, the president must not be beholden to any particular group, whether aristocratic or democratic, Federalist or Republican.[12]

Such was his philosophy, but could President Adams—or anyone—hold himself to it when confronted with real-life political contests?

The next four years would serve as a field test for his theory of government, anchored and highlighted by a transcendent, nonpartisan chief executive. Through his own agency, he had the opportunity to prove by positive example that a republican government under strong and impartial leadership could in fact beat back, in his words, "that fiend, the Spirit of Party."[13]

John Adams's presidential "honey moon"—a term used and perhaps coined by Jefferson—proved short, even by today's standards. This did not surprise his vice president, who alleviated the disappointment of his own defeat with this somber realization: "I know well that no man will ever bring out of that office the reputation which carries him into it. The honey moon would be as short in that case as in any other, & its moments of exstacy would be ransomed by years of torment & hatred." That gloomy prospect consoled Jefferson perfectly. "I protest before my god, that I shall, from the bottom of my heart, rejoice at escaping."[14]

Adams, however, had not escaped. On March 6, 1797, two days after his inauguration, he sounded out his cabinet (all holdovers from Washington's administration) on the idea of including Madison, a leader of the opposition party, in a three-man peace mission to France. His goal was to depoliticize international negotiations, but his closest advisers unanimously rejected the idea, arguing that Madison, demonstrably pro-France, would be a weak negotiator. That evening, as the new president and vice president walked home from a dinner with Washington, Adams informed Jefferson that he would heed his cabinet's advice and not tap Madison for the job, while Jefferson informed Adams that Madison was not interested in any case. As Jefferson recalled years later, bipartisan cooperation ceased that very instant, only two days into Adams's term in office: "We came to Fifth street, where our road separated, his being down Market street, mine off along Fifth, and we took leave; and he never after that said one word to me on the subject, or ever consulted me as to any measures of the government." Although the "enthusiasm" of the inauguration had led Adams to forget "party sentiments" for the moment, he immediately "returned to his former party views." That was Jefferson's version, but Adams later confirmed the substance of the story. "Party passions had so deep and extensive roots," he recalled, that every member of his own cabinet threatened to resign if he appointed Madison to the mission.[15]

The fuss over France continued. The ruling French Directory, claiming that Jay's Treaty violated the 1778 alliance and that the United States had not yet paid its wartime debts, refused to receive the American minister and declared that American vessels trading with Britain would be considered fair prey for privateers. In May, President Adams, in a special address to a joint session of Congress, rebuked France and called on lawmakers to rejuvenate the navy and raise a "Provisional Army." This infuriated Republicans, who unleashed a frontal assault in the press and fought against military preparations in Congress. Late in June, less than four months into Adams's term, Jefferson reported the mood in Philadelphia, the nation's capital, to Edward Rutledge:

> The passions are too high at present, to be cooled in our day. You & I have formerly seen warm debates and high political passions. But gentlemen of different politics would then speak to each other, & separate the business of the Senate from that of society. It is not so now. Men who have been intimate all their lives, cross the streets to avoid meeting, & turn their heads another way, lest they should be obliged to touch their hats. This may do for young men with whom passion is enjoyment. But it is afflicting to peaceable minds. Tranquillity is the old man's milk.[16]

It would only get worse. The hawkish secretary of state, Timothy Pickering, announced to Congress that France had seized over three hundred American vessels. Adams's three new envoys to France were met by agents who tried to bribe them. France's belligerence favored Federalists, who took advantage of the militaristic mood to pass legislation that suppressed dissent (Sedition Act), expelled immigrants considered "dangerous to the peace and safety of the United States" or simply hailed from an enemy nation (two Alien Acts), and made it more difficult for foreigners to become American citizens (Naturalization Act). This legislative package further angered Republicans, who resisted in every conceivable manner. Newspapers refused to be silenced, even at the risk of legal prosecution. The Republican legislature in Kentucky, working from a draft penned by Jefferson, declared the Sedition Act "void, and of no force," while the Virginia legislature, on Madison's instigation, protested that the acts were "palpable and alarming infractions of the Constitution," and to keep "the present republican system of the United States" from becoming "an absolute, or, at best, a mixed monarchy," it affirmed its right to "interpose" between the federal government and the people. As Adams's administration neared its end, the partisan divide had grown wider than ever, and the Union itself seemed threatened.[17]

How did Adams figure in all this? Washington had done what he could to avoid war with Britain, and he had succeeded, but in doing so, he had antagonized France. Now his successor faced the challenge of avoiding a new war, and that in the midst of a partisan political environment that poisoned his every act. Any move toward peace would leave him open to Federalists' charges of being too soft, but if he maneuvered in the other direction, promoting military measures that might deter French advances, Republicans would put up an equally staunch resistance. The middle road was narrower than ever, nearly impossible to locate.

Adams's personal vendetta with Hamilton further complicated his tasks. In July 1798, amid fears of a French attack on American soil, Congress passed a bill that authorized the president to raise an "Additional Army" headed by none other than George Washington. Washington accepted the appointment under two conditions: he would be able to choose his own officers, and he would "not be called into the field until the Army is in a situation to require my presence." He then presented to President Adams a list of principal officers he wished Adams to appoint, topped by Alexander Hamilton, Charles Cotesworth Pinckney, and Henry Knox, ranking in that order.[18]

Knox immediately protested his low ranking. During the Revolution, he had held a higher rank than Hamilton, and now he refused to serve under an inferior officer. President Adams, who would make the final decision, sided with Knox over Hamilton, ostensibly because of military protocol but clearly for fear that Washington would be little more than a figurehead and Hamilton would wind up in charge of an army of some twelve thousand soldiers. This frightened Adams almost as much as it did Republicans. When urged by his secretary of war (James McHenry) and secretary of state (Timothy Pickering), both Hamilton supporters, to go with Washington's list, Adams held firm: "General Washington has through the whole, conducted with perfect honor and consistency. I said and I say now, if I could resign to him the office of President, I would do it immediately and with the highest pleasure, but I never said I would hold the office & be responsible for its exercise, while he should execute it." Adams, not Washington, was president, and the "power and authority" rested with him. "Knox, Pinckney, Hamilton" would be the order of command.[19]

Refusing to admit defeat, McHenry and Pickering engaged others to present their case, and they finally prevailed on Washington himself to write to Adams. When accepting command of the additional army, the first president reminded his successor, he and others had understood he was to determine his chief officers, and accordingly he had prepared a list that stipulated rank, but Adams had reordered them "the last to be first, and the first to be last." The Senate and most of all "the public" would be disappointed if "deprived of the services of Coll. Hamilton in the military line," Washington wrote. Was Adams's "determination to reverse the order" absolutely final?[20]

Washington's appeal turned out not to be necessary because Adams had already caved to the pressure, allowing the nominations to proceed as first intended. The political risk of crossing Washington was too great, the cost of holding firm too high. In his response to Washington he tried to save face by reaffirming that "by the present Constitution of the United States, the President has the authority to determine the rank of officers," but by his own discretion the president would allow "you as Commander in Chief" to resolve any complaints about rank, and if anyone should object to "the judgment of the Commander in Chief," Adams would "confirm that judgment." The wording was curious. In Article II, Section 2, the Constitution stated clearly that the president was to be "Commander in Chief" of the army, navy, and all state militias when called into service, but in his message to Congress on July 2, Adams had signed that title away: "I nominate George Washington, of Mount Vernon, to be Lieutenant General and Commander in Chief of all the armies raised, or to be raised, in the United States." With that move, Adams essentially lowered himself from first to a distant fourth in the military/political chain of command, behind not only Washington but also Hamilton and the president's own cabinet, all of whom supported Hamilton. "His Elective Highness" had fallen mightily. Having already lost control of his party, which he rebuked in any case, he no longer had the political clout to control his own appointees.[21]

If High Federalists (as Hamilton and his allies came to be called) were hard on Adams, tougher yet were his Republican critics, who made no distinction between Adams, who was still trying to avoid war with France, and Hamilton and company, who sought it. A Virginia correspondent warned Hamilton to "take care of yourself" because people in his state wanted "the heads of JOHN ADAMS, and ALEXANDER HAMILTON; & some few others perhaps." Republican rage was fueled not only by the push for war with France but also by the measures needed to pay for it. States were required to raise funds, and when a small army of tax collectors in Pennsylvania started visiting each home to assess its size, building materials, and the dimensions of its windows, people banded together to hound the tax men and decry everything Federalist, from the house tax to the Alien and Sedition Acts, from Congress and President Adams to "all friends of government, because they were all tories." Although Adams was able to suppress this incipient rebellion, named after one of its leaders, John Fries, he could not suppress all dissent, much of it directed his way. In the Republican press, the president of the United States was mocked as "His Rotundity"—a far cry from the exalted title Adams would have preferred.[22]

How could he not take this personally? Like Washington, Adams struck back at his detractors. The Alien and Sedition Acts gave him legal sanction not only to demean critics, as Washington had done, but also to suppress them. Adams did not instigate these repressive measures; in fact, he worried they would be considered war measures (the Alien and Sedition Acts were passed simultaneously with the authorization of the additional army) and consequently "a hurricane of clamor would be raised against them." Yet believing "there was need enough for both," he consented to the bills, and once they became law, his administration prosecuted fourteen high-profile cases under the Sedition Act that triggered, in his words, a "fierce and violent" opposition. Despite his best intentions, Adams, like his predecessor, had become a partisan player. With other Federalists, he treated criticisms leveled against himself, his administration, or the Federalist-dominated Congress as assaults on legitimate government under the Constitution. It is not difficult to see how this backfired, broadening the base of the opposition. Republicans gained considerable ground by complaining that the Federalists' repressive measures were intended to "perpetuate their authority and preserve their present places."[23]

Each of the first two presidents had aspired to transcendent governance, yet each failed to produce the intended result: the settlement of differences without flagrant discord. This is not to say the first twelve years under the Constitution ended in failure, as we might infer if we look only at the tone of political discourse. The nation restored its credit and was solvent. The national debt and balance of trade had stabilized. Exports increased from $20 million in 1790 to $70 million in 1800, and population in that decade grew by 35 percent. All this was possible, in part, because there were no costly military conflicts. Jay's Treaty avoided war with Britain, and while the scuffles with France included several naval confrontations, both France and the United States backed off; the "Quasi-War" ended with the Convention of 1800, which established American neutrality. In the end, the partisan divide paid some dividends: Francophiles and Anglophiles in a sense canceled each other out, each group resisting war with its favored nation. Both Washington and Adams, in their respective negotiations with Britain and France, managed to buy enough time to prevent hawks at home from driving the agenda and declaring war. To accomplish this, they did not have to assume exceptional powers; they only needed to assert their constitutionally guaranteed authority to appoint ambassadors, which they did.[24]

It comes as no surprise that Washington, who arrived at the office with more political capital than any subsequent president, could accomplish this much, but Adams came with little capital and faced headstrong opposition almost from the outset. Unlike Washington, he was in no position to expand or even define presidential powers. The aggressive acts taken by Federalists during his administration— raising and supporting a large federal army and passing the Alien and Sedition Acts—were pushed through by High Federalists in Congress and within his own cabinet. Presidential leadership was not required. Although Adams possessed the trappings of the presidency, he did not have the support necessary to lead the nation in the manner he had hoped and perhaps expected; he could hardly arbitrate between conflicting parties when neither party paid him much respect. To be a strong president required more than exercising the powers granted by the Constitution and augmented during Washington's administration. This legal authority was necessary but not sufficient to exert leadership, Adams inadvertently demonstrated. Although it was nowhere written, an effective president would need to build greater support and command higher esteem than his office alone guaranteed.

That said, Federalists and Republicans alike realized they could not possibly achieve their goals *without* capturing the presidency. Since party-line voting had solidified in Congress, overriding a presidential veto by a two-thirds vote of both houses became nearly impossible, and that, in effect, gave the president an absolute "negative" over any legislation—a warrant that the framers had rejected. The power to appoint ambassadors had given the president the lead role in foreign relations, and this turned out to have commercial as well as military implications. Cabinet officers, whom the president appointed and could dismiss at will, had come to play a major role in shaping policy, functioning in some ways as the executive council the framers never created. These powers, when considered together, were too great to wind up in the hands of the opposition, so electing the president superseded all other goals. In 1800, as Adams entered the fourth and final year of his first term in office, both sides readied for an epic battle. All the political struggles of the 1790s would be rolled into one: Which party could place its own man in the highest office in the land?

Ironically, anticipation of the election in some ways softened dissent. The Virginia legislature had appealed to other states to follow its lead in declaring the Alien and Sedition Acts "unconstitutional," but none did. The rebels in Pennsylvania had hoped others would join them in resisting wartime taxes, but none did. Instead, with the election looming, most Republicans chose to alter their tactics, preferring electoral politics over direct or violent confrontation; playing too strong a hand, they reasoned, would only hurt their chances at the ballot box. Here was a payoff for free and reasonably frequent elections, which not only prevented dictatorship but also provided an alternative to revolutionary upheavals. Yet the election would not proceed along the lines the delegates to the Federal Convention had intended, because they had failed to predict the hardening of party lines. Viewing the presidency as a winner-take-all affair, each side, of necessity, tried to muscle its way into power, pushing the limits of the system stipulated in the Constitution.

The jockeying began at the state level. Since electors were to be chosen in a manner determined by state legislatures, Republicans and Federalists alike realized that to elect a president, they would have to organize locally and secure majorities in those bodies. Organizational techniques varied from state to state, but partisans had previously figured out ways to solidify support for candidates to state offices and

Congress. Legislative leaders in Massachusetts, New York, and Virginia caucused to nominate candidates and strategize. Party activists in Delaware and New Jersey gathered in state conventions. In Pennsylvania and Maryland, local party committees coordinated efforts to select slates and bring out the vote. By 1800, these fledgling party organizations were poised to tackle the much larger task of electing a president.[25]

Several states were not competitive, but a few were. In Pennsylvania in 1799, Republicans prevailed in a close gubernatorial election, but the state senate remained in the hands of Federalists, and the two parties couldn't agree on the manner of selecting electors. Confident they had a majority, Republicans favored statewide elections that would give them all of Pennsylvania's fifteen electors, but Federalists pushed for district elections, in which they would capture several spots. Fearful that the new governor, Thomas McKean, would try to rig the system in favor of the Republicans, the U.S. senator James Ross, the Federalist whom McKean defeated, introduced a bill in Congress that would allow a committee of thirteen—six senators, six representatives, and one representative selected by the Senate—to judge the eligibility of contested electors from any state.[26]

Republicans immediately cried foul. Both the Senate and the House were under Federalist control, and if Ross's bill passed, Federalists could police the election in such a manner as to produce a president of their own persuasion. Republican senators tried amending the bill to make it less conspiratorial; committee members should be chosen by lot, they said, and the proceedings should be open to the public. The Federalist majority rejected both amendments, and the bill proceeded through its first and second readings.[27]

On the third and final reading, the South Carolina Republican Charles Pinckney (son of Thomas Pinckney's cousin) took the floor and assailed the bill as "even more alarming than the alien and sedition law." His central argument was irrefutable: "By the Constitution, electors of a President are to be chosen in the manner directed by the State Legislatures—this is all that is said. . . . There is not a single word in the Constitution which can, by the most tortured construction, be extended to give Congress, or any part of our Federal Government, a right to make or alter the State Legislature's directions on this subject." This was true not only in the letter of the law but in the spirit as well. Pinckney, who had been a delegate to the Federal Convention, reminded the House that he and his colleagues, when writing the Constitution, had intentionally stripped Congress of its authority to choose the president, except when electors could not produce a majority winner. They had done this in the hopes of preventing intrigue and ensuring presidential independence, but if Ross's bill passed, intrigue would be the inevitable result, and the president would become a creature of Congress. In a contested election, he predicted, "party spirit" would "govern every decision." Losers at the state level would raise objections that their friends in Congress would uphold, thereby invalidating their opponents' electors. Free elections would thus become farcical. "Give the power of deciding on their votes, and of rejecting or receiving them as they please, to thirteen men, all of the same political description, all wishing the same men, sitting behind closed doors, and whose deliberations are removed from the public eye, and you will find it difficult to avoid suspicion." Citizens would understandably lose faith in "the integrity of government"—the bedrock of a republican nation.[28]

It was a carefully prepared and persuasive speech, but fortunately for the bill's proponents there was no need for a reasoned rebuttal. Immediately after Pinckney relinquished the floor the question was called, and Ross's bill passed the Senate along strict party lines, 16 to 12.[29]

The House, though, killed the measure by making alterations the Senate did not accept. Members there had their own reasons for not going along with the Senate's plan. According to the Constitution, the House would choose the president if electors produced no clear winner, but Ross's bill would effectively give control of the election to the Senate, which determined the majority of the committee's thirteen members. Further, moderate Federalists in the House faced elections by the people every two years, and once the Republican newspaper *Aurora* pirated a copy of the bill and published it, congressmen who supported it would do so at their peril.[30]

Defeat of the Ross bill averted a national disaster, for it would have undercut the authority of the president by delegitimizing the electoral process. But other dangers lurked. The contentious political environment that produced the Ross bill and allowed it to advance as far as it did would produce another crisis not so readily circumvented.

To understand the election of 1800, we need to know the playing field and the time line. Congress had stipulated that electors would meet at their respective state capitals to cast their votes on December 3. Since each state was at liberty to decide how and when electors would be chosen, "election day" in 1800 could be anytime before then. Four years earlier, eight states had permitted the people to choose their electors, but now that number had dwindled to five. In these states the election could be as late as November, but in the eleven states in which the legislatures chose electors, the people's only say in the matter would come during the annual election for state legislators, which could be up to a year earlier; after that, the choice of electors, and therefore the president, was in the hands of those we would today call politicians.

In several states, politicians in the legislatures altered the rules of the game to favor their particular party, which, under the Constitution, they were perfectly entitled to do. In Massachusetts and New Hampshire, Federalist legislatures took the decision out of the hands of the people and gave it to themselves, thereby ensuring a complete slate of Federalist electors. The Republican legislature in Georgia did likewise. In Virginia, the Republican-dominated legislature changed from district voting to statewide voting to keep Federalists from capturing a few seats. The Federalist legislature in Maryland wanted to eliminate popular elections by district, which had produced a split group of electors in 1796, and choose the electors themselves to produce a Federalist sweep, but this itself became a major campaign issue, and in October Republicans gained control of the legislature. In Pennsylvania the Republican assembly quarreled with the Federalist senate, and only at the last minute did the two bodies arrive at a compromise that split the state's electors almost equally, eight Republicans and seven Federalists.[31]

New York was a special case, and very consequential. As the law stood early in 1800, electors were to be chosen by the legislature, which Federalists controlled. Unless that changed, New York would end up totally in the Federalist column, as it had in 1796. Hoping to take a few votes this time around, Republicans took the high ground and pushed for district elections by the people, but the Federalist legislature held firm. Then, in the April state election, aggressive door-to-door campaigning by Republicans placed the legislature unexpectedly in their hands. Each party immediately switched its position: Federalists favored district elections so they could capture a few seats, while Republicans thought it best to keep the decision with the legislature. Real-world politics trumped political theory. What counted was the result, not the process.

Alexander Hamilton took the shift of power in his home state hard. Like any astute observer at the time, he saw that the loss of New York's twelve electoral votes would be difficult to make up elsewhere and his party might very likely lose. In a panic, he wrote to the state's governor, John Jay, his friend, political ally, and co-author of *The Federalist*. Immediately, Jay should call an emergency session of the outgoing Federalist legislature in order to institute district elections, Hamilton proposed, thereby preempting the appointment of electors by the incoming Republicans. Recognizing his blatantly political proposal might be viewed harshly, he tried to muster some semblance of a moral argument to support it:

> I'm aware there are weighty objections to the measure; but . . . in times like these it will not do to be overscrupulous. It is easy to sacrifice the substantial interests of society by a strict adherence to ordinary rules. . . . The scruples of delicacy and propriety . . . ought to yield to the extraordinary nature of the crisis. They ought not hinder the taking of a *legal* and *constitutional* step, to prevent an *Atheist* in religion and a *Fanatic* in politics from getting possession of the helm of the State.

Pressuring Jay as best he could, Hamilton concluded, "Appreciate the extreme danger of the crisis, and I am unusually mistaken in my view of the matter, if you do not see it right and expedient to adopt the measure." The governor saw it differently. At the bottom of Hamilton's letter he scribbled, "Proposing a measure for party purposes wh. I think it wd. not become me to adopt."[32]

While much of the political maneuvering in the early going was independent of the actual candidates, neither party could succeed without settling on a standard-bearer; if either party split its votes, it would likely lose. Selecting a candidate, of necessity, was an insiders' game. The framers had tried to decentralize the choice of president by requiring electors to meet separately and simultaneously in the state capitals, but the emerging parties undercut their intention. If parties were national, as they had to be in order to have any chance of success, they needed to gather in some central location to nominate candidates, and the most logical place was Philadelphia, the nation's temporary capital. There, congressmen separated into their respective parties and caucused. On May 3, Federalists gathered within the Senate chamber and decided to support John Adams for president and Charles Cotesworth Pinckney for vice president, and they discussed strategies to get them elected. On May 11, at Maraché's boardinghouse nearby, Republicans tapped Thomas Jefferson for president and Aaron Burr for vice president.

Jefferson's nomination was uncontested. He was currently vice president, he had almost been elected president four years earlier, and he was willing. As in 1796, Burr was added to provide regional balance, but this time his inclusion seemed to make more sense, for he had played a major hand in delivering New York to the Republicans. His nomination did present one problem, however. In the previous election, numerous southern Republicans had balked and left him off their tickets, and if they did so again, John Adams might come in second and become vice president, which no Republican wanted. Party loyalty was therefore paramount, and Republicans vowed to make sure their electors voted for both nominees.

Adams proved more problematic. He had softened his stance on France and disbanded the additional army, thereby widening the rift with High Federalists, but he had strong support in New England, and by avoiding a war with France, he had even placated some moderate Republicans. To leave the sitting president off the ticket would be suicidal, the caucus concluded—but could they get him elected? As they had done four years earlier, they tried to make inroads into the Republican South by nominating a Pinckney from South Carolina for vice president—not Thomas Pinckney this time, but his brother. Yet Adams's supporters worried, with good reason, that Hamilton and his allies might try to play the same trick as they had in 1796, when they tried to get Pinckney elected over Adams. At the caucus, New Englanders vowed to hold true and get their electors to vote for both candidates, but would that happen? What if it did, and Pinckney outpolled Adams in South Carolina to elevate him to the presidency? The alliance between moderate Federalists, dubbed Adamsites, and High Federalists, led by Hamilton, was tenuous at best.

Note the featured factors in these debates and decisions: nominating caucuses, tickets with regional balance, party loyalty, pledged electors. None of these had been anticipated at the Federal Convention, yet all would become fixtures in presidential politics.

So thorough was the obsession with capturing the presidency that it competed with actual governance. "Our parties in Congress seem to regard the approaching election as the only object of attention," wrote Fisher Ames, a High Federalist. A year before electors were to meet and cast their votes, Speaker of the House Theodore Sedgwick offered proof of Ames's assessment in a letter to a fellow Federalist: "In all our measures, we must never lose sight of the next election of President."[33]

By mid-October elections had been held in all eleven states in which legislatures chose the electors, but the national outcome was still very much in doubt. The five states with popular elections had yet to weigh in, while the results in Pennsylvania and South Carolina had been indecisive. Voters in Pennsylvania had produced a Federalist senate and Republican assembly, and unless these two bodies could agree, Pennsylvania would have *no* electors—a major loss to Republicans, who had carried the state in 1796. South Carolinians had given Republicans a slim edge in the legislature, but party loyalties there were more tenuous than elsewhere, and nobody could safely predict whether Republican electors would vote for Pinckney and possibly even his running mate.

Then suddenly, on October 24, Alexander Hamilton reentered the mix. On that day the *New-York Gazette and General Advertiser* published a fifty-four-page pamphlet titled *Letter from Alexander Hamilton, Concerning the Public Conduct and Character of John Adams, Esq., President of the United States*. It was a remarkably vindictive work and potentially a game changer. Instead of promoting the virtues of his party's candidate for president, he issued a damning indictment:

> There are great and intrinsic defects in his [Adams's] character, which unfit him for the office of Chief Magistrate. . . . He is often liable to paroxysms of anger, which deprive him of self command. . . . He has made great progress in undermining the ground which was gained for the government by his predecessor, and . . . it might totter, if not fall, under his future auspices.

Although the campaign of 1800, like that of 1796, was replete with character assassination and negative campaigning, shots were usually fired in the direction of the opposing party. That Hamilton would treat the Federalists' nominal leader in such a manner seemed at first glance to constitute a serious breach of party discipline—but that's not how Hamilton saw it. In its own convoluted way, his letter presented a reasoned argument, even if embedded within a free-flowing stream of inflammatory rhetoric.

Hamilton's diatribe was as much a vindication of his own behavior as a denunciation of Adams's. He told how he had wanted to give Thomas Pinckney an "equal chance" in the previous election to ensure a Federalist victory, but his warning had been ignored by those supporting Adams, and this allowed Jefferson to become vice president and almost president. Adams's resistance to running equally with Pinckney created "in a great measure . . . the serious schism which has since grown up in the Federal Party," Hamilton claimed. For several pages, he defended the Pinckney brothers and himself from charges of being under "British influence." He then indicted the president for ignoring "the advice of his Ministers" and firing two of them—Hamilton's allies McHenry and Pickering—not for "misconduct" but for "collateral inducements," or what we might call today political gain. (This contradicted his earlier position; Hamilton had supported giving the president the discretionary power of removal when the issue was debated in the First Federal Congress.) Finally, Hamilton admitted to his own reasons for "personal discontent" with Adams's actions. Contrary to "the *express stipulation* of General WASHINGTON," Adams had resisted making Hamilton second-in-command of the additional army, and upon Washington's death the president had refused to promote him to the top spot.

Now for the clever logic, evident to Hamilton but confusing to readers then and now. Despite all these reasons *not* to support Adams, Hamilton still would. Torn between "the unqualified conviction of his [Adams's] unfitness for the station contemplated, and a sense of the great importance of cultivating harmony among the supporters of the Government [Federalists], on whose firm union hereafter will probably depend the preservation of order, tranquility, liberty, property, [and] the security of every social and domestic blessing," he would choose the latter. Party unity trumped all other considerations, even the "unfitness" of the president. So if he was willing to go that far to preserve "harmony" among Federalists, shouldn't *all* Federalist electors support the *full* party ticket, Adams *and* Pinckney? That was his closing argument. Explicitly, his intent was to keep Federalist electors in line; implicitly, he no doubt hoped that after hearing about Adams's shortcomings, one or two might choose Pinckney and *not* Adams, thereby delivering the presidency to his preferred candidate.[34]

Hamilton's argument, logical as it was, obviously backfired. Adams supporters were furious, High Federalists embarrassed, and Republicans elated. Unwittingly, Hamilton endangered the support Pinckney already enjoyed and gained him no more, and he certainly did Adams no favors. If Hamilton had meant to mend the schism that divided Federalists, he didn't. As one Federalist put it, "Gen. Hamilton's letter on the conduct & character of the President . . . will administer *oil* rather than *water* to the fire."[35]

Hamilton's letter probably had little impact on the popular elections in Virginia, North Carolina, Maryland, Kentucky, and Rhode Island, all held between November 3 and 19, nor in the ongoing contest within the Pennsylvania legislature, which ended in a virtual stalemate that yielded eight Republican and seven Federalist electors. Yet the letter might have played some role, even if indirectly, in South Carolina, where the election would eventually be decided.

Without South Carolina, each party had in its column precisely sixty-five electors. While Jefferson and Adams could count on that many votes from their parties, some votes for their running mates might still be "thrown away." All this would come into play in Columbia during the ten days preceding the December 3 deadline, when electors would cast their ballots. In and out of chambers, legislators debated and caucused in preparation for choosing electors. Charles Cotesworth Pinckney, popularly known as General Pinckney or C.C., was certainly a local favorite, a low-country patrician with as much prestige and honor as any in the state and connected to nearly everybody who wielded power or influence. Opposing him, though, was the U.S. senator Charles Pinckney, the vice presidential candidate's cousin who had argued so vociferously against the Federalist-sponsored Ross bill in Congress. Absenting himself from the national body in order to participate in the wrangling, "Blackguard Charley" (as his Federalist family and peers called the Republican renegade) lobbied against his own kin. With allegiances torn, the most popular alternative was to put forth electors pledged to a split ticket of Pinckney and Jefferson, a result that would have pleased Hamilton. Yet Hamilton had made that impossible. Such a ticket would need the support of General Pinckney himself, and after the controversial letter, he was boxed in; at the risk of appearing Hamilton's tool, he needed to retain strict party loyalty. Without the candidate's assent, the compromise faltered, and on December 2,

with not a day to spare, the South Carolina legislature chose eight electors, all pledged to Jefferson and Burr. Even in South Carolina, where
party organization and allegiances were weaker than anywhere else in
the nation and personal connections particularly strong, party trumped
family and local loyalties.[36]

On December 3, electors met as stipulated in their state capitals, and
though the voting was supposed to be secret until ballots were opened
on the Senate floor two months hence, this constitutional stipulation
had been ignored from the time of the first presidential election. As
soon as communications across distances would permit, within weeks
rather than months, everybody knew the results: the Republicans had
prevailed by exactly eight votes.

Note the plural, *Republicans*. Jefferson and Burr had garnered 73 votes
each, Adams 65, and Pinckney 64. It was an amazing display of party
unity on both sides. Back in 1796, 46 of 138 electors had voted for candidates not on their party's ticket. In 1800, only one did—an elector from
Rhode Island who voted for John Jay rather than Pinckney to ensure
that Adams and Pinckney would not wind up in a tie. Republicans,
recalling how Federalists had lost the vice presidency in 1796 by not
staying united, failed to take that precaution. Every single one voted
diligently for the two candidates, and that produced a result the framers had not foreseen but Hamilton had during the very first presidential
election: the avowed winner would have to face a runoff with his presumed vice president in the House of Representatives, as required by
Article II, Section 1, Paragraph 3 of the Constitution.

This would have been merely a technical glitch, easily rectified by
a simple vote in the House of Representatives, if parties had not rigidi-
fied. In a winner-take-all game, however, all strategies make sense, as
long as one plays by the rules, and there was nothing in the rules that
prevented Federalists in Congress from voting for Burr over Jefferson.
With Burr they would have considerable influence, with Jefferson none.

The rest of the story is legion and need not be detailed here; a
simple outline will suffice to reveal the stark truths. The Constitution
stipulated that voting in the House would be by state delegations and
that a majority was necessary to produce a winner. Of the sixteen delegations, eight were Republican, six Federalist, and two evenly divided.
To gain the critical ninth vote, Republicans needed to persuade just a

single Federalist from either of the divided states, or a few from one of the others, *not* to back Aaron Burr for president. This they could not do, even though Burr had neither the personal credentials nor the political persuasion that would normally appeal to them. All that mattered was foiling their political opponents.

One prominent Federalist refused to play along with this game. Long opposed to Burr for a multitude of personal and political reasons, Alexander Hamilton sounded the alarm to his fellow Federalists: Burr was altogether without "public principles," an opportunist who would "plunder" his country, "disturb our institutions," and seek for himself "permanent power." Much as he had preferred Adams to Jefferson even though he detested them both, he now argued that Jefferson was "by far not so dangerous a man" as his longtime antagonist from New York. "For heaven's sake," he pleaded, "let not the Foederal party be responsible for the elevation of this man." (Four years later, when Burr ran for governor of New York, Hamilton again derided him in public; this time Burr challenged Hamilton to a duel, Hamilton accepted, and Burr prevailed.)[37]

Nobody listened to Hamilton's latest tirade. Burr's character was not the issue. "He is ambitious—selfish—profligate. His ambition is of the worst kind—it is a mere love of power," Speaker of the House Sedgwick admitted. Yet Burr held "no pernicious theories," and because of his obvious inadequacies "Burr must depend on good men for his support & that support he cannot receive but by a conformity to their views." A Burr presidency, in short, would give Federalists access to centralized power, and that was worth fighting for.[38]

Since the first presidential election, Hamilton had been willing and even eager to exploit the "defect in the constitution" to achieve his party's ends, yet now, when Federalists found themselves with a special opportunity to do so, he reneged. Was it honor that caused him to back off? Personal vendetta? Sound judgment? Whatever his reasons, Federalists in Congress did not share them. They had learned too well from their master: party loyalty came first.

The first vote to break the Jefferson-Burr tie was taken in the Capitol building, under construction in the swampy town of Washington, at 1:00 p.m. on Wednesday, February 11. Predictably, eight states voted for Jefferson, six for Burr, and two delegations, splitting evenly, cast no votes. Members caucused, offered deals, and voted again, but the result remained unchanged. Into the night they voted and caucused, and at 8:00 the following morning, after casting twenty-seven ballots, the House finally recessed. Voting resumed on Friday and again on Saturday. Not until Sunday, the Sabbath, did members take a full break. By then they had voted thirty-three times.

On that day, a frustrated Jefferson wrote to his ally James Monroe, currently governor of Virginia. Federalists, he said, had talked of passing "a law for putting the government into the hands of an officer" of their own choosing if the election were not settled by March 4, when Adams's term as president ended. Jefferson and the Republicans countered with force: "We thought it best to declare openly and firmly, one & all, that the day such an act passed, the middle states would arm, & that no such usurpation, even for a single day, should be submitted to."

While the prospect of armed resistance to federal authority "shook them," Jefferson reported, Federalists were even more "alarmed" by the next volley: Republicans threatened to call a convention "to re-organize the government, & to amend it." That truly hit its mark. "The very word convention gives them horrors, as in the present democratical spirit of America, they fear they should lose some of the favorite morsels of the constitution." For years, Federalists had complained that Republicans were warmed-over Anti-Federalists bent on destroying the Constitution, and now their worst fears might come true. A new convention, they knew, might well throw out the old rules altogether, just as the Federal Convention of 1787 had done.[39]

Neither threat was idle. A new constitutional convention could and probably would have been called if Jefferson were not elected, and military preparations were already under way in at least two key states. Governor McKean of Pennsylvania later assured Jefferson, "Militia would have been warned to be ready, arms for upwards of twenty thousand were secured, brass field pieces etc. etc. and an order would have been issued for the arresting and bringing to justice every member of Congress and other persons found in Pennsylvania . . . concerned with the treason." In Virginia, Governor Monroe had already placed a militia guard around a large storehouse of arms in New London, halfway between the state capital in Richmond and Washington, to keep it from the hands of the national government. Fears of disunion struck a chord with the Delaware Federalist James Bayard, who announced he would withhold his vote for Burr rather than "hazard the Constitution upon which the political existence of the state depends." A few others followed Bayard's lead, and at noon on Tuesday, February 17, on the thirty-sixth ballot, the House of Representatives voted ten states to four, with two abstaining, for Jefferson.[40]

The nation had come to the brink of dissolution not simply because of one small "defect" in the Constitution; that flaw was easily remedied by the Twelfth Amendment, which required electors to distinguish between votes for president and votes for vice president. The real cause of near collapse was the manner in which that defect was exploited, and the deeper cause of that was the breakdown of honest governance, as the framers construed it. Once positioning for a presidential election had become the main concern of the national legislature, and once the Speaker of the House of Representatives had supported for the presidency a man he believed to be utterly without virtue and susceptible to influence, the dream had died.

The villain in this narrative could be called "faction" or the "spirit of party," so universally assailed by all the principal players, but factions and parties are not in themselves bad, and besides, as Madison and others readily affirmed, they would always be around. The task of devising workable rules for government was to *contain* factions and parties, not eliminate them. In *The Federalist* 10, Madison revealed the Constitution's basic containment policy—to keep any single faction from dominating the government:

> If a faction consists of less than a majority, relief is supplied by the republican principle, which enables the majority to defeat its sinister views by regular vote. It may clog the administration, it may convulse the society; but it will be unable to execute and mask its violence under the forms of the Constitution. When a majority is included in a faction, the form of popular government, on the other hand, enables it to sacrifice to its ruling passion or interest both the public good and the rights of other citizens.

By coming together as a body politic that extended across state and regional lines, Madison argued, Americans could ensure they would not live under the dominion of one particular group.

The creation of the presidency, and in particular the manner prescribed for the president's selection, undermined that strategy. So too did the strengthening of the presidency during Washington's administration and the establishment of national political parties. By 1800, the president was the presumed leader in setting foreign policy, he and his cabinet not only enforced domestic law but also helped shape it, and he possessed what amounted to an absolute veto. (Party politics made a veto override unlikely unless one party controlled at least two-thirds of both houses of Congress but not the presidency, an implausible occurrence. Not until 1845 did Congress override a presidential veto, and not until Reconstruction, when radicals in Congress battled President Johnson, was the override used as a formidable political tool.) The incentives to capture this office were too great for any interest group to ignore, but to have a realistic chance of success required organizing on a national level. This effectively marginalized minor factions, leaving only two top contenders. When one of these mega-parties proved victorious, it naturally wanted to remain in power, and to satisfy its "ruling passion," it was indeed tempted to sacrifice "the public good and the rights of other citizens." Such is the simple logic of must-win contests that require absolute majorities. The very event that Madison most feared had come to pass, courtesy of the Constitution.[41]

Though the elector system had facilitated the development of national parties with the ability to command discipline and ultimately control public policy, it didn't have to be that way. Imagine for a moment that James Wilson had been successful in his bid to institute popular elections for president. Parties would still have formed, and to increase their chances of success, they would have nominated candidates, but the general voting population would not have exercised nearly the discipline evidenced by electors. Would Aaron Burr, a northerner with no particular appeal in the South, really have carried the day in that region? Of course not. Theoretically, electors were supposed to vote according to their own discretion, but by 1800 they didn't; citizen voters, on the other hand, would have been guided only by their personal political preferences, and this would likely have resulted in a plethora of candidates, each the darling of some interest group. High Federalists might well have abandoned Adams after he disbanded the army and concluded peace with France. Northern farmers and artisans, although Republican, might have pushed candidates who were not from the southern slavocracy. Southern Federalists would have been free to vote for General Pinckney if they pleased. Such a wide-open field would likely have resulted in the pluralistic checks Madison had envisioned, making it more difficult for one group to command trans-regional allegiance and therefore take control of the presidency. Instead, the framers inadvertently created a narrow road to the assumption of centralized power, ensuring that a candidate favored by one of the mega-parties would take the presidency.

In the emergent two-party system there was still a check on the ruling party's ability to elect a president of its choosing—but just a single check, the opposing party, and that might not always suffice. What if Ross's bill, which would have allowed a partisan Congress to override state voting results, had passed, as it almost did? Federalists would have been in a position to ensure their own party's success. Could they have repeated this over and over, as we have seen so often in other nations? If so, it might have taken another revolution, or at least another constitutional convention, to change the rules and the rulers.

CHAPTER TEN

Jefferson Stretches the Limits

The election of 1800 might have been ugly, and it certainly did not proceed as the framers intended, but in the end it did produce a chief executive who was the clear choice of presidential electors. Better yet, power changed hands peaceably. Despite the fears of Federalists, the people they labeled Jacobins did not retaliate with a reign of terror. Instead of initiating a wholesale attack on the Constitution, the ascendant Republicans found little incentive to dismantle the governmental machinery they had just inherited, nor were they able to dismantle the opposition. Federalists continued to participate as a minority party in Congress, and they maintained control of the federal judiciary. A shared government was not what either party had imagined. Each assumed that the winner would prevail not merely for a single election cycle; once victorious, it would actually *vanquish* the defeated party. That in large measure explains the intensity of the passions during the election.

Jefferson's victory fell short of apocalyptic expectations precisely because the framers had established some balance among the separate branches of government. No judges were elected or unseated by the federal election of 1800. Republicans did turn a fifty-six-to-forty-nine deficit in the House of Representatives into a commanding sixty-five-to-forty majority, but Federalists retained nearly half the Senate seats, safely beyond the threshold they would need to negate a treaty. Jefferson would not be governing alone.

In addition to constitutional limits on his authority, the incoming president would be restrained by the very resistance to centralized power that led to his victory. How could a Republican president be an effective leader of a strong national government while remaining true to his ideological roots? That would be a difficult task, perhaps impossible. Many Federalists at the time accused Jefferson of inconsistency; before coming to power, they claimed, he had wanted to rein in the presidency, but once in command he proceeded to expand the office in numerous ways. Alexander Hamilton, however, did not go along with this politically expedient interpretation. Thinking back on their shared time in Washington's cabinet, Hamilton recalled that while Jefferson had always wanted to limit centralized powers, he had not begrudged the chief executive his fair share of authority *within* the federal government. "While we were in the administration together," Hamilton recalled early in 1801, when justifying his preference for Jefferson over Burr, "he was generally for a large construction of the Executive authority & not backward to act upon it in cases which coincided with his views. Let it be added, that in his theoretic ideas he has considered as improper the participation of the Senate in the Executive authority."[1]

The full story is more complex than any summary interpretation. Both before and during his presidential tenure, Jefferson struggled to reconcile the apparent discrepancy between republican principles, which favored deliberations among elected representatives over executive prerogatives, and the efficacy of a strong executive office unencumbered by such deliberations. His struggle is our struggle too. To this day, Americans understand that much is to be gained and lost by allocating powers to a single man who can make critical decisions swiftly and efficiently. Which authorities *should* be entrusted exclusively to the president, and which should be checked? The Constitution provided a bare-bones outline. Some details were filled in during the terms of the first two presidents, both Federalists, but several issues remained unresolved, and the manner in which these were handled by a president who resolutely espoused republican philosophy would highlight the difficulties in applying theory to real-life exigencies.

Jefferson's thoughts and feelings about executive power, shaped by America's Revolutionary experience, followed a familiar trajectory. In his 1774 *Summary View of the Rights of British America*, he urged King George III to "reflect" that he was "no more than the chief officer of the people, appointed by the laws, and circumscribed with definite powers, to assist in working the great machine of government, erected for their use, and consequently subject to their superintendance." Two years later, in the Declaration of Independence, Jefferson hurled invectives at "the present King of Great Britain." Simultaneously, while in Philadelphia, he composed a draft for Virginia's first constitution that referred to the state's chief executive not as "governor" or "president" but as "administrator," the weakest imaginable appellation. Upon serving his one-year term, the administrator would be ineligible for the next three. If Jefferson's constitution had been adopted, Virginia's chief executive would have been specifically prohibited from vetoing laws, dissolving or proroguing the legislature, declaring war, concluding peace, raising an army, coining money, erecting courts, establishing corporations, laying embargoes, or exercising several other powers that in the British government were prerogatives of the Crown. There should be no vestige of kingly authority here in America, Jefferson believed.[2]

Jefferson started questioning this view in 1781, when serving as Virginia's governor during the British invasion. His calls for the militia to muster were largely ignored, causing him to complain that "mild laws," which contained inadequate provision for executive "coercion," prohibited him from raising and supporting the armed force he needed to put up a defense. "We can only be responsible for the orders we give and not for their execution," he grumbled to Baron von Steuben, who himself had complained when only 12 unarmed Virginians reported for duty one day instead of the 104 who had been promised. Governor Jefferson asked the legislature for additional executive powers and for a declaration of martial law in zones proximate to the British forces, but it was too late. His term in office expired on June 2, 1781, and the following day Jefferson and the legislators fled the advancing British forces. When the assembly reconvened, it narrowly defeated a proposal to appoint a "dictator." The dramatic swing of the pendulum, from too little executive power to too much, horrified Jefferson. In *Notes on the State of Virginia*, written immediately after his governorship, he decried the absence of an independent executive office. With all power vested in the legislature, Virginia was ruled by a "despotic government." Echoing the cries of prewar Tories, he declared, "One hundred and seventy-three despots would surely be as oppressive as one." Indeed, for want of "a few votes," the legislature had almost abdicated its responsibility to represent the people and placed all power into "a single hand." "In lieu of a limited monarchy," he exclaimed, the legislature had nearly created "a despotic one."[3]

The crisis in leadership could have been prevented had Virginians not eschewed all executive authority. Jefferson understood why this happened—he had certainly added his voice to the anti-executive clamor—but now it was time to create an independent and more powerful executive office. In June 1783, in a second attempt to draft a state constitution, he proposed a more open-ended role for the state's chief executive, whom he now called "governor." Instead of being elected annually by the legislature, he would serve a single five-year term, thereby lessening his dependence. He would have "powers only, which are necessary to execute the laws (and administer the government), and which are not in their nature either legislative or judiciary," but the precise enumeration of those powers was not to be determined in advance. "The application of this idea must be left to reason," his draft stated flatly.

There were limits, among which were erecting courts, establishing corporations, and laying embargoes. These had also been placed off-limits in his 1776 draft, but this time he allowed the governor other powers. Declaring war, concluding peace, contracting alliances, raising an army, building forts, constructing armed vessels, and other such functions "we leave to be exercised under the authority of the confederation," but if the confederated government did not claim jurisdiction in a particular case, authority in these fields "shall be exercised by the governor," subject to regulation by the legislature. This reversed the existing order of operations. If Virginia were to be invaded again, the governor could act as he saw fit, even though the legislature could rein him in later. Recognizing that the creation of a stronger executive might frighten those who had just fought a war to rid themselves of a king, Jefferson included an interesting disclaimer: "By executive powers, we mean no reference to those powers exercised under our former government by the crown as of its prerogative, nor that these shall be the standard of what may or may not be deemed the rightful powers of the governor."[4]

This draft, like the one in 1776, never received serious consideration, but four years later, when George Washington sent him a copy of the document produced by the Federal Convention, Jefferson offered again his thoughts on the executive office. Writing from Paris to John Adams and James Madison, he exploded at the provision allowing the chief executive to serve an indefinite number of terms. "Their President seems a bad edition of a Polish king," he complained to Adams, who had also missed the convention. "Experience concurs with reason in concluding that the first magistrate will always be re-elected if the constitution permits it," he told Madison. "He is then an officer for life." This, with his frustration at the lack of a Bill of Rights, caused him to "stagger," although he supported most other features and generally approved the work of the convention. Two other caveats deserve note in light of his later positions. He would have preferred that the judiciary be granted veto power over legislation, either with the president or separately, and he believed that congressional representatives, because they were elected by popular vote, were "very illy qualified to legislate for the Union, for foreign nations &c." He did not oppose popular elections per se; indeed, they were absolutely necessary if Congress were to have the power of taxation. He just thought that people so chosen "will not be adequate to the management of affairs either foreign or federal." Who, then, *would* be adequate? The Senate? The president? Other executive officers? Jefferson did not elaborate.[5]

Jefferson's first musings on the Constitution were offered from a distance; he was neither responsible for its contents nor positioned to change them. Soon, though, he would take more than an abstract interest in the allocation of powers. First as secretary of state, then as leader of the opposition party, and finally as president, he would come to view the Constitution through lenses colored by political strife.

In 1790, when Washington consulted Secretary of State Jefferson on whether the Constitution required the president to seek the advice of the Senate before dispatching foreign emissaries, Jefferson replied:

> The transaction of business with foreign nations is Executive altogether. . . . The Senate is not supposed by the Constitution to be acquainted with the concerns of the Executive department. It was not intended that these should be communicated to them; nor can they therefore be qualified to judge of the necessity which calls for a mission to any particular place . . . which special and secret circumstances may call for. All this is left to the President. They are only to see that no unfit person be employed.[6]

The implications of this reasoning were profound. If the Senate had no legitimate access to foreign communications, it certainly could not involve itself with setting foreign policy. Not only diplomatic missions were to be "left to the President," but all relations with foreign nations, save only for declarations of war and ratifying formal treaties.

Yet in 1793, when Hamilton expressed a similar view in his Pacificus essays—the executive is the sole "organ of intercourse between the nation and foreign nations," Hamilton argued, and with the exception of declaring war and ratifying treaties, "the EXECUTIVE POWER of the Union is completely lodged in the President"—Jefferson strenuously objected. By then the political landscape had changed. Pro-France representatives held a slim majority in the House, and Jefferson did not want this body to be excluded from setting foreign policy.[7]

While Jefferson had always maintained there were two exceptions to the president's authority in the realm of foreign relations, declaring war and ratifying treaties, in 1796 he suddenly discovered a third exception. Since Jay's Treaty dealt with commercial affairs, and since the Constitution granted Congress the power "to regulate Commerce with foreign Nations," it followed that the treaty required approval not only from the Senate but from the House of Representatives as well. To James Monroe he wrote:

> We conceive the constitutional doctrine to be that though the President and Senate have the general power of making treaties, yet wherever they include in a treaty matters confided by the Constitution to the three branches of legislature, an act of legislation will be requisite to confirm these articles, and that the House of Representatives, as one branch of the legislature, are perfectly free to pass the act or to refuse it, governing themselves by their own judgment whether it is for the good of their constituents to let the treaty go into effect or not. On the precedent now to be set will depend the future construction of our Constitution.[8]

There were actually two issues here, one theoretical and the other practical. First, and most generally, the Constitution stated that treaties were to be treated as "the supreme Law of the Land," and since all other laws needed to pass through both houses of Congress, treaties should have to go through the same process. If that did not convince, a second argument hit more directly. A cardinal principle of republican governments, including this one, was that no expenditures of the people's money could be made without approval from the people's direct representatives, assembled in the House.

In order to affirm or deny the treaty, Jefferson and other Republicans argued further, Congress should have access to papers relevant to the negotiations. When a speech by Representative Albert Gallatin arguing for the requisition of documents from the executive branch appeared in the *Aurora*, Jefferson told Madison it was "worthy of being printed at the end of the *Federalist*, as the only rational commentary on the part of the constitution to which it relates." In 1787, upon first view of the Constitution, he had complained that representatives in the House were "very illy qualified" to deal with foreign affairs, but now he was insisting they do so. In 1790, as secretary of state, he had maintained that the Senate was "not supposed by the Constitution to be acquainted with the concerns of the Executive department" and "it was not intended that these should be communicated to them," but now he reasoned that a simple majority of the House and the Senate could declare virtually any treaty "constitutionally void" and that representatives and senators had a legitimate right to access any materials they wished so they could make up their minds.[9]

Jefferson's argument in this case was historically weak but logically strong. According to Madison's notes of the Federal Convention, when James Wilson moved on September 7 to give the House of Representatives as well as the Senate the power of advice and consent in treaty making, the motion was resoundingly defeated ten states to one; the convincing argument was the "necessity of secrecy in the case of treaties," which even Wilson acknowledged. Yet the Constitution *did* declare treaties to be the law of the land, and more particularly it required that expenditures in any matter whatsoever receive House approval. The framers had clearly wanted the House not to be involved in treaty making, yet they had established rules which, if strictly followed, required that it would. This provided fertile ground for debate and turned constitutional arguments into political ones. Soon, as president, Jefferson would face the question of House approval for a treaty of his own doing, the Louisiana Purchase, and he would assume a very different stance when the House demanded papers from the executive department regarding his embargo.

President Jefferson would face other constitutional issues as well. Always, he had advocated a firm separation of powers, but what would he do when the judiciary, controlled by Federalists, exerted its own independence from the executive? He had been one of the most forceful advocates for the Bill of Rights and a leading opponent of the Alien and Sedition Acts, but could he stay within the limits of the Constitution while enforcing legislative acts and presidential policies? Addicted to careful reasoning, the nation's third chief executive would have no shortage of arguments to support the positions he took, but walking that fine line between executive authority and republican principles would be no easier for him than for others. The delineation of executive powers "must be left to reason," Jefferson had declared in his 1783 draft for a state constitution, but for a man exerting power in real-world situations, reason could and would turn fickle.

Shortly after noon on Wednesday, March 4, 1801, before some 1,140 dignitaries and commoners (154 were women) assembled beneath the arched roof in the new and spacious Senate chamber, Thomas Jefferson, dressed as "a plain citizen, without any distinctive badge of office," delivered "in so low a tone that few heard it" an eloquent call for unity that would serve as a model for future inaugural addresses. The incoming president entreated his audience to "bear in mind this sacred principle":

> That though the will of the majority is in all cases to prevail, that will to be rightful must be reasonable; that the minority possess their equal rights, which equal laws must protect, and to violate would be oppression. Let us, then, fellow-citizens, unite with one heart and one mind. Let us restore to social intercourse that harmony and affection without which liberty, and even life itself, are but dreary things. And let us reflect that having banished from our land that religious intolerance under which mankind so long bled and suffered, we have yet gained little if we countenance a political intolerance, as despotic, as wicked, and capable of as bitter and bloody persecutions.

With words that have been cited countless times since, Jefferson declared, "We have called by different names brethren of the same

principle. We are all Republicans, we are all Federalists." He then enumerated a list of "federal and republican principles" that would shape
his administration: "attachment to union and representative government," "equal and exact justice to all men," "the right of election by the
people," "a wise and frugal government," "the supremacy of the civil
over military authority," and so on. A few of these—"the honest payment of our debts," "the support of the state governments in all their
rights," and "encouragement of agriculture, and of commerce as its
handmaid"—could be construed as oblique jabs at Hamiltonian policies, but even these were phrased in ways that would not stir dissent.
One, though, did appear pointed: "absolute acquiescence in the decisions of the majority," a not-too-subtle reminder to Federalists of their
recent electoral defeat and an enjoinder not to force the issue.[10]

How, exactly, would "we are all Republicans, we are all Federalists"
translate into the business of governance?

Governance in the early Republic was not what we have come to
expect today. Congress typically met in early December (sometimes
a few weeks earlier), did its business, then adjourned in the spring.
Sessions lasted three to six months; for the remainder of the year, the
executive department, headed by the president, conducted all affairs of
state. When Jefferson assumed office, the special session of Congress
that had been called to usher him immediately adjourned, and members
would not convene again for another eight months. Jefferson was left
to administer the federal government under laws passed by Federalists.

His main task during that time was to appoint civil officers. Presumably, the president was to avoid partisan considerations and base
his decisions solely on personal qualifications, but circumstances were
not what the framers had imagined. After the bitter election and the
Republicans' ascension to power, all executive actions would be gauged
politically. Should Jefferson try to mollify his opponents or satisfy his
base? He received contradictory counsel. Some advised "giving offices
to some of their [Federalist] leaders, in order to reconcile." Others
urged him to appoint only Republicans and remove Federalists already
in office. William Branch Giles, the Republican Party leader in the
House, advocated "a pretty general purgation of office." Conciliation,
he argued, "would produce general and lasting disgusts in its [the
administration's] best friends, and revive the hopes and enterprises of
its enemies, for they are not dead.—They only sleep."[11]

Jefferson tried to satisfy both camps. He promised to give new appointments "only to republicans," but he shied from a wholesale purge of Federalist officeholders so as not to provide a rallying point for the opposition. He would, however, conduct a few "deprivations of office," taking care to do so "gradually, & bottomed on some malversation or inherent disqualification"; the firings should not appear "to be made on the ground of political principle alone." This strategy he announced to James Monroe on March 7, three days after taking office. Always, he stated, incoming Republicans should be "balancing measures according to the impression we perceive them to make." In the end, he removed exactly sixteen Federalist officers "on political principles alone . . . to make room for some participation for the republicans," he confessed to Joseph Nicholson, a Republican leader in the House. He would fire no more, for fear of jeopardizing "our object of harmonizing all good people of whatever description."[12]

If Jefferson's tactics were politically motivated, his hand was to some extent forced. Back on December 12, news had arrived in Washington that South Carolina had voted Republican, thus assuring Adams's defeat, and for the next eighty-two days, until 9:00 in the evening of March 3, the outgoing president and Federalists in Congress worked at a feverish clip to overload the government with new appointees, all of their persuasion. On March 2 alone, Adams sent forty-two nominations to the Senate; the following day these were confirmed and sent hastily back to the president so he could sign them before relinquishing the office at midnight. This angered Jefferson exceedingly. Over and over in his letters, he recounted how "mr A" had "crouded in" his appointments "with whip & spur from the 12th of Dec. when the event of the election was known, (and consequently that he was making appointments, not for himself, but his successor) until 9. aclock of the night, at 12. aclock of which he was to go out of office." It was an "outrage of decency," he proclaimed, and he would consider every one of these appointments "nullities."[13]

Except judges who had been appointed for life. These were "irremovable" by direct acts, Jefferson conceded, but that did not prevent him from removing them indirectly. During the eight-month interlude between the inauguration and the first session of the Seventh Congress, Jefferson and the Republicans plotted a multipronged attack on the Federalist-controlled judiciary.

First, Jefferson removed Federalist marshals and court attorneys who had been "packing juries and prosecuting their fellow citizens with bitterness of party hatred." While he couldn't touch the judges, he could redirect the "executive" arm of the courts. He could also withhold a handful of commissions to Adams's "midnight" appointees that had slipped through the cracks and never been delivered, a move that led to the landmark case *Marbury v. Madison* discussed on pages 243–45.[14]

Next, after Congress reconvened, it would repeal the Judiciary Act recently enacted by lame-duck Federalists. This measure increased the number of district and circuit courts, enabling Adams to grant new judgeships to Federalists, and reduced the number of seats on the Supreme Court from six to five, thereby making it less likely that Jefferson would be able to appoint a justice of his persuasion. Repealing the Judiciary Act was perfectly legal, Republicans argued. If the Constitution allowed Congress to "ordain and establish" new courts, it also permitted Congress to abolish them.

Third, to postpone legal challenges they expected from Federalists, the Republican Congress canceled two sessions of the Supreme Court. By the time the Court met again early in 1803, the Judiciary Act would already have been repealed and the new courts abolished.

Finally, Republicans vowed to impeach Federalist judges. To do this, they would need to show cause, and as the other assaults progressed, they eyed likely targets.

President Jefferson had his hand in all of this. In his first State of the Union address, he called Congress's attention to "the judiciary system of the United States, and especially that portion of it recently erected." Nobody could mistake the reference to the Judiciary Act of 1801. Were new courts really needed? He had gathered lists of the courts' business, which he "now lay before Congress" so members could judge for themselves whether the expansion was necessary. Clearly, he believed it was not, but he let the data speak for itself.[15]

Meanwhile, he worked with Republicans in both houses of Congress to craft a repeal and strategize for pushing it through. This would be the featured battle in "our winter campaign," as Jefferson phrased it: "the suppression of useless offices, and lopping off the parasitical plant engrafted at the last session on the judiciary body." Today, we expect the president to take a leadership role in drafting legislation, but this was not what the framers had envisioned, and it was what Anti-Federalists had feared. Indeed, Hamilton's participation in the legislative process had been one of the triggers to the formation of an opposition party, and a cornerstone of the Republican platform was to limit executive interference with the people's direct representatives. Consequently, Jefferson had vowed not to interfere with Congress, and openly he did not, but starting with the campaign to repeal the Federalists' Judiciary Act, and continuing through his two terms in office, he bonded closely with congressional party leaders to enact his agenda. Federalists noted this with disdain. "The Executive as completely rules both Houses of Congress as Bonaparte rules the people of France," complained the Massachusetts congressman Manasseh Cutler as debate on the repeal neared conclusion.[16]

Repeal of the Judiciary Act passed the Republican-dominated House handily, but in the Senate the razor-thin Republican majority temporarily disappeared when two senators reported absent due to illness. The task of introducing and managing the bill fell to John Breckinridge, who had ushered Jefferson's resolutions opposing the Alien and Sedition Acts through the Kentucky legislature three years earlier. Opposition to repeal was led in part by one of the Senate's most recent members, Gouverneur Morris.

Morris was staging a comeback of sorts after a twelve-year absence from domestic politics. He had sat out the ratification debates, calling them only half-jokingly a "dull subject." In 1789, to further the business interests of Robert Morris and himself, he traveled to France, just in time to take in the first phase of that nation's Revolution. Washington then asked him to perform a diplomatic task in Britain, which he did, and after returning to France, on the morning of December 6, 1791, Gouverneur Morris brashly completed his trilogy of constitutions—the first one for New York, the next for the United States, and this one for a Continental European giant clearly in need of some guidance. Adjusting for the change in venue, Morris's French constitution, unlike those he helped author in America, featured a hereditary monarch; "the proper form of government" for any state, he wrote, depended on "the habits and manners of its citizens." Morris's weak attempt to salvage the French monarchy got nowhere, but he soon learned that President Washington had appointed him to serve as minister to France. Over and above the objections of French sympathizers such as Jefferson and Monroe, the Senate approved the appointment. As minister, Morris did not shy from dealing with the new revolutionary government, but simultaneously he sheltered refugee aristocrats and tried to help the royal family escape. In 1794, French revolutionary officials demanded his recall, and he spent the next four years touring Europe. After that he returned to his original home at Morrisania, delivered New York's official eulogy to President Washington, and early in 1800 was appointed by the state legislature to fill the remaining term of the U.S. senator James Watson, who resigned to accept one of John Adams's lame-duck appointments.[17]

Reentering the political fray, Morris found himself fighting a rearguard action against a less cataclysmic "revolution" than France's, this one merely trying to reverse the policies of the previous administration. A Federalist by temperament and philosophy, by class and business interests, and by any other measure, Morris would have to adjust whatever views he had expressed in his previous incarnation as an American statesman to reflect the political contingencies of the moment. At the Constitutional Convention in 1787, he had engineered the transfer of appointive powers from the Senate to the president, fearing that the Senate would be "subject to cabal." Now, sitting in that body, he looked upon the Senate more favorably and the presidency, now in Republican hands, less so. On January 14, in a lengthy address opposing presidential appointive powers without consent of the Senate, he entreated senators to stay true to their constitutional mission and not repeal the Judiciary Act. "*We*, the Senate of the United States, are assembled here to save the people from their most *dangerous* enemy, to save them from themselves; to guard them against the baneful effects of their own precipitation, their passion, their misguided zeal. 'Tis for these purposes that all our Constitutional checks are devised." To allow repeal would "plunge us all into the abyss of ruin," he decried. "Do not, I beseech you, . . . commit the dignity, the harmony, the existence of our nation to the wild wind. Trust not your treasure to the waves. Throw not your compass and your charts into the ocean. Do not believe that its billows will waft you into port."[18]

Morris's rhetoric, extended metaphors and all, had no effect on party-line voting. Although Vice President Aaron Burr, as president of the Senate, cast a tie-breaking vote on a procedural issue with the Federalists, no other Republican broke ranks, and when all had returned to duty, the repeal bill narrowly passed. President Jefferson signed it into law on March 3, 1802, the last day of his first year in office. Stage one of the assault on the Federalist judiciary was completed, but it had required the expenditure of political capital. "I hope to see them [the people] again consolidated into a homogeneous mass, and the very name of party obliterated from among us," Jefferson had written to Robert Morris two days after taking office. "I will do anything to obtain it short of abandoning the principles of the revolution." Following his "principles," though, had shattered the dream of unity. Federalists might have lost the battle, but their argument that Jefferson and the Republicans were attempting to destroy the Constitution by crushing the independence of the judiciary only grew stronger, galvanizing opposition to the administration. To what lengths would the ruling party now go, once "Jefferson's measure" (as his opponents tagged the repeal) had passed?[19]

Among the forty-two "midnight" appointees were four men chosen for the relatively inconsequential positions of justices of the peace: William Marbury, Robert Hooe, Dennis Ramsay, and William Harper. Although John Adams had signed their commissions in the waning hours of his presidency and Secretary of State John Marshall had quickly affixed the Great Seal of the United States, James Marshall, the secretary's brother, in his haste had failed to include them with others he delivered to the appointees. Presumably, this minor administrative oversight could be straightened out, but Jefferson, upon assuming office, refused to deliver the commissions that had already been signed and sealed. Teaming up with the Federalist Charles Lee, a former attorney general under Washington and Adams, Marbury, Hooe, Ramsay, and Harper took Jefferson's secretary of state, James Madison, to court. Madison was required by the Judiciary Act of 1789 to hand over their commissions, they argued, but the defendant refused to produce the documents or even show up in court.

The case, *Marbury v. Madison,* was tried before the all-Federalist Supreme Court, with Chief Justice John Marshall presiding. Marshall and the associate justices faced a political dilemma. If they ruled in favor of the plaintiffs and ordered Secretary of State Madison to deliver the commissions, Jefferson would likely order Madison to disobey the Court, thereby setting up a constitutional showdown that Jefferson and the Republicans, at the height of their popularity, would win. On the other hand, the Federalist justices did not want to bow to Republican pressure and deny the plaintiffs their rightful offices.

Having sealed the original commissions when he was secretary of state, Marshall could easily have recused himself and let the other judges struggle with the problem, but instead he conceived a masterful exit strategy. First, he explained point by point why Madison, by law, should deliver the commissions, but he stopped short of ordering him to do so. Instead, he determined that the Supreme Court was not empowered to hear the case. The Constitution, he said, gave original jurisdiction to the Supreme Court only in cases "affecting ambassadors, other public ministers and consuls, and those in which a state shall be a party," so this suit did not qualify. Further, since the Judiciary Act of 1789 had stated a case like this *should* qualify, that act was *unconstitutional*. Marshall purposely lost the battle in order to win the war. Yes, Jefferson could deny the plaintiffs their commissions, but in this and all future issues brought before it, the Supreme Court would make the final determination on the constitutionality of laws. It was certainly a bold move, and perhaps it was not even "constitutional," since nowhere in the Constitution is the Supreme Court granted the explicit authority to make such a determination, but Marshall's prevailing opinion in *Marbury v. Madison* has withstood the test of time and become a central canon of our legal system.

Today, in our texts, we treat Marshall's decision in *Marbury v. Madison* as establishing what we call judicial review, but historically the matter was not so cut-and-dried. Although Marshall headed the Court for another third of a century, he never again overturned federal law. President Jefferson, meanwhile, refused to accept Marshall's pronouncement. True, he did not directly challenge the decision, which technically ruled in the administration's favor by dismissing the plaintiff's case, but privately he fumed. To Abigail Adams, eighteen months after *Marbury v. Madison* was concluded, he wrote, "The opinion which gives to the judges the right to decide what laws are constitutional, and what not, not only for themselves in their own sphere of action, but for the legislature & executive also, in their spheres, would make the judiciary a despotic branch." A key word here is "would"; for Jefferson, the matter was by no means settled. The notion that the judiciary could interfere with an action of the executive department seemed a clear violation of the basic principle of independent branches, which he had long espoused and the Constitution, he thought, had incorporated. The president, duly elected, clearly should have the final say in executive matters, not appointees from a different branch of government, while Congress itself should decide whether proposed legislation was constitutional. Each branch, Jefferson believed, must determine its own responsibility to the Constitution, subject only to the will of the people. The Constitution, after all, had required Jefferson to take an oath pledging to "preserve, protect and defend the Constitution of the United States," and how could he do this without determining for himself what the Constitution really meant?[20]

Separation of powers under the Constitution was not absolute, however, and this might work in Jefferson's favor. Federalist judges, if they overreached their authority, could potentially be impeached. Although the power of impeachment belonged to the legislative branch, Jefferson was the de facto leader of the party that controlled Congress, and he did not turn a blind eye to the possibility of utilizing this constitutionally approved technique for removing Federalist judges. The problem, though, was that "civil Officers of the United States" could only be impeached for "Treason, Bribery, or other high Crimes and Misdemeanors." Could Federalist judges be proven guilty on any of those counts?

Jefferson believed one could. The Supreme Court justice Samuel Chase had evidenced clear bias when trying cases under the Sedition Act. He bullied defense attorneys and tried to stack juries; once, he allegedly asked the marshal to remove from the jury panel "any of those *creatures* or people called democrats." Repeatedly, Chase preached his brand of Federalism from the bench, and his instructions to a grand jury in Baltimore in May 1803 caught Jefferson's attention. "I can only lament that the main pillar of our State Constitution has already been thrown down by the establishment of universal suffrage," Judge Chase told the jurors. "Our republican constitution will sink into a mobocracy, the worst of all possible governments. . . . The modern doctrines by our late reformers, that all men in a state of society are entitled to enjoy equal liberty and equal rights, have brought this mighty mischief upon us." When Jefferson read Chase's words in a newspaper, he wrote immediately to Joseph Nicholson, who was then managing the impeachment trial of a Federalist judge who had literally become insane: "You must have heard of the extraordinary charge of Chase to the Grand Jury at Baltimore. Ought this seditious and official attack on the principles of our Constitution, and on the proceedings of a State, to go unpunished? And to whom so pointedly as yourself will the public look for the necessary measures? I ask these questions for your consideration, for myself it is better that I should not interfere." The president's message to this Republican stalwart was clear: Chase should be impeached, but the president should not be implicated.[21]

Nicholson and John Randolph, the eccentric Republican "whip" who attended congressional sessions booted, spurred, and with riding whip in hand, drew up eight articles of impeachment, which the House of Representatives readily approved. Yet despite marshaling dozens of witnesses who attested to Chase's political excesses while serving in an official capacity, Nicholson and Randolph were unable to maintain party-line discipline in the Senate. Had all Republican senators toed the party line, Chase would have been removed from office, but just enough moderates joined with the outnumbered Federalists to acquit Chase on all counts.

Chase's impeachment trial was both a setback for Jefferson and a rare repudiation of partisanship. While the framers had established high standards for impeachment—"Treason, Bribery, or other high Crimes and Misdemeanors"—they also decriminalized the procedure by insisting that "Judgment in Cases of Impeachment shall not extend further than to removal from Office" and disqualification from holding future offices. While Chase had certainly broken no law, a good case could be made that he had violated his judicial charge of impartiality. Everybody knew, however, that had Chase been convicted, other impeachments would certainly follow. Not only would the judiciary be politicized even more than it was, but it would also become forever beholden to Congress, which could and likely would judge the judges habitually. That's why several moderate Republicans, fearful of setting a dangerous precedent, balked. (The exact number varied with the eight articles of impeachment.) With Chase's acquittal, the judiciary became *more* independent of Congress and, indirectly, the president. Jefferson had hoped impeachment would chasten the judiciary for its usurpations, but instead the judicial branch emerged stronger yet. No Supreme Court justice has been tried for impeachment since.

The borderlands between executive and judicial authority were explored yet one more time during Jefferson's presidency. On January 22, 1807, the president sent a special message to Congress announcing that Aaron Burr, "whose guilt is placed beyond question," had spearheaded a western conspiracy with "two distinct objects, which might be carried on either jointly or separately, and either the one or the other first, as circumstances should direct. One of these was the severance of the Union of these states by the Alleghany mountains; the other, an attack on Mexico." The first constituted treason, and the second a violation of treaty and law, since Spain was nominally on friendly terms with the United States. Although two grand juries in the West had failed to return indictments, the president vowed to bring Burr to justice closer to the center of national authority.[22]

This he did, but the case wound up in the federal district court in Richmond, Virginia, where the presiding judge was none other than Chief Justice John Marshall (at that time, Supreme Court justices presided over lower courts as well), and Jefferson did not trust Marshall or any other Federalist judge to oversee a fair trial. "What loophole they will find," he wrote to William Branch Giles, "we cannot foresee." Old wounds had not healed. To Giles the president did not bother to conceal his disdain for Federalist opponents, who "give all their aid, making Burr's cause their own, mortified only that he did not separate the Union and overturn the government." If Burr had succeeded in his secessionist efforts, he continued, "they would have joined him to introduce his object, their favorite monarchy, as they would any other enemy, foreign or domestic, who could rid them of this hateful republic for any other government in exchange." More than six years into his presidency Jefferson was still consumed with venom, but he did have a somewhat rational backup plan should Burr be acquitted. "The nation will judge both the offender & judges for themselves," he predicted. "They will see that one of the great co-ordinate branches of the government, setting itself in opposition to the other two, and to the common sense of the nation, proclaims impunity to that class of offenders which endeavors to overturn the Constitution." The folly of allowing judges to set traitors free would alert people to the need for reining in the judiciary, which could be done with a constitutional amendment. No longer would judges, with "impunity," be allowed to "overturn the Constitution."[23]

As the proceedings began, Jefferson tried to direct the prosecution by issuing frequent and specific instructions to George Hay, U.S.

attorney for the District of Virginia, who was charged with handling the case. Writing from Washington, he told Hay how to examine witnesses, administer their oaths, and pay them. "Go into any expense necessary for this purpose, & meet it from the funds provided by the Attorney general for other expenses," the president wrote.[24]

On June 2, in his third letter within a week, Jefferson told Hay how he should respond to the defense's citation of *Marbury v. Madison:* "I think it material to stop at the threshold the citing that case as authority, and to have it be denied to be law." He pointed out the essential inconsistency of the ruling—the Court said how the case should be decided, even though it "disclaimed" authority to rule on it because it did not have original jurisdiction—and then proceeded to argue his side once again to Hay. Since Jefferson, not Marshall, had interpreted the case correctly, and since the Court had transcended its authority by interfering with the internal affairs of the executive branch, the president felt no obligation to follow any aspect of the Court's ruling, particularly the assumption that it could declare an act unconstitutional. Jefferson's defiance is worth noting at some length:

> I shall ever act . . . against any control which may be attempted by the judges, in subversion of the independence of the executive and Senate within their peculiar department. . . . [W]here our decision is by the Constitution the supreme one, & that which can be carried into effect, it is the Constitutionally authoritative one, and that . . . by the judges was *coram non judice* [literally, "before one who is not a judge," indicating an improper venue or lack of jurisdiction], & unauthoritative, because it cannot be carried into effect. I have long wished for a proper occasion to have the gratuitous opinion in *Marbury v. Madison* brought before the public, & denounced as not law; and I think the present a fortunate one, because it occupies such a place in the public attention. I should be glad, therefore, if, in noticing that case, you could take occasion to express the determination of the executive, that the doctrines of that case were given extrajudicially & against law, and that their reverse will be the rule of action with the executive.[25]

Four years after Marshall had asserted final authority in interpreting the Constitution, Jefferson was still claiming that authority as well, and now the trial of Aaron Burr provided yet another occasion for the chief justice and the chief executive to assert the supremacy of their respective branches. When Burr requested that the court subpoena documents from the president, Marshall considered the matter carefully and then agreed to do so. Unlike the British king, who was said to be above the law and therefore could not be compelled to answer a subpoena for documents, the American president, in the eyes of the law, was still a citizen and therefore subject to the court, Marshall determined. For a Federalist, it was a strangely Republican argument, while the response by the Republican president was more in keeping with Federalist philosophy. Jefferson agreed to submit "whatever the purposes of justice may require," but as head of the executive branch he alone would determine which documents those might be, and no court could order otherwise. "*Voluntarily,*" he said, he would send the requested documents, but while doing so, he insisted it was "the necessary right of the President of the U S to decide, independently of all other authority, what papers, coming to him as President, the public interests permit to be communicated, & to whom." During the debate over Jay's Treaty more than a decade earlier, when President Washington had resisted demands by Congress to hand over documents, Jefferson had protested, but now, as president, he was as willing as any Federalist to fight for the autonomy of his office.[26]

As Jefferson feared but expected, Burr, like Chase, was acquitted. Marshall accepted Burr's argument that to prove a person treasonous, the prosecution must first show that an actual act of treason had occurred, and the Constitution stipulated that only "levying War" against the United States or giving "Aid and Comfort" to the nation's enemies qualified as treason. In this case, there had been no war or armed insurrection, nor had Burr aided an enemy. Whether or not he had hoped, planned, or conspired to do so was not at issue in this trial, Marshall informed the jury, which then had no choice but to set Burr free.

Historically, Marshall was on firm ground. At the Federal Convention, on August 20, the framers had deliberately tightened the definition of treason to prevent political prosecutions. It was "essential to the preservation of liberty to define precisely and exclusively what shall constitute the crime of Treason," Gouverneur Morris said then, and although Madison wanted to give Congress "more latitude" in defining the crime, George Mason's motion to allow less latitude prevailed, with only Delaware and Georgia dissenting. None of this had yet been made public, but Marshall was certainly acting in accordance with the intentions of most framers.

To Jefferson, though, Marshall had simply found a "loophole" in order to acquit Burr. Only because the government had intervened had Burr's treasonous designs not been set into motion. Jefferson was as upset with the suppression of evidence as with the acquittal. Marshall had deemed the testimony of 140 government witnesses immaterial since there had been no actual treasonous act, but Jefferson now insisted affidavits from these witnesses "be laid before Congress, that they may decide, whether the defect has been in the evidence of guilt, or in the law, or in the application of the law, and that they may provide the proper remedy for the past and the future." Since the judicial branch—"our Foreign Department," he later called it in disdain— had neglected its proper duty, he would take the matter to the people, through their elected representatives. Accordingly, on October 27, in his Seventh Annual Message to Congress, he submitted for the members' consideration evidence from the court proceedings "together with some evidence not there heard." The "framers of our constitution," he noted, had wished both to guard their government from "destruction by treason" and to protect citizens "against oppression under the pretence of it." Had those ends been served? In essence, he was asking Congress to evaluate the court's performance and, if the framers' goals had not been obtained, to determine "by what means, more effectual, they may be secured." The president, of course, had already made up his mind on the matter and declared the courts "guilty." His original draft of the address asked suggestively "whether there is not a radical defect in the administration of the law" and whether the trial did not "induce an awful doubt whether we all live under the same law," but not wanting to appear heavy-handed, he left this loaded language out of his final version and assumed the evidence would speak for itself.[27]

True to Jefferson's request, Congress did hold hearings on the Burr affair, but these failed to produce either a constitutional amendment that would make judges accountable to the people or any other remedy for what Jefferson believed was judicial overreach. To the end of his life, Jefferson considered the failure to contain the judiciary a near-fatal flaw in the Constitution. "It is a misnomer to call a government republican, in which a branch of the supreme power is independent of the nation," he wrote in 1821. His answer was a constitutional amendment that would grant judges commissions for defined six-year terms "with a reappointability by the president with the approbation of both houses." Judges would have to answer to the president rather than vice versa, had Jefferson's view prevailed.[28]

In both Burr's trial and Chase's impeachment, Jefferson and the Republicans entertained a looser interpretation of the Constitution than did their Federalist opponents, whether Chase and his attorneys or Chief Justice Marshall. Again, this marked a radical reversal in stated principles. Republicans, when resisting what they considered Federalist overreach in the 1790s, had insisted on a tight construction of the Constitution, while Federalists, and in particular Hamilton, had argued that the founding document needed to be interpreted more liberally. On multiple counts, the change in power delivered by the election of 1800 was effecting a sort of polarity shift in ideology, with each side arguing the other's previous position. Such was, and is, the grammar of politics when power changes hands. In this case, a Republican president defended and tried to expand the executive office more aggressively than a Federalist president, after the problems encountered during Adams's administration, might dare.

On one key point Jefferson remained absolutely consistent: since governmental authority rested in the people, all officers must be made accountable to them, and that very accountability vested elected officials with a great deal of power, for they acted on behalf of the people. This take on republican theory became increasingly apparent as Jefferson himself executed what he considered the people's will. The administration of unspecified powers for the good of the nation, done in the name of the people, could be for better or worse, as two defining episodes in Jefferson's presidency, the Louisiana Purchase and the Embargo, indicate.

In his first inaugural address, Jefferson had called the United States "a rising nation, spread over a wide and fruitful land," but that nation could neither rise nor spread without access to the port that controlled North America's great interior waterway, the Mississippi River. "There is on the globe one single spot, the possessor of which is our natural and habitual enemy," Jefferson wrote to Robert R. Livingston, his minister to France. "It is New Orleans, through which the produce of three-eighths of our territory must pass to market, and from its fertility it will ere long yield more than half of our whole produce and contain more than half our inhabitants." New Orleans had just changed from Spanish to French hands, and under Napoleon's leadership France's possession of New Orleans presented a serious threat to American interests. Of necessity, the United States would have to ally itself with Britain to oppose France, and no Republican savored that prospect. Consequently, Jefferson instructed Livingston to negotiate a sale of lower Louisiana to the United States and dispatched the special envoy James Monroe to aid him.[29]

Where, exactly, did the Constitution empower the president to purchase territory from a foreign nation? This question nagged Jefferson, whose predilection for a strict interpretation of the Constitution had anchored his political beliefs before assuming the presidency. In January 1803, before any deal had been made, the president queried his cabinet about the constitutionality of a purchase. Attorney General Levi Lincoln, from Massachusetts, advised that a constitutional amendment would be necessary before adding any territory to the United States and incorporating it into the Union, but Albert Gallatin, the Treasury secretary, held that the United States "as a nation have an inherent right to acquire territory" and that the president's authority to negotiate treaties gave him ample authority to purchase land. Jefferson agreed with Gallatin's line of reasoning as "a matter of expediency," but he remained uncertain "whether, when acquired, it may be taken into the Union by the Constitution." It would be "safer not to permit the enlargement of the Union but by amendment of the Constitution," he concluded.[30]

Passing a constitutional amendment, though, would have to come after the fact. Negotiations were already under way, and by April they were concluded. Preferring to focus on European rather than American expansion, Napoleon offered to sell not only New Orleans but France's entire claims on the North American mainland. For $15 million Jefferson could double the size of the nation—*if* he accepted the offer. Would those pesky doubts about the Constitution interfere, causing him to reject the deal? Of course not. To do so would betray the interests of the nation, with which he had been entrusted. In the president's mind acquiring New Orleans was necessary at any price—even stretching the "construction" of the Constitution, itself a cardinal sin.

While Jefferson rejoiced at the news from Paris, he still fretted over the apparent discrepancy between what he was doing and what he believed the Constitution permitted him to do. The key point here is not whether his actions were or were not constitutional, but that he *believed* them not to be. In several letters written between early July, when the news of the purchase arrived in the United States, and October, when Congress was slated to convene and consider ratification and funding, Jefferson vacillated between principle and expediency, arguing forcefully for each and finally settling on a solution that in retrospect was politically fanciful. To John Dickinson, who had drafted the Articles of Confederation and helped frame the Constitution, he wrote: "There is a difficulty in this acquisition which presents a handle to the malcontents among us, though they have not yet discovered it. Our confederation is certainly confined to the limits established by the revolution. The general government has no powers but such as the constitution has given it; and it has not given it a power of holding foreign territory, & still less of incorporating it into the union." Jefferson repeated this refrain to John Breckinridge, whom he was counting on to steer ratification of the purchase through the Senate, and then added bluntly, "The executive in seizing the fugitive occurrence which so advances the good of their country, have done an act beyond the Constitution." Even so, Congress must leave "behind them metaphysical subtleties" and "ratify and pay for it," then "throw themselves on their country" for acting in an "unauthorized" manner.[31]

Five days after writing to Breckinridge, Jefferson received two letters from Livingston, still in Paris, that suggested any delay in ratification could kill the deal. The president immediately wrote again to Breckinridge, alerting him to keep the president's musings about the Constitution confidential. In order not to give Napoleon "a pretext for retracting," Jefferson needed to rush ratification through the Senate with minimal debate. To this end, he urged Breckinridge to gather "every friend of the treaty on the first day of the session." Simultaneously, he cautioned Secretary of State Madison, Attorney General Lincoln, and Thomas Paine not to divulge the qualms he had expressed to them: "I infer that the less we say about constitutional difficulties respecting Louisiana the better, and that what is necessary for surmounting them must be done sub silentio," he wrote to Madison.[32]

Three weeks later Jefferson covered the gamut in a letter to a fellow Virginian, Senator Wilson Cary Nicholas, who believed that incorporating the new territory into the Union was perfectly in keeping with the Constitution. Jefferson, of course, thought otherwise. He did not want his views to slow down the ratification process, and Nicholas, like Breckinridge, was in a position to speed it up, but he also did not wish to cede to Nicholas's loose construction of the Constitution. So back and forth he went:

> There is reason, in the opinion of our ministers, to believe, that if the thing were to do over again, it could not be obtained, and that if we give the least opening, they will declare the treaty void. . . . Whatever Congress shall think necessary to do, should be done with as little debate as possible, and particularly so far as respects the constitutional difficulty. . . .
>
> But when I consider that the limits of the United States are precisely fixed by the treaty of 1783, that the Constitution expressly declares itself to be made for the United States, . . . I do not believe it was meant that they might receive England, Ireland, Holland, etc., into it, which would be the case on your construction. When an instrument admits two constructions, the one safe, the other dangerous, the one precise, the other indefinite, I prefer that which is safe and precise. I had rather ask an enlargement of power from the nation, where it is found necessary, than to assume it by a construction which would make our powers boundless. Our peculiar security is in the possession of a written Constitution. Let us not make it a blank paper by construction.

It was a firm stand against broad construction, but not long maintained. Jefferson concluded, "If, however, our friends shall think differently, certainly I shall acquiesce with satisfaction; confiding, that the good sense of our country will correct the evil of [broad] construction when it shall produce ill effects."[33]

Jefferson never got the amendment he hoped would right the wrong he had done, but he did prepare a draft. It was a curious piece with three components, only the first of which was necessary to bring his actions clearly in line with the Constitution. "Louisiana, as ceded by France to the U.S. is made part of the U.S.," it commenced, and its "white inhabitants shall be citizens." In the next part, the amendment established an east-west line at the mouth of the Arkansas River, north of which no settlement would be permitted. Had the measure ever been seriously considered, this provision, reminiscent of King George III's Proclamation of 1763, would certainly have doomed it. Finally, it allowed for Florida to become part of the Union, "whenever it may be rightfully obtained." For reasons Jefferson well understood, and partly by his own doing, the amendment was never presented to Congress; its primary function was to ease its author's mind. Instead, at the very moment the Louisiana Purchase came before the Senate, that body was working out the details for quite a different refinement of the Constitution. That one, what is now the Twelfth Amendment, did not deal with "metaphysical subtleties" of interpretation. The Constitution simply needed to distinguish between votes for president and votes for vice president to avoid a repetition of the 1800 election.[34]

In the end, despite his serious misgivings, Jefferson did indeed "make our powers boundless" by ceding to a broad construction of the Constitution. This stalwart Republican had resisted as strongly as anyone could expect, but even he succumbed. What president would have done otherwise, when offered the chance to nearly double the size of the nation? By placing one man at the helm, the framers had invited this response. Nowhere did it appear in the Constitution, nowhere *could* it appear, but the temptation for a president to loosen his grip on constitutional scruples would prove nearly irresistible.

If Jefferson had overreached his constitutional powers by purchasing Louisiana, as he suspected and feared, he paid no price. Few others seemed to care. The ends, enormously positive by most accounts, eclipsed the means. Soon, though, he would embrace a broad construction of presidential powers that led to a more questionable outcome, and in that case his sacrifice of republican principles would become all too evident.

By 1807 the Napoleonic Wars sweeping Europe had altered the tone of the nation's foreign relations and domestic politics. Britain and France were locked in combat as usual, but the stakes had been raised, and both nations preyed freely on any vessels doing business with the enemy. That meant American ships were not safe anywhere, and commerce suffered accordingly. This changed party-line alignments; no more did Federalists favor Britain across the board, nor Republicans favor France. The anger against both nations was nearly ubiquitous, and both political parties were equally susceptible to outbreaks of war fever.

On June 22 the British warship HMS *Leopard*, while blockading two French vessels that had pulled in to the Chesapeake Bay, fired on the American frigate *Chesapeake* for fifteen minutes, killing three sailors and injuring eighteen. A boarding party then searched the *Chesapeake* and came up with four alleged deserters from the British navy, three of whom were Americans by birth. The *Chesapeake* Affair, as it was and still is called, raised the ire of the American public to a new level because the frigate had scarcely cleared its harbor before the *Leopard* followed it out to sea, then battered it.

Like his two presidential predecessors, Jefferson was faced with the difficult task of keeping his nation from a destructive and costly fight against a European superpower. War, he reasoned, would undermine Republican policies by increasing taxes and making it more difficult to retire the national debt, but fortunately there was an alternative to military conflict: economic warfare. In the decade before the Revolution, colonials had voluntarily abstained from purchasing British goods, and that had caused the imperial government to back down. Now, if Americans refused to export as well as import goods, they could starve Britain and force it to back down once again. Further, by treating France in the same manner, the United States could persuade that nation too to stop its predation on American ships, and the seas would be safe once again. To achieve this goal, Jefferson proposed an absolute embargo on all American trade; anything short of that would be easily circumvented. True, an embargo would involve some sacrifice, but the president was confident "the conveniences of our citizens shall yield reasonably" in light of the "importance" of "the present experiment" in furthering the national interest without warfare. Further, as in Revolutionary days, an embargo would promote self-reliance, encourage Americans to develop their own manufactures, and lead them away from decadent imports. It was a familiar refrain.[35]

In truth, Jefferson did more than propose an embargo; he engineered it, hurriedly pushed it through Congress, and enforced it with an iron hand. On December 17 he gathered his cabinet to present the idea, but he did not seem open to a thorough investigation of the potential impacts. The following morning his closest adviser on economic matters, Secretary of the Treasury Gallatin, weighed in against the "doubt-ful policy," as he called it. "I prefer war to a permanent embargo," he told Jefferson bluntly. "Government prohibitions do always more mis-chief than had been calculated; and it is not without much hesitation that a statesman should hazard to regulate the concerns of individuals as if he could do it better than themselves." If Jefferson remained fixed on an embargo, Gallatin counseled, it must be only temporary, to buy some time for a diplomatic settlement. That would never work, Jeffer-son responded. If other nations knew the embargo was temporary, they would simply wait it out until it was repealed.[36]

At noon that same day, December 18, Jefferson sent an exception-ally brief message to Congress, presenting for "consideration" his plan for "an inhibition of the departure of our vessels from the ports of the United States." That same afternoon, meeting in secret session, the Senate submitted the idea to a special committee that immediately churned out a terse bill conforming to Jefferson's wishes. Within hours of receiving the president's message, the full body then suspended the rule requiring any bill to be read three times "on three different days" and approved the embargo by a vote of 22 to 6. The House took a bit longer. Representatives discussed the bill for three days, added some minor amendments, defeated a call to make the embargo temporary, and passed the measure 82 to 44 on December 21. The following day the Senate approved the House's amendments, and the president affixed his signature. That was the extent of the nation's deliberation of Jeffer-son's embargo policy, since the whole matter was conducted in secret.[37]

"The Embargo" (the word is usually capitalized and preceded by the definite article, signifying the uniqueness of the event) would affect American commerce more directly and completely than any piece of legislation in the nation's history before or since, yet it never received a serious hearing by Congress, much less the public. Was this as the framers intended? At the Federal Convention, before August 24, the working draft stated that the president "may recommend to their [Congress's] consideration such measures as he shall judge necessary, and expedient." At Gouverneur Morris's urging, "may" was changed to "shall," thereby strengthening the president's hand, but that did not alter the chain of command: the president recommends, Congress con-siders and then decides. Twenty years had passed, however, since the Constitution was drafted, and political divisions had altered the very fabric of that document. Now the president was the leader of a party as well as the nation, and if his party held over 80 percent of the seats in both houses of Congress, as the Republicans did in 1807, he could do as he pleased. There would be no effective check.

As the Embargo took hold on the ground, Gallatin's warning became prophecy. With livelihoods threatened and eliminated, the "mischief" commenced. Since the Embargo Act applied only to vessels "bound to any foreign port or place," merchants loaded coastal crafts and sent them to Canada or the West Indies, where they could be reloaded onto more worthy ships and sent on their way. This prompted a second Embargo Act that clamped down on coastal shipping and provided for penalties, which the initial act, prepared in haste, had neglected to do. Still, though, exporters skirted the law by sending goods overland to Canada, thus prompting a third Embargo Act forbidding export by land as well as sea; even goods or produce intended only for Canada became contraband.

The tighter the grip, the greater the impulse to resist. Communities along the Great Lakes and in northern New York and New England, linked by geography to the St. Lawrence and Lake Champlain watercourses, could no longer take pigs or lumber to market across an imaginary international boundary that disrupted the daily flow of commerce. Understandably, they became alienated from restrictions conceived in some distant place and enforced with a strong hand by a central government that did not appear to reflect or even acknowledge their interests. What, exactly, was the difference between shutting down all commerce in these border communities and closing the port of Boston in 1774? Jefferson had assumed that Americans would unite in common cause behind the Embargo, much as they had done in their resistance to British imperial policies during the nonimportation agreements of the 1760s, but the context was altogether different this time around. Back then, enforcement was by local committees, the very people who had fashioned the agreements; now the rules were made and enforced by a faraway government that through its actions had lost the confidence of local people.

As increased enforcement triggered greater resistance, that resistance in turn led the president and Congress to clamp down more tightly yet—a feedback cycle with no apparent end. On April 25, acting as hastily as it had when instituting the Embargo four months earlier, Congress passed the Enforcement Act of 1808, also known as the Fourth Embargo Act, which authorized government officials to detain any "vessel, flat, or boat"—thus including a simple lake barge—"which there may be reason to suspect" of violating the Embargo. What might such a "reason" be? That was left to the "opinions" of the customs collectors or gunboat officers. Federal agents should suspect "unusual deposites of provisions, lumber, or other articles of domestic growth or manufacture," but that was their only guidance, other than the port of landing. No vessel was to be granted clearance "for any other port or district of the United States, adjacent to the territories, colonies, or provinces of a foreign nation . . . without special permission from the President of the United States." Communities proximate to Canada or the Gulf Coast were thereby forbidden to receive any domestic produce, unless the president himself granted an exemption. While the Embargo was intended to starve Britain and/or France into submission, it would henceforth starve American communities as well—or instead.[30]

The day Congress passed this draconian measure it adjourned for six months, leaving the execution of the act to President Jefferson. Although the Fourth Embargo Act was in clear violation of the Fourth Amendment, which required "Warrants . . . upon probable cause" before searches, and the Fifth Amendment, which guaranteed that no citizen be deprived of property "without due process of law," it did not lead Jefferson into any paroxysms of constitutional soul-searching. Instead, he embraced the unprecedented powers he believed Congress had given him. As he viewed it, he now had the authority to detain violators, seize vessels and cargoes, and levy fines as he pleased; these would serve as his means to accomplish a "great public object." In letters to Gallatin, to whom he entrusted on-the-ground enforcement, he revealed a sense of relief and even delight that the executive department would not be "trammeled by legal rules of evidence" that "may embarrass judges and juries." These were "to have no weight with us to whom the law has referred to decide according to our discretion." The president did not wish to formulate "precise rules" that could be "evaded," preferring instead to use his broad powers "freely that we may, by a fair experiment, know the power of this great weapon, the embargo." Gallatin was to decide as many cases on his own as he could, and "where in doubt, consider me as voting for detention." In localities known for resistance he was to reverse the burden of proof, assuming guilt unless proven otherwise. "We may fairly require positive proof that the individual of a town tainted with a general spirit of disobedience, has never said or done anything himself to countenance that spirit," he instructed Gallatin. The most extreme or difficult cases, of course, the president would decide himself.[39]

One of those towns "tainted with a general spirit of disobedience" was Alburg, Vermont, just south of the Canadian border on Lake Champlain. In June, after a militia company captured a large raft hauling lumber to market in Canada, the owner hired some sixty local lumberjacks to sneak past the militia guard in the dead of night and recapture the raft and its payload. After accomplishing their task, they collected their pay from the raft's owner and returned to their homes. When Jefferson heard of the incident, he wrote immediately to Gallatin, "We must try to harass the unprincipled agents, and punish as many as we can." After the lumberjacks were rounded up and placed on trial for treason, Jefferson wrote to Gallatin again: "If all these people are convicted, there will be too many to be punished with death. My hope is that they [the U.S. circuit court in Burlington, where the case was being tried] will send me full statements of every man's case, that the most guilty may be marked as examples, and the less so suffer long imprisonment under reprieves from time to time." The president not only sought executions but assumed that he would be the one to determine which of the accused should die.[40]

Brockholst Livingston, the presiding circuit court judge whom Jefferson had appointed to the Supreme Court the previous year, refused to play along. Expressing his "astonishment" at the government's case, Livingston instructed the jury that "treason," as defined by the Constitution, must involve "levying war" against the United States or giving aid and comfort to the enemy, but the defendants, after seizing the raft, had simply returned to their homes, "not suspecting they had a war on their hands, with any power, and least of all with the government of their own country," and the United States was at war with no nation, so the defendants could not possibly have given aid and comfort to the enemy. They might be guilty of some lesser crime, but to convict these men of treason would establish a "precedent so dangerous" that it would permit "every abuse . . . in times of public agitation."[41]

Livingston was not the only Republican judge to rebuke the president for his enforcement of the Embargo. William Johnson, also a Jefferson appointee to the Supreme Court, declared in the U.S. circuit court at Charleston that the president had violated the Fourth Embargo Act, which Jefferson and Gallatin had helped draft, by proclaiming in advance that all shipments be denied clearance; the law actually gave the discretionary power of clearance in the case under consideration to customs collectors, not the president, Johnson maintained. "The officers of our government, from the highest to the lowest, are equally subjected to legal restraint," he chided from the bench. While these Republican judges thought Jefferson had stretched the limits of his power too far, the Federalist judge John Davis, presiding over the U.S. district court for Massachusetts, disagreed with the contention made in his court that the Embargo was unconstitutional on the grounds that Congress possessed only the authority to regulate commerce, not suspend it. Like Hamilton, and unlike the pre-presidential Jefferson, Davis favored a broad construction of federal powers.[42]

That Jefferson would be scolded by Republican judges and supported by a Federalist judge is hardly as curious as it might seem, for his enforcement of the Embargo had led to a marked extension of executive authority. Indeed, Jefferson had become rather Hamiltonian in his thinking. "Congress must legalize all *means* which may be necessary to obtain its *end*," he told Gallatin (the emphases are his); Hamilton would have had no problem with that line of reasoning, although his ends would certainly have been different. Was there no limit? "We may consider as further means, how it might do to destroy all boats and canoes on our side of the [St. Marys] river, paying for them?" he queried Gallatin. (The St. Marys River separated Georgia from East Florida, then under Spanish dominion.) That could not be done "without being authorized by law," Gallatin replied, and Congress was not likely to grant its assent.[43]

Together, Jefferson and Gallatin went back to Congress for a fifth time, hoping to remedy the "defects" that stood in the way of even tougher enforcement, and this final Embargo Act, which did receive a full airing in Congress, exceeded all others:

- Shipowners were required to post bonds of six times the value of the cargo in order to gain clearance, retrievable only when the vessel landed in a domestic port, cargo intact. Fines were also raised to four times the value of the cargo.

- Federal agents were authorized to confiscate anything contained in "vessels, carts, wagons, sleighs, or any other carriage . . . *apparently* on their way toward the territories of
  a foreign nation, or the *vicinity thereof,* or to a place where
  such articles are *intended* to be exported." (Emphasis added.)
  Alleged intent to break the law was equivalent to breaking it.

- The president could issue orders binding on all agents, cir-
  cumventing Judge Johnson's ruling. Jefferson could thereby
  judge all cases in advance and shut down any suspect port in
  its entirety.

- The president was authorized to use not just the militia
  but the U.S. Army and Navy to enforce "the laws laying an
  embargo." This is precisely what Anti-Federalists in 1787–88
  and Republicans in 1798–99 (including Jefferson) had warned
  against: a standing federal army, led by the chief executive,
  empowered to enforce laws during peacetime and suppress
  U.S. citizens.[44]

Here was a Republican nightmare come true, under the leadership of a Republican president. How had it come to this? Near the
close of the Federal Convention, on September 7, Madison had moved
that treaties of peace could be authorized by two-thirds of the Senate "without the concurrence of the President." Potentially, he said, a
president could "derive so much power and importance from a state
of war that he might be tempted, if authorised, to impede a treaty of
peace." Something akin to this was happening now. Jefferson had so
identified his presidency with the Embargo that he could not relin-
quish it, despite the hardships it produced (tens of thousands of seamen
unemployed and widespread food shortages), its divisive impact, and its
failure to effect any kind of diplomatic advances with Britain and
France. "Agriculture, commerce, [and] navigation," he said, must "bow"
before "the great leading object" of the times, the Embargo; they
amounted to "nothing when in competition with that." This stance, oft
repeated and rigidly held, made it impossible for him to retreat. The
Embargo was Jefferson's war, and he had become a wartime president,
assuming the extra powers often granted to an executive during such
times.[45]

Yet by the time Jefferson left office on March 4, 1809, the nation had given up on the Embargo, even if Jefferson hadn't; Congress repealed all acts as of that date. Justifying the apparently failed policy to himself and others proved not so difficult a task for the outgoing president as it might seem. Practically, the Embargo had bought extra time and allowed the nation to prepare for war, if war should come. It "gave us time to call home our seamen, ships and property, to levy men and put our seaports into a certain state of defence," Jefferson wrote at the very close of his term. Morally, he felt on solid ground too, for at least he had tried an alternative to war.

What about his philosophy of governance? Had he sacrificed cherished Republican principles by centralizing authority, increasing the powers of the executive, and widening the role of a standing army and navy? There too he had an answer. The president is entrusted with the security of the nation, and to fulfill his task and be true to the American people, he must sometimes assume powers he would not ordinarily possess. Eighteen months after leaving office, when asked by a friend "whether circumstances do not sometimes occur, which make it a duty in officers of high trust, to assume authorities beyond the law," he answered that the solution was "easy . . . in principle, but sometimes embarrassing in practice." Elaborating, he wrote:

> A strict observance of the written laws is doubtless *one* of the highest duties of a good citizen, but it is not the *highest*. The laws of necessity, of self-preservation, of saving the country when in danger, are of higher obligation. To lose our country by a scrupulous adherence to written law, would be to lose the law itself . . . thus absurdly sacrificing the end to the means.[46]

This did not apply to lesser public officers "charged with petty duties," he continued, but "it is incumbent on those only who accept great charges, to risk themselves on great occasions, when the safety of the nation, or some of its very high interests are at stake."

Although Jefferson conjoined them, there were actually two sets of contingencies here: "the safety of the nation" and "some of its very high interests." At the Federal Convention, on August 17, delegates had agreed that the president should possess "the power to repel sudden attacks" without waiting for Congress to convene. (That is why they required congressional approval if the nation were to "declare war" but not if the president was forced by an invasion to "make war.") Here indeed was a case of "self-preservation," to use Jefferson's term, but imagine the outcry at the convention if a delegate had moved that the president should be empowered to act as he saw fit, without consulting Congress, anytime he claimed the nation's "very high interests are at stake." With few exceptions, they would have recoiled in an instant. George Mason and Elbridge Gerry would not have been the only ones to demand a more precise explication for what "high interests" might entail and expound on the dangers of allowing the president to define them as he pleased. There was no surer path to the destruction of republican government. Had the convention occurred in 1807 instead of twenty years earlier, speakers undoubtedly would have observed that Napoleon had risen to power and ended republican dreams in France by claiming to promote the high interests of his nation.

Yet who among the delegates, had he subsequently served as president under the Constitution he helped to create, would have *rejected* using the muscle of his office to further what he supposed to be the high interests of the nation, as Jefferson did with the Louisiana Purchase and the Embargo? It should come as no surprise that a president, once in office, comes to favor a broad construction of the sparse list of powers granted him by the Constitution. Specifically, he is empowered to command the armed forces but not raise them or determine when and why they go to war. He can recommend legislation and veto it, but he is not directly authorized to shape it. He can grant reprieves and pardons only for federal offenses. He can negotiate treaties but not execute them without the approval of a supermajority of senators. Finally, he can appoint ambassadors and judges, again with Senate consent, but the Constitution does not directly state that these appointees are to function as his underlings; judges certainly shouldn't, and ambassadors, by a strict reading of the Constitution, are as beholden to the Senate as to the president. By contrast, Congress possesses a long list of sweeping powers that include taxation, coining and borrowing money, regulating commerce, raising armed forces and declaring war, and so on, coupled with the authority "to make all Laws which shall be necessary and proper for carrying into Execution the foregoing Powers." Little wonder, then, that presidents interpret their authority liberally. A president is expected not by law but by common wisdom to be "the general guardian of the National interests" (Gouverneur Morris's words), yet how can he accomplish this task without expanding his reach beyond the strictures of the short list of his designated powers?

This does not mean that a president who interprets the Constitution broadly, as even Jefferson did in the end, is necessarily abusing his office, for that document does contain one sentence that can be pushed to almost any limit: "The executive Power shall be vested in a President of the United States of America." We do not have to agree with Hamilton that this single statement vests the president with near boundless power to understand its importance; rather, we have only to look at popular expectations. By creating a single executive, the framers fashioned an office that would literally personify the government. Before, under the Articles of Confederation, the "United States" was embodied by "the United States in Congress assembled," but now one man was at the helm, a figurehead for the nation. That George Washington was the office's first occupant accentuated this aspect of the presidency. The president was a quasi-king, stripped of much of the pomp and many of the powers of his British counterpart but still filling a similar, if lesser, symbolic function. That in part explains the intensity of the contested elections of 1796 and 1800; allegedly, the winner would *be* the nation, the loser not.[47]

Partly, then, the expansion of presidential powers under the first three administrations can be explained by the symbolic nature of that office, which the Constitution did not and could not adequately convey. There are contributing factors as well. These start with the prestige of the first president, who at the outset of his term could not be opposed without suffering political harm. Then, as the office fleshed out during Washington's occupancy—the president's control of his appointees, his dominance in foreign relations, executive leadership in setting a domestic agenda—it became increasingly clear that no group could prevail and no policy could be implemented without the president joining in. Practically as well as symbolically, presidential elections became do-or-die affairs, and this in turn accelerated the formation of a two-party system. Finally, once the president had become the head of his party as well as the nation, he had every incentive to stretch the limits of his powers to overcome political opposition. These interrelated aspects of the office—symbolic, practical, and political—combined to create a feedback system that functioned like a ratcheted tool: the presidency would expand but not contract by its own doing. Only if the ratchet were released by some countervailing agent, whether the courts, Congress, or public outcry, would expansion be checked.

Viewed in this light, Jefferson's free use of executive powers, despite his previous attachment to a strict construction of the Constitution, reveals the natural trajectory of the office, not merely a self-serving shift in one man's ideology. The presidency was becoming more than any of the framers except Hamilton had called for; even Gouverneur Morris might have been amazed, although not necessarily disappointed, in the increasing sweep of presidential authority. From the time George Washington took office on April 30, 1789, the presidency embarked on an evolutionary course that would take it well beyond the strictures of the original rule book.[48]

We could continue to explore the expansion of the presidential office in subsequent administrations, but the end of Jefferson's administration affords a natural resting spot. By then a particular form of executive leadership had been debated, refined, set in writing, and tested by the generation we know today as the founders. Both the original parameters and the direction in which the office was likely to evolve had been established. In later years, the growth of the nation would further extend the scope of presidential reach in both absolute and relative terms. The president would become more powerful not only because his nation was but also because the expansion of government would have a more direct effect on executive functions than on legislative ones; a nation that would grow fortyfold from Jefferson's time did not require forty times as many laws, but it did need a vastly expanded administrative machinery. Further, with the increase of nationalism and revolutions in media, people would focus more attention on their nationally elected leader than on local representatives, whom the framers had assumed would be the people's closest tie with government. Already more dominant than the framers had expected, the presidency was certain to continue its ascendant course.

Although the framers could not be expected to foresee the various transformations that increased the president's power and prominence, they themselves were partly responsible for the later growth of the presidency. Once they had approved James Wilson's motion for a single chief executive and rejected George Mason's attempt to diffuse executive authority with an independent council, and once they had ceded to Gouverneur Morris's relentless push to free the chief executive from

Congress and permit reelection, the presidency was bound to take on a life of its own. In the real world, if not on paper, that meant the president must become a political actor in his own right, and this in turn encouraged him to maximize his powers to the extent that was politically feasible. The precise stipulations in the Constitution were only a starting point. Equally important in the long run were the hidden yet in some sense natural repercussions of creating a single, independent chief executive.

Then and Now—Translations

On October 15, 1789, as President Washington set out from New York with two aides and six servants to tour through New England, he observed firsthand everyday life in the nation he was expected to lead. After crossing from Manhattan on King's Bridge, he traveled through what is now the Bronx and home to some 1.4 million people, mostly living in buildings taller than any tree Washington passed by. That evening in his diary the president described the first leg of his journey:

> The road for the greater part, indeed the whole way, was very rough and stoney, but the land strong, well covered with grass and a luxurient crop of Indian corn intermixed with pompions [pumpkins] which were ungathered in the fields. We met four droves of beef cattle for the New York market (about 30 in a drove) some of which were very fine—also a flock of sheep for the same place. We scarcely passed a farm house that did not abd. in geese. Their cattle seemed to be of a good quality and their hogs large but rather long legged.

A farmer himself, Washington was pleased. The following day in Connecticut, on the road from Norwalk (now home to Xerox Corporation) to Fairfield (where General Electric is headquartered), he noted,

> The superb landscape . . . is a rich regalia. We found all the farmers busily employed in gathering, grinding, and expressing the juice of their apples; the crop of which they say is rather above mediocrity. The average wheat crop they add, is about 15 bushels to the acre from their fallow land—often 20 & from that to 25. . . . The principal export from Norwalk & Fairfield is horses and cattle—salted beef & porke, lumber & Indian corn, to the West Indies—and in a small degree wheat and flour.[1]

If the country Washington observed was very different back then, so too was the manner in which he observed it, close-up and literally on the ground, experiencing every stone and pebble on his way and accompanied only by a party of eight—no Air Force One, no Secret Service, no advance team, no press corps. Personal contact was still possible in a nation inhabited by fewer than four million people; now, with our numbers grown eightyfold, we encounter a president's image daily but not the man himself. Back then, no prior presidents had shown the way; now forty-four men have held the office and precedents abound. In Washington's time, the president of the United States still struggled for international recognition; now he leads the world's premier superpower. How can all these changes *not* affect the nature of the presidency, and further, how can they not affect our understanding of how the people of the founding era viewed the office they had just created?

When we think of what the presidency signified to post-Revolutionary Americans and now connotes to us, we must account for such differences in context and therefore meanings. "The past is a foreign country," wrote the novelist L. P. Hartley. "They do things differently there." We cannot assume their moral and political language translates directly to ours, yet despite all the differences, and in some sense even because of them, Americans today hark back to those early times hoping to reaffirm a national identity. With so much to be lost in translation, this is risky business, yet we can hardly do otherwise. Veneration of a family's ancestors or a society's founders is key to cementing social bonds, and the United States, more than most nations, has a clearly demarcated founding generation to revere. Further, because our government is bound by a written constitution, we have a legal obligation to investigate the terms of that contract as understood by the people who ratified it, granting their assent in proxy for ours. These two reasons, societal bonding and legal obligation, drive us to listen closely to the framers, but when we do, how can we be sure we understand what we hear? Was the presidency that they created the same as the one we infer? These are not abstract or academic concerns, for they drive a question we cannot help asking, even if there is no sure way of providing an answer: How would the framers, and their fellow Americans who ratified the Constitution, regard what the presidency has become?

Any attempt at cross-time translation will encounter serious problems, not the least of which is the absence of absolute verification. None of the nation's founders are around to tell us, "Yes, this is exactly what we meant," or "No, you are off base when you read our words that way." Since no hypotheses can be confirmed once and for all, the best we can hope for is that our interpretations are not inconsistent with any of the available evidence from those times.

To avoid reading history backward or at least minimize its inherent dangers, we must explore the similarities and differences between the presidency as it was originally intended and the office today. A likely starting point is to ask, in very general terms, what goals for executive functioning we share with the founding generation and how our goals differ. If we wish to evaluate both the framers' performance in creating a viable office—what they got right and what they got wrong—and the performance of subsequent generations in carrying out their wishes, we need to be clear about whose standards we are using, ours or theirs.

The framers believed, and we do too, that the chief executive should facilitate efficient governance. We might not choose the term they used, "vigor," but we expect the same results. Efficiency, though, should not be used to justify an overreach of executive authority. Although rule by committee had proved cumbersome during Revolutionary days, monarchical rule was even worse. Limits must be placed on executive prerogatives. Patronage should not go unchecked. On the other hand, the chief executive should be able to check legislative overreach. Balanced government was and is the ideal.

The president is the head of state, representing American interests with foreign nations. Simultaneously, he (now he/she) is to set a high moral tone within the nation. Only because a president does not seek power for its own sake can he be entrusted to command the armed forces.

The presidency must be anchored by a credible electoral process that has the people's trust. Unless losers as well as winners accept the results, the office will not function properly.

These goals, general as they are, provide some commonality across time. To deny any, then or now, would be to venture beyond the limits of acceptable discourse.

In several ways, though, our values have changed over time, and expectations of the presidency have evolved accordingly. Most notably, of course, we no longer allow our government to sanction slavery, as framers of the Constitution did. While this dramatic turn does not directly affect views of the presidency per se, it both highlights the differences over time and hints at other changes that do. Doubtless, nobody at the Federal Convention imagined that any American citizen, including women, blacks, and those without property, could enjoy the franchise, that white males would someday constitute only a minority of those casting votes for the president, and that a person of color or a woman might actually run for or even occupy the highest office in the land. This revolution in the composition of the civic body, as sweeping as it is, signifies even more than an expansion of the president's constituency. The role of the electorate, both in choosing and in influencing the president, has changed. Today the people, not presidential electors, effectively choose the president. (Although residual peculiarities of the elector system still allow for the election of a president who does not win the popular vote, the electors themselves have nothing to do with this. It would be unconscionable for a member of the Electoral College to vote according to his own discretion, as the framers assumed he would do.) Further, once in office the president is expected to follow the "mandate" granted him by the voters, or at least not to cross them; the people place limits on discretionary governance. In short, the framers did not perceive the historical thrust toward democracy, a plausible and even logical evolution of their own notion of popular sovereignty.[2]

In a related vein, eighteenth-century Americans held to a different ethic of campaigning. Self-promotion and pandering to voters—the framers deemed these dishonorable, and even more dishonored would be a president who bowed to the desires of those who financed his campaign. Indeed, the very act of bankrolling a campaign would have been viewed as evidence of corruption; the president ought never to be bought, either before or after his election. Today, we accept the melding of money and politics with a grain of salt, but accept it we do, and that probably marks the largest difference between our view of the presidency and that of the founding generation.

The framers also believed that the ideal president should be nonpartisan in every sense of the word, representing no party, region, or interest group. At the Federal Convention, the goal was to create an office that would lessen differences, not accentuate them. During ratification debates, the prospect of a nonpartisan presidency under Washington provided at least a weak palliative to calm Anti-Federalists. We have not totally forsaken this ideal, but it is increasingly difficult to locate. To gain a party's nomination, a presidential candidate must convince fellow Democrats or Republicans that he/she will vanquish the opposition, and then in the general election the candidates, or at least their surrogates, routinely vilify each other. Eventually, the winner will issue the presumptive "I will be a president for all Americans" pronouncement, but even then a president who takes bipartisanship seriously and acts on that principle is accused of being too weak and told to start "acting like a Democrat" or "acting like a Republican." We put forth mixed messages, causing a president to fall short no matter which path he or she follows.[3]

Such are the basic parameters of the presidency, then and now. Keeping both the framers' values and our own in mind, where they merge and where they diverge, we can compare what they believed they created with the presidency of today. Has the office achieved what they expected of it?

In several ways that we often take for granted, it has. The president's role as commander in chief, a provision that frightened Anti-Federalists in 1787–88, has indeed helped to ensure civilian control of the military. Elsewhere in the world, political turmoil often leads to military takeovers, but we don't worry about that in the United States. Civilian control has produced immeasurable dividends, and the very fact that we forget to acknowledge it constitutes a tribute to its success.

The presidential veto, also of concern to Anti-Federalists, has not produced, by itself, executive abuses of power. It is invoked rarely, albeit threatened more often, yet it has still served to check the power of

Congress, as the framers intended. The veto and the override, in conjunction, have furthered the interests of balanced governance, precisely the framers' intention.

Similarly, the provision for impeachment of the president has not destroyed the balance of powers, as some contemporaries had feared. Twice, in the cases of Andrew Johnson and Bill Clinton, the ruling majority in the House of Representatives has issued articles of impeachment, but in both instances the Senate determined that the charges fell short of the tough standards for conviction the framers had set: "Treason, Bribery, or other high Crimes and Misdemeanors." Only once, when Richard Nixon clearly broke the law, did the likely prospect of impeachment and conviction cause a resignation. The notion behind impeachment was that even the president must somehow be held accountable but that the means of dismissing him should not be amenable to political manipulation. Although some still might argue that Johnson had in fact committed an impeachable offense, he was acquitted in large measure because of the fear of setting a precedent for political manipulation of the impeachment process, which the framers had hoped to prevent. Impeachment, in short, has toed the fine line they hoped it would.

With one glaring exception, the election of Abraham Lincoln, the transition from one president to the next has been peaceful. Losers have accepted the results, even when they had reason to do otherwise. This too was not guaranteed at the outset. Anti-Federalists feared that a president who failed to be reelected would find some means of remaining in power, but George Washington, the nation's first president, *voluntarily* became its first ex-president, and then John Adams, after coming up short in the contested election of 1800, quietly boarded a stage to return home on the eve of his successor's inauguration. All subsequent presidents who were defeated at the polls have lived with the results, as the framers hoped and we now assume.

Again with only one exception, presidents have not sought to repeat in office more than once. The framers did not stipulate a limit on the number of presidential terms, but many Anti-Federalists wanted such a constraint, and finally, more than a century and a half later, their concern was answered in the form of the Twenty-Second Amendment. Before that, seven presidents followed Washington's precedent and retired after two terms; only Franklin Delano Roosevelt, facing a war of historic proportions, sought a third term. Delegates to the Federal Convention wanted to create a strong executive leader who had no expectation of lifetime tenure, and in this they had their way.

Understanding they could not define the office of the presidency beyond the broadest outline, the framers expected details to be worked out later, as in fact they were. If the president and the Senate combined to make appointments, did that mean they had to concur in removing the officials they had appointed? In treaty making, what, exactly, would the "Advice and Consent" of the Senate entail? Answers would have to be honed by subsequent statesmen. Whether or not those later formulations reflected the framers' true intentions, answers were provided, fleshing out the office more fully than anyone could possibly have done in advance. This organic evolution did not violate the framers' wishes but embodied them. The last thing they wanted was for their new government to be completely codified, unable to adjust to the needs of the people it was intended to serve.

Yet political, societal, and even technological changes in later years have not only fine-tuned the office the framers conjured but altered it in significant ways. The framers, of course, cannot be held responsible for alterations due to causes they did not and in many cases could not foresee, but to understand the differences between the presidency as it was originally intended and the office it was to become, we need to take stock of these various transformations.

Consider the immediate distortion of the framers' most unique contribution to governmental forms—the system of presidential electors—and the political realities that prevent it from being altered or abolished. The partisan divide in the 1790s made clear from the outset that the system could be gamed, thus negating individual discretion and undermining the entire scheme. This much the framers might have foreseen had they asked tougher questions, and indeed, judging from the lukewarm support of many Federalists—"it's not perfect, but it's the best available option"—they would not have been surprised to see their complicated formula modified, as it was in 1804 with passage of the Twelfth Amendment, which allowed electors to vote separately for president and vice president. Yet they could not have been expected to predict that the nation would be saddled indefinitely with the rest of their elector scheme because of the political difficulties in gaining the approval of three-quarters of the states, the threshold for amending the Constitution. Three types of states have vested interests in preserving what we now call the Electoral College—small states, battleground states, and early primary states—and while the framers did notice that the system gave small states a slight advantage, they failed to anticipate the significance of battleground states, and they had no conception of what early primary states might be, much less how these would help preserve their dubious creation.

The framers understood the dangers that state and regional rivalries posed in electing a president, and they tried to mitigate these by requiring each presidential elector to cast at least one of his votes for a person from outside his own state. This was not nearly enough to prevent regional interests from driving presidential elections, and worse yet, another provision highlighted regional rivalries: the notorious three-fifths clause, which increased representation from the South not only in the House of Representatives but also in the Electoral College. With this added benefit, slave states in the early Republic were able to capture the presidency by picking up only a handful of electoral votes north of the Mason-Dixon Line. The impact on the nation's political complexion, and specifically on the presidency, can be gleaned from some basic statistics. Without the extra electors resulting from the three-fifths clause, Jefferson would have dropped at least twelve electoral votes in 1800, resulting in his defeat; in effect, he was elected by slaves who could not vote, an ironic outcome not lost on Federalists who labeled him "the Negro president." Before 1850, slaveholders held the presidency for all but twelve years. The five presidents who repeated in office—Washington, Jefferson, Madison, Monroe, and Jackson—were all slaveholding southerners, and this was no accident. Presidential candidates at that time were determined by congressional caucuses within each party, and the three-fifths clause increased the relative strength of southerners within the Republican caucus. No Republican could receive his party's support without the full concurrence of its pro-slavery majority, which helped determine both the party's and the president's agenda.[4]

Once in office, these slaveholding presidents strengthened their regional grip on the federal government by filling half the high offices with southerners, even though the South accounted for just over one-third of the free population. Of the thirty-one presidential appointees to the Supreme Court prior to 1850, eighteen owned slaves. Presidential actions were influenced by inflated numbers of southerners in the House of Representatives, who killed measures that banned slavery from the territories. When Jefferson purchased Louisiana, Monroe annexed Florida, and Polk went to war with Mexico, each was aiding slavery's expansion and through the three-fifths clause further increasing the number of southern votes in presidential elections. Even Washington, who more than any other tried *not* to be a regional president, supported southern interests on at least one hotly contested issue. In 1793 the Federalist Congress, to conform with the 1790 census, passed a reapportionment bill that gave the North a net gain of four seats in the House. When considering whether or not to sign the measure into law, Washington consulted his closest advisers. Hamilton and Knox supported the bill, but Jefferson, Madison, and Randolph opposed it and argued for an alternate construction of the numbers more generous to the South. Despite his reluctance to cross Congress, Washington sided with his fellow Virginians and delivered the nation's first presidential veto.[5]

The three-fifths clause only heightened the regionalism that created it. Delegates to the Federal Convention were already divided along regional lines, and few would have been surprised to see that rift widened by their own doing. They understood the compromise for what it was, a measure grounded in political realities rather than in solid republican theory.

The framers would more likely have been surprised by the rapid expansion of executive positioning relative to Congress in the first twenty years. As much as they admired George Washington, they had no way of foreseeing that every contested authority during his administration would be determined in favor of the president, nor that their initial decision to create a single chief executive, coupled with their later resolution to limit Congress's role in selecting him, would result in a power trajectory that leaned strongly in the executive's direction. Madison certainly didn't see this trend coming, and he soon found himself resisting it. Jefferson, who was not present at the convention, hesitated to grant his assent to a presidential office unbounded by any temporal limits. He seems to have sensed that a president's power would tend to expand, but even he would have been surprised if informed by some soothsayer of his own high-handed enforcement of the Embargo two decades later. Would the framers have been pleased or displeased with these developments? Answers would no doubt have varied across the spectrum, from hearty approval by Hamilton to scolding disapproval by the already disgruntled Gerry.

Over time, the premier expansion of the president's authority has been his ability to "make war," in the framers' words, without approval from Congress. At the Federal Convention, immediately following James Wilson's proposal for a single chief executive, Charles Pinckney pronounced he "was for a vigorous Executive" but feared his powers "might extend to peace & war &c., which would render the Executive a monarchy, of the worst kind, to wit an elective one." Today, the president does indeed possess de facto powers of war and peace. The movement in that direction started in 1793 with Washington's proclamation of neutrality, which, its critics argued, prevented Congress from exercising its constitutional authority to declare war. Then came the Quasi-War with France, which hinted at a breakdown in the demarcation between declared and undeclared wars. In the nineteenth century the United States engaged in military actions across the globe without declarations of war, and not since World War II has a single American soldier gone into battle under a formal declaration. Constitutional law has yet to catch up with this turn of events, which has placed the president front and center and forced Congress to resort only to the power of the purse to have any real say in matters of "peace & war." Occasionally, as with the War Powers Resolution of 1973, Congress tries to reaffirm that fundamental principle of republican governance that the framers thought they had safely embedded within the Constitution: citizens cannot be forced to sacrifice their blood and treasure in warfare without the consent of their direct representatives. Yet even at best, Congress's role has become reactive, not proactive. It receives reports of policies and actions the president has already put in place and is then asked to grant its assent and finance the measures. Has this created "a monarchy," as Pinckney warned? Not exactly, but the increasing complexities of international relations and the complete breakdown of eighteenth-century standards for what differentiates war from peace have certainly altered the balance between the executive and the legislative branches.

Would the framers be pleased with this reallocation of authority? Once more, opinions would differ, but Hamilton, who was out of sync with the rest at the time, does seem to have had the last say in this matter as well—or almost the last say. There is no telling if or when Congress will again insist on taking a larger role, how vigorously the executive will object if it does, or what the results of that intra-governmental struggle might be.

Finally, the presidency has been transformed by the restructuring of political life. In 1787 delegates to the Federal Convention begrudged democracy and did their best to contain it by the "successive filtrations" (Madison's term) they placed between the people and governmental leaders, but Americans today embrace democracy as their guiding principle; no modern political figure, in public, would dare come forth with the kinds of statements denigrating popular government that were common currency among the framers. Yet democracy itself has been profoundly altered due to the combined effects of concentrated wealth and technological advances in communications. The perpetual mega-campaign of today, driven by hundreds of millions of dollars and extending by television, radio, print, and the Internet into the daily lives of every potential voter, bears little resemblance to the town meeting/county convention democracy of Revolutionary days. Money, media, and influence constitute the very grit of politics. The old-fashioned ideal of a statesman's "honor," which in the founding era required independence from outside influence, is no longer a prerequisite for public life.

Lest we become too nostalgic, we should understand that the founding generation was not so politically naïve as to think that what we call influence, and they considered a form of corruption, would not pose a threat to their experiment in republican government. John Adams, for one, predicted that democracy would inevitably revert to aristocracy because some men would learn to command the votes of others. "By an aristocrat," he wrote in 1814, "I mean any man who can command or influence *two votes, one besides his own*." Aristocracy, or rule by the few, did not have to be marked by "artificial titles, tinsel decorations of stars, garters, ribbons, golden eagles and golden fleeces, crosses and roses and lilies, exclusive privileges, hereditary descents, established by kings or by positive laws of society." Instead, his "aristocrat" might command or influence votes "by his virtues, his talents, his reserve, his face, figure, eloquence, grace, air, attitude, movements, wealth, birth, art, address, intrigue, good fellowship, drunkenness, debauchery, fraud, perjury, violence, treachery, pyrrhonism [skepticism], deism, or atheism; for by every one of these instruments have votes been obtained and will be obtained."[6]

Today, Adams's various means of influence, more often devious than virtuous, are embodied in the political vernacular of campaign advertisements. Had he foreseen the transformative reach of concentrated wealth and mass media, he would not be so surprised by the degradation of political dialogue. Even so, he and his contemporaries would of course be disappointed that the office of the presidency has not been able to rise to a higher level. With hindsight, we can easily see why it has not. Almost from the outset, presidential politics both reflected and augmented partisanship. "Our parties in Congress seem to regard the approaching election as the only object of attention," wrote Fisher Ames toward the beginning of election season in 1800. Now, with partisanship magnified by the infusion of money and stirred to a frenzy by media, this obsession never ceases for a moment. Instantly after a presidential election, the jockeying and scheming commence for the next. This has turned the framers' dream of a transcendent president nightmarish. Since the political fate of a sitting president is directly linked to the well-being of the nation, and since the party that does not control the presidency figures it will never get its way until it captures that office, that party assumes a vested interest in seeing the nation fail. Further, if leaders of that party follow the inexorable logic of game theory, which many do, they will act on this premise. The framers had hoped for enlightened governing; instead, in our current political landscape, governing is held hostage to politics.[7]

The challenge we and the president face is to change the game and break the cycle. For the citizenry, this would entail suspending the frequent and visceral assault on the very idea of government, an attack that amounts to a sweeping negation of the framers' work. For the three branches of government, it would mean finding some means, consistent with the First Amendment guarantee of free speech, of containing the impacts of unlimited political expenditures and perpetual campaigns, which together have tarnished our democracy. For the president, it would mean trying to maintain a reasonable balance between governance and politics, admittedly a difficult task if undertaken unilaterally. While the ideal of a truly transcendent presidency was not realized in the founding era and appears even more implausible today, this is not to say that ideal was without valid purpose. Imagine for a moment the consequences had Washington not even aspired to that high goal; the new nation, frail and divided, might well have split apart at the outset. Imagine, too, if a modern president were successful in using his

or her immense powers to place political operatives in positions authorized to oversee fair elections, thereby perpetuating one party's control
of the government indefinitely. As frightful as a complete politicization
of the presidency could be, any movement in the opposite direction
is equally uplifting. While the presidency has not turned out entirely
as the framers intended, we would still do well to embrace the values of
governance they expected the chief executive of the United States, in
whom they placed great trust, to exemplify.

Why the Story Has Not Been Told

The narrative of Gouverneur Morris's relentless push to free the executive from Congress can be readily surmised from James Madison's *Notes of Debates in the Federal Convention of 1787,* yet strangely, in the 225 years that have passed since the Constitutional Convention and 172 years since the first publication of Madison's *Notes,* it has never before been chronicled in full detail. This gives cause for wonder and calls for some explanation.

To uncover Morris's role, a researcher needs only to ask, "How did the presidency develop day by day, speech by speech, and vote by vote at the Federal Convention?" Yet not many have journeyed down that path, and to understand why they haven't, we need to look at the different genres in which the subject might be raised: academic studies of the origins of the presidency, biographies of Gouverneur Morris, and narrative accounts of the Constitutional Convention.

Scholarly treatments of the presidency at the convention tend to be studies, not narratives. Typically, they elucidate the positions of the various delegates and use these as organizing principles. By conjoining what was said by a given person at different points in time to construct a coherent philosophy, they miss the day-by-day and even minute-by-minute dynamics of the dialogue. Concerned more with theory than process, they fail to utilize narrative as an analytical tool, which is the only way to access this story. Gouverneur Morris favored a strong and independent executive, they all observe. He opposed selection by Congress. True, all true, but dissecting his speeches and expounding on his positions will not reveal his influence. Only close scrutiny of the interchange, keeping the exposition in strict chronological order, can demonstrate his agency.[1]

Since biographies, by nature, are narratives, we might expect Morris's several biographers to have picked up on the story, and perhaps they would have, had Morris not penned the final draft of the Constitution. This low-hanging fruit, impossible to resist, has obscured other fruit just a bit harder to see; one recent title, for example, is *Gentleman Revolutionary: Gouverneur Morris, the Rake Who Wrote the Constitution*. Morris's rewording of the preamble has provided biographers with a clear and dramatic theme that anchors the single chapter each devotes to the convention. Eager to move on to subsequent chapters, which dramatically place Morris in the midst of the French Revolution and the Reign of Terror, they let his "authorship" of the final draft of the Constitution define his participation at the convention. While they do state his arguments for a strong and independent executive, they divorce these from the vibrant give-and-take that would reveal his influence and importance.[2]

Narrative accounts of the convention, because they must cover the full sweep of topics, breeze through the messy, looping, we-can't-decide debates on the presidency. Slavery, federalism, the small-state/large-state controversy, defining the powers of Congress, and fine-tuning a system of checks and balances require extensive treatment, complicating the narrative arc. Of course all authors deal with the creation of the presidential office, but the back-and-forth chronology of this story does not present a clean, linear progression, and dealing with the befuddling daily minutiae would slow down the telling. Authors generally credit Morris for his authorship of the final draft, his heartfelt speech against slavery, his ardent nationalism, and his advocacy of an independent executive—shouldn't that suffice? They have fifty-four other framers to include and a few they need to feature; so much to discuss in so little space. Again, the genre sets its own limits.[3]

Whether or not they adopt a narrative form, authors who address the origins of the presidency develop protagonists of some sort, and Morris, for various reasons, is not their top choice. Many turn to

Washington, the first occupant of the office, who set precedents and established the tone. Although Washington did not say much at the convention, he exerted influence by his very presence; the office might have looked very different had delegates not assumed Washington would be the first president. This line of reasoning, although not incorrect, diverts attention from the dialogue at the Federal Convention that actually created the presidency.

Others turn to Hamilton, who allegedly defined the office in his *Federalist* essays more completely than the framers had done in the Constitution. As discussed on pages 149–52, however, *The Federalist* was an argument, not an exposition; it did not create the office, it expressed private views only, and it enjoys no unique claim to constitutional authority. As Treasury secretary under Washington, Hamilton did in fact help shape the executive office, but that too steers attention from the Federal Convention, where he expressed extreme views that actually limited his effectiveness.

Treatments of the convention inevitably feature Madison, the so-called Father of the Constitution, but that appellation contributes to our story's neglect by minimizing the impact of others. In fact, Madison did not drive the debate on the presidency, which he acknowledged as his weak suit. At the outset of the convention on June 1, he suggested the "extent of executive authority" should be "to carry into effect national laws, to appoint to offices in cases not otherwise provided for, and to execute such other powers 'not Legislative nor Judiciary in their nature,' *as may from time to time be delegated by the national Legislature*" (emphasis added). Executive powers were clearly derivative, not constitutionally vested. As the convention progressed he changed his stance, but his ideas respecting executive authority were repeatedly defeated. If Madison had had his way, the president, with some members of the judiciary, would enjoy absolute veto powers; impeachments would be tried by the Supreme Court, not the Senate; the executive department would include an independent council; and the Senate could conclude treaties of peace without the consent of the president. Of course all delegates had some ideas that were not adopted, but if we look at how the major components of the presidency came to fruition, we see Madison as only one of many key players. The "Father of the Presidency" he was not.

That title is sometimes bestowed on James Wilson, who made the motion for a single executive, first introduced the notion of presidential electors, named the office, and served on the Committee of Detail, which gave the presidency some sense of definition in early August. Further, to the delight of modern authors, he pushed doggedly for popular elections, a notion that was shunned by most of his peers but is common currency today. Wilson presaged the modern presidency, it is said, although that is reading history backward.

While Wilson did much to shape the executive office, his story masks that of Gouverneur Morris. In part, that is because of their differences in style. Wilson adopted concrete positions and held them firmly, making his participation easier to follow and recount. Morris, by contrast, was admittedly all over the map. Fickle, he is called, too clever by half. In the words of one recent author, "For lawyerly sophism, Morris had few peers." This reputation tempts commentators to dismiss him out of hand. One recent author wrote that Morris, "having temporarily taken leave of his senses," suggested that each presidential elector vote for two candidates, one from outside the elector's home state—a seemingly sensible proposition at the time and one that found its way into the Constitution.[4]

There was reason to Morris's madness, but that reason requires close scrutiny to detect. Inconsistency does not preclude influence. When Morris suddenly repudiated life tenure for the president in favor of repeatable two-year terms, other delegates listened, even if later commentators have not. Morris's argument on July 19 altered the thrust of the convention, albeit but briefly. On August 24 and 31, he maneuvered cleverly to recapture ground he had gained but then lost. Within the Committee of Eleven he held sway, and when a report emerged that turned the presidency on its head, the convention finally acquiesced. None of this can be captured by saying, "Gouverneur Morris believed this," or "Gouverneur Morris believed that," the way Wilson is treated. The static view must give way to a more dynamic approach.

This is not to say Morris was more of a "father" to the presidency than Wilson, or vice versa. That sort of tiering is pointless and even counterproductive, concealing the collective nature of the enterprise and the interactive dialogue that fosters ideas and generates solutions. The Constitutional Convention was in fact a deliberative body, and understanding deliberations, which are inherently fluid, calls for a fluid narrative.

Accounts of the origins of the presidency cannot be rigidly structured. Debates bordered on the farcical at times, and they demand our patience. Through the chaos we search for a story line, and as we do, we find human actors, protagonists who appear to drive the agenda and without whom the story cannot be told. Gouverneur Morris is one of these, as is James Wilson. The dramatic tension cannot be disclosed without paying attention to George Mason, Edmund Randolph, James Madison, Elbridge Gerry, John Rutledge, and others who make key appearances. These are the players, and as we watch them interact, the story reveals itself. There are no shortcuts, just as there were no pat solutions to the troublesome problems the framers faced. When undertaking this book, I had no idea that a peg-legged, haughty lawyer viewed today as too clever by half would play such a role, but there he was, day after day, espousing his agenda and conniving for its acceptance. His ideas evolved with the situational dynamics of the moment, but in the end his actions helped determine much of the presidency as we know it.

Gouverneur Morris does not own this story; in fact, after the convention he virtually disappears, even as the debates continue. Others would determine whether or not the Constitution would be ratified, who could remove appointees, who would shape foreign policy, and how far executive authority might extend in myriad situations. But to discuss the origins of the presidency within the walls of the Pennsylvania State House in the summer of 1787 without accounting for Gouverneur Morris's influence will inevitably lead, and has always led, to distortions of the historical record.

A Note on Capitalization

I have eliminated some of the capitalization within quotations to make the words and thoughts of the authors appear less archaic. Although most scholars prefer to retain all original capitalization, I see no useful purpose in this practice, which often reflects idiosyncratic handwriting or casual contemporary transcription and has little if any significant effect on content. On the other hand, I retain all the original spelling, which contributes to our understanding of the etymology of words and therefore has historical import.

I do preserve capitalization when it appears to conform to conventional usage at the time. In reading documents contemporary to the founding era, I have noted some patterns in capitalization, an informal grammar of sorts. Words denoting governmental constructs, bodies, or offices (e.g., "Government," "National," "State," "Union," "Colonies," "Executive," "Monarchy," "King," "President," "Magistrate," "Chief Magistrate," "Legislature," "Assembly") were generally capitalized. So too were words denoting geographic constructs and directions (e.g., "Continent," "Country," "East," "Western") and individuals to whom deference was given (e.g., "Chairman," "Gentlemen"). When a word is capitalized within a source document that conforms to such unwritten rules, I let the capitalization stand. I have also maintained the original when the text suggests that the author purposely used capitalization for emphasis. In this manner I have tried to strike a middle ground between seemingly random capitalization, which would slow readers down and perhaps interfere with comprehension, and a complete modernization of texts, which would falsely suggest there were no linguistic differences between those times and ours.

Previously, when source documents were difficult to access, it was important for scholars not to alter quotations in any way, but readers today who wish to consult sources directly will have little trouble doing so. All quotations in this book are cited; many sources can be located on the Internet and most are available in printed collections at almost any university.

I have retained the original capitalization when quoting from documents that the nation has enshrined: the Declaration of Independence, the Articles of Confederation, and the Constitution.

Notes

SHORTENED REFERENCES

Adams, *Works*: Charles Francis Adams, ed., *The Works of John Adams* (Boston: Little, Brown, 1856).

Annals: *Annals of Congress,* formerly *The Debates and Proceedings in the Congress of the United States, 1789–1824,* Library of Congress, American Memory, A Century of Lawmaking for a New Nation, http://memory.loc.gov/ammem/amlaw/lwac.html.

DHRC: Merrill Jensen et al., eds., *Documentary History of the Ratification of the Constitution* (Madison: State Historical Society of Wisconsin, 1976–).

Farrand, *Records*: Max Farrand, ed., *The Records of the Federal Convention of 1787* (New Haven, Conn.: Yale University Press, 1911). Farrand includes not only Madison's notes but also the convention's official journal and less comprehensive notes taken by Robert Yates, Rufus King, James McHenry, William Pierce, William Paterson, Alexander Hamilton, and George Mason, as well as committee reports, printed drafts, and numerous letters from delegates. Farrand can also be accessed at Library of Congress, American Memory, A Century of Lawmaking for a New Nation, http://memory.loc.gov/ammem/amlaw/lwfr.html.

Franklin, *Papers*: Leonard W. Labaree and William B. Willcox, eds., *The Papers of Benjamin Franklin* (New Haven, Conn.: Yale University Press, 1959–).

Hamilton, *Papers*: Harold C. Syrett, ed., *The Papers of Alexander Hamilton* (New York: Columbia University Press, 1961–87).

JCC: *Journals of the Continental Congress,* Library of Congress, American Memory, A Century of Lawmaking for a New Nation, http://memory.loc.gov/ammem/amlaw/lwjclink.html.

Jefferson, *Papers*: Julian P. Boyd, Charles T. Cullen, John Catanzariti, and Barbara B. Oberg, eds., *The Papers of Thomas Jefferson* (Princeton, N.J.: Princeton University Press, 1950–). Although this is the most recent and authoritative collection, it is far from finished and must be augmented by the older Ford and Lipscomb/Bergh collections listed below.

Jefferson, *Works*: Paul Leicester Ford, ed., *The Works of Thomas Jefferson* (New York: G. P. Putnam's Sons, 1904–5). This pagination will differ from the earlier edition of Ford's collection, dated 1892–99 and titled *Writings* instead of *Works*.

Jefferson, *Writings*: Andrew A. Lipscomb and Albert Ellery Bergh, eds., *The Writings of Thomas Jefferson* (Washington, D.C.: Thomas Jefferson Memorial Association, 1904).

LDC: *Letters of Delegates to Congress*, Library of Congress, American Memory, A Century of Lawmaking for a New Nation, http://memory.loc.gov/ammem/amlaw/lwdglink .html.

Maclay, *Journal*: *The Journal of William Maclay, 1789–1791*, Library of Congress, American Memory, A Century of Lawmaking for a New Nation, http://memory.loc.gov /ammem/amlaw/lwmj.html. Also in Kenneth R. Bowling and Helen E. Veit, eds., *The Documentary History of the First Federal Congress* (Baltimore: Johns Hopkins University Press, 1988), vol. 9.

Madison, *Notes*: James Madison, *Notes of Debates in the Federal Convention of 1787*, ed. Adrienne Koch (New York: W. W. Norton, 1987). Unless otherwise noted, all references to the Constitutional Convention are from Madison's *Notes*. Since these are published in so many forms and places, the easiest way to demark any particular reference is simply by date. Where the date is mentioned in the text, I provide no further reference; if not mentioned, my note will read: Madison, *Notes*, and the date. An easy-to-use online access to Madison's *Notes*, organized by date, is Yale Law School's Avalon Project, http://avalon.law.yale.edu/. Click "18th Century," then "Madison's Notes on Debates."

Madison, *Papers*: Robert A. Rutland et al., eds., *The Papers of James Madison* (Chicago: University of Chicago Press, 1962–; and Charlottesville: University Press of Virginia, 1977–). The volumes are arranged in four series: Congressional, Secretary of State, Presidential, and Retirement.

Mason, *Papers*: Robert A. Rutland, ed., *The Papers of George Mason* (Chapel Hill: University of North Carolina Press, 1970).

Sparks, *Gouverneur Morris*: Jared Sparks, *The Life of Gouverneur Morris, with Selections from His Correspondence and Miscellaneous Papers* (Boston: Gray & Bowen, 1832).

Washington, *Diaries*: Donald Jackson and Dorothy Twohig, eds., *The Diaries of George Washington* (Charlottesville: University Press of Virginia, 1976–79).

Washington, *Papers*: W. W. Abbot and Dorothy Twohig, eds., *The Papers of George Washington* (Charlottesville: University Press of Virginia, 1983–). The volumes are numbered in separate series: Colonial, Revolutionary War, Confederation, Presidential, and Retirement. Although this is the most recent and authoritative collection, it is far from finished and must be augmented by the older Fitzpatrick collection (listed below) and the Washington papers in the Library of Congress.

Washington, *Writings*: John C. Fitzpatrick, ed., *The Writings of George Washington from the Original Manuscript Sources, 1745–1789* (Washington, D.C.: U.S. Government Printing Office, 1931–44). Also at http://etext.virginia.edu/washington/fitzpatrick/.

PROLOGUE: A PREGNANT MOMENT

1. Madison to Washington, April 16, 1787, in Madison, *Papers*, 9:384–85.

CHAPTER ONE: "LITTLE GODS ON EARTH"

1. Richard L. Bushman, *King and People in Provincial Massachusetts* (Chapel Hill: University of North Carolina Press, 1985), 24.

2. *Boston Gazette*, December 29, 1760.

3. Bushman, *King and People,* 21.

4. *Boston News-Letter,* January 1, 1761.

5. Bushman, *King and People,* 22.

6. John Dickinson, *Letters from a Farmer in Pennsylvania,* letter 3, Online Library of Liberty, http://oll.libertyfund.org/?option=com_staticxt&staticfile=show.php%3Ftitle=690&chapter=102302&layout=html&Itemid=27.

7. William Lincoln, ed., *The Journals of Each Provincial Congress of Massachusetts in 1774 and 1775, and of the Committee of Safety, with an Appendix, Containing the Proceedings of the County Conventions* (Boston: Dutton and Wentworth, 1838), 601–5. Resolves from the other rebellious counties in Massachusetts (606–60) also contained angry phrases coupled with deference to the king.

8. King George III to Lord North, November 18, 1774, in *The Spirit of 'Seventy-Six: The Story of the American Revolution as Told by the Participants,* ed. Henry S. Commager and Richard B. Morris (Indianapolis: Bobbs-Merrill, 1958), 1:61; Robert Middlekauff, *The Glorious Cause: The American Revolution, 1763–1789* (New York: Oxford University Press, 1982), 262; Washington, *Papers,* Revolutionary War Series, 1:90, 171, 274, 280, 447; 2:161, 187, 282, 392, 585. Only when referring to British soldiers in Canada did Washington use the term "King's troops" (Washington, *Papers,* Revolutionary War Series, 2:73).

9. "Petition to the King," July 8, 1775, in *JCC,* 2:158–62.

10. "King George III's Address to Parliament, October 27, 1775," Library of Congress, American Memory, American Revolution, http://www.loc.gov/teachers/classroommaterials/presentationsandactivities/presentations/timeline/amrev/shots/address.html.

11. Thomas Paine, *Common Sense,* reprinted in *Thomas Paine Reader,* ed. Michael Foot and Isaac Kramnick (New York: Penguin Books, 1987), 72–79.

12. Henry Laurens to John Laurens, February 22, 1776, in *The Papers of Henry Laurens,* ed. Philip M. Hamer (Columbia: University of South Carolina Press, 1968–2003), 11:115.

13. Warren M. Billings, ed., *The Old Dominion in the Seventeenth Century: A Documentary History of Virginia, 1606–1700* (Chapel Hill: University of North Carolina Press, 2007), 35–41; Kermit L. Hall, ed., *Major Problems in American Constitutional History: Colonial Era Through Reconstruction* (Lexington, Mass.: D. C. Heath, 1992), 30–34.

14. Evarts B. Greene, *The Provincial Governor in the English Colonies of North America* (New York: Russell & Russell, 1966), 67–68.

15. Ibid., 61–62.

16. Ibid., 46–47.

17. Warren M. Billings, John E. Selby, and Thad W. Tate, *Colonial Virginia: A History* (White Plains, N.Y.: KTO Press, 1986), 104; William M. Billings, "Thomas Culpeper," in *Oxford Dictionary of National Biography* (Oxford: Oxford University Press, 2004), 14:606.

18. Patricia U. Bonomi, *The Lord Cornbury Scandal: The Politics of Reputation in British North America* (Chapel Hill: University of North Carolina Press, 2000).

19. Benjamin Labaree, *Colonial Massachusetts: A History* (Millwood, N.Y.: KTO Press, 1979), 254.

20. Washington to Richard Henry Lee, December 26, 1775, in Washington, *Papers,* Revolutionary War Series, 2:553, 611.

CHAPTER TWO: REVOLUTION AND THE RETREAT FROM EXECUTIVE AUTHORITY

1. *JCC,* 1:79.
2. Ibid., 15–24, 30.
3. James Duane, Notes on Debates, September 5, 1774, in *LDC,* 1:25.
4. John Adams, Diary, September 2, 1774, in *LDC,* 1:7; Silas Deane to Elizabeth Deane, September 10, 1774, in *LDC,* 1:61; Randolph to Henry Tazewell, February 3, 1775, cited in Jack Rakove, *The Beginnings of National Politics: An Interpretive History* (New York: Alfred A. Knopf, 1979), 51; Randolph to Mann Page Jr., Lewis Willis, and Benjamin Grymes Jr., April 27, 1775, cited in Michael A. McDonnell, *The Politics of War: Race, Class, and Conflict in Revolutionary Virginia* (Chapel Hill: University of North Carolina Press, 2007), 60; Adams, Diary, September 2, 1774, in *LDC,* 1:7.
5. John Adams to Abigail Adams, October 9, 1774, in *LDC,* 1:164. On October 24, Adams expressed even greater frustration in his diary: "In Congress, nibbling and quibbling—as usual. . . . There is no greater mortification than to sit with half a dozen witts, deliberating upon a petition, address, or memorial. These great witts, these subtle criticks, these refined genius's, these learned lawyers, these wise statesmen, are so fond of shewing their parts and powers, as to make their consultations very tedius" (in ibid., 236).
6. *JCC,* October 22, 1774, 1:94.
7. Ibid., June 2, 1775, 2:78.
8. Ibid., June 3, 1775, 79.
9. Committee of Secret Correspondence Statement, October 1, 1776, in *LDC,* 5:273. Emphasis appears in Franklin, *Papers,* 22:637.
10. Morris to Deane, December 20, 1776, in *LDC,* 5:627; Ellis P. Oberholtzer, *Robert Morris: Patriot and Financier* (New York: Macmillan, 1903), 293.
11. *JCC,* 6:1042, 1032.
12. Ibid., November 15, 1777, 9:921–22.
13. The various state constitutions can be viewed online at Yale Law School's Avalon Project, "The American Constitution: A Documentary Record," http://avalon.law.yale.edu/subject_menus/constpap.asp.
14. The only new constitutions without an executive council were those of New Hampshire, which had no executive branch at all but did have a legislative council to temper the authority of its president, and New York, which transferred some appointive powers to a chancellor and others to a special committee that included himself and four members of the senate.
15. South Carolina's provisional constitution, drafted before independence, granted its president an absolute veto power, but after independence an amended constitution eliminated the executive veto.
16. Allan Nevins, *The American States During and After the Revolution, 1775–1789* (New York: Macmillan, 1924), 374; McDonnell, *Politics of War,* 462–65, 469.
17. Hamilton to Duane, September 3, 1780, in Hamilton, *Papers,* 2:400–18.
18. *JCC,* February 7, 1781, 19:126.
19. Reed to Greene, November 1, 1781, in *The Papers of Robert Morris, 1781–1784,* ed. E. James Ferguson (Pittsburgh: University of Pittsburgh Press, 1973), 1:21.
20. Clarence Ver Steeg, *Robert Morris: Revolutionary Financier* (New York: Octagon Books, 1972), 166–67.
21. Madison, *Papers,* Congressional Series, 9:385.

CHAPTER THREE: FIRST DRAFT

1. For the cool spring, see James Madison to Thomas Jefferson, May 15, 1787, and Rufus King to Henry Knox, June 3, 1787, in Farrand, *Records,* 4:20, 64. For the weather on June 1 and other dates, see William Johnson, Diary, in ibid., 552.

2. This concluding phrase, and the concept, are explicated and defended by Max M. Edling in *A Revolution in Favor of Government: Origins of the U.S. Constitution and the Making of the American State* (New York: Oxford University Press, 2003).

3. Farrand, *Records,* 3:88–89; Madison, *Notes,* June 1.

4. Madison, *Notes,* June 6.

5. Farrand, *Records,* 3:94.

CHAPTER FOUR: SECOND GUESSES

1. Hamilton, *Papers,* 4:186. Hamilton's written notes to himself, along with his "Plan of Government" and Madison's, John Lansing's, and Rufus King's rendition of his speech, appear in ibid., 178–211. His "Draft of a Constitution," an elaboration that he handed to Madison near the end of the convention, appears in ibid., 253–74. His June 18 "Plan for Government" also appears in Madison, *Notes,* under that date.

2. Farrand, *Records,* 1:301.

3. Hamilton, *Papers,* 4:186.

4. Yates's account is in Farrand, *Records,* 1: 363.

5. King's account is in ibid., 366. Morris's recollection is from Morris to Robert Walsh, February 5, 1811, in ibid., 3:418. Johnson's claim that nobody came forth in support of Hamilton might have been correct at that moment, but on June 29, eight days after Johnson made that remark and eleven days after Hamilton delivered his speech, one delegate, George Read of Delaware, expressed support for Hamilton's national system, proclaiming that the Virginia Plan, still the working draft, had "too much of a federal mixture in it." Read wished that Hamilton's plan, which was "truly national," could be "substituted in place of that on the table." Nobody came to Read's defense, however, just as nobody had initially supported Hamilton. Perhaps it was coincidental, but the morning after Read spoke in his behalf and received no response from other delegates, Hamilton departed the convention. Note that even Read, who agreed with Hamilton's extreme nationalism, said nothing in support of Hamilton's preference for a lifelong American "monarch."

6. Ibid., 3:89.

7. Ibid., 92.

8. Morris to Thomas Penn, May 20, 1774, Gouverneur Morris's Letters, http://www.familytales.org/dbDisplay.php?id=ltr_gom4502, accessed November 11, 2009.

CHAPTER FIVE: GOUVERNEUR MORRIS'S FINAL PUSH

1. Farrand, *Records,* 2:134, 137, 145, 163, 171.

2. Clinton Rossiter, *1787: The Grand Convention* (New York: Macmillan, 1966), 202.

3. New York's three delegates had all gone back to their home state. Hamilton left because he was always outvoted by the antinationalists John Lansing and Robert Yates, and Lansing and Yates left shortly after because they were always outvoted by the rest of the convention.

4. Morris's comments here are taken from the notes of James McHenry, in Farrand, *Records,* 2:407.

5. This committee is often called the Committee on Postponed Matters, the Committee on Postponed Parts, or the Committee on Remaining Matters, but these are later appellations. I use here the contemporary designation, the Committee of Eleven, following the convention's official journal, Madison's *Notes,* and how the committee referred to itself, even though the name repeats that of an earlier committee.

6. Dickinson to George Logan, January 16, 1802, in *Supplement to Max Farrand's "The Records of the Federal Convention of 1787,"* ed. James H. Hutson (New Haven, Conn.: Yale University Press, 1987), 300–301. The following year, in a private letter, Pierce Butler wrote: "His [the president's] Election, the mode of which I had the honor of proposing in the Committee . . ." (Pierce Butler to Weedon Butler, May 5, 1888, in Farrand, *Records,* 3:302). Some historians have taken this passing remark, within a dependent clause of a private letter, as sufficient evidence to attribute exclusive authorship to Butler. Although Butler might conceivably have moved the final proposal, he did not own this plan. All elements had been suggested before. On July 25, Dickinson had suggested a two-part process, a nomination procedure and a final vote. Also on July 25, Williamson had suggested that each elector vote for three candidates, at least one from a state not his own, and Morris had refined that process to a two-candidate system that the committee finally adopted. The original elector plan had come on June 2 from Wilson, who was not on the committee. Butler probably helped synthesize the elements, but his fellow foes of legislative selection no doubt had their say, while Sherman must have spoken on behalf of the runoff within Congress, and the small-state delegates certainly pushed for disproportionate representation. This was a politically motivated process, not the instantaneous brainstorm of Butler, Dickinson, Morris, or any other individual.

7. While the necessity for compromise helps us understand the complexities of the plan, it does not explain why that plan was preferred over some form of popular election. For that we must look to the deep resistance to popular elections ingrained in the minds of most delegates. Some historians, unwilling to acknowledge the antidemocratic proclivities of the Constitution's framers, claim they really had no choice in the matter. It would have been impossible to create an election machinery on a national scale, they say, and any attempt to develop a uniform franchise requirement would have torn the convention asunder. This defense begs the question. The Committee of Eleven could have called for popular elections in each state without a federal machinery; such elections could be conducted by state governments and open to voters enfranchised by local standards. The framers had no difficulty in reverting to state standards in legislative elections, and they could have done the same for executive elections. Further, to prevent a state from achieving undue influence by expanding its electorate and boosting its vote totals, the Committee of Eleven could have weighted each state's popular votes according to a preexisting formula, just as it did in its elector plan, and that formula might well have been the same as that of the final system, based on the total number of representatives and senators from each state. One handy way of doing this would have been to give each state a certain number of "electors" but, rather than allow these electors to make their own decisions, bind them to the results of popular elections, as is the custom today. Expecting representatives to follow instructions from their constituents was common in New England and practiced to some

extent elsewhere during the Revolutionary era, so it would not have been a stretch to build on this custom and have the populace instruct electors. (See Ray Raphael, "The Democratic Moment: The Revolution in Popular Politics," in *The Oxford Handbook of the American Revolution* [New York: Oxford University Press, forthcoming].) In sum, there was no objective or mechanical reason to institute an intermediate level of decision makers between the people and the president; that was a discretionary decision to keep the people from voting directly for the president. Although five states (New York, Massachusetts, New Hampshire, Connecticut, and Rhode Island) chose their governors through popular elections, selecting the nation's chief executive was too critical a task to be left to an untutored electorate, most delegates believed.

8. We have direct evidence of further small-state/large-state negotiations that figured into this compromise. Back on July 16, as part of the so-called Great Compromise that established proportional representation in the House and equal voting in the Senate, delegates had stipulated that all money bills must originate in the House. That provision had been overturned on August 8, however, and this caused great consternation in the minds of some delegates from large states. Accordingly, the Committee of Eleven reversed the decision of August 8, returning to the original compromise of July 16. When the committee's reversal was discussed on September 5, Gouverneur Morris commented, "It had been agreed to in the Committee on the ground of compromise." Later that day, Rufus King "observed that the influence of the small States in the Senate was somewhat balanced by the influence of the large States in bringing forward the candidates; and also by the concurrence of the small States in the Committee in the clause vesting the exclusive origination of money bills in the House of Representatives." To this Madison affixed a rare and revealing footnote: "This explains the compromise mentioned above by Mr. Govr. Morris. Col. Masson Mr. Gerry & other members from large States set great value on this privilege of originating money bills. Of this the members from the small States, with some from the large States who wished a high mounted Govt endeavored to avail themselves, by making that privilege, the price of arrangements in the constitution favorable to the small States, and to the elevation of the Government." In short, the compromise that gave large states greater influence in the first stage of the election process but small states greater influence in the Senate runoff was linked to even more sweeping negotiations.

9. Dickinson, on the following day, managed to ensure that the Senate's appointive powers extended no further than ambassadors and Supreme Court justices, but he did not challenge these.

10. Morris's fingerprints can be found on other changes emerging from the Committee of Eleven. The idea of voting for two candidates was his, first suggested on July 25. When the committee inserted a fourteen-year residency requirement for the president, it did not pull that number out of a hat—back on August 9, Morris had pushed that requirement for senators.

11. Hamilton to King, August 10, 1787, in Hamilton, *Papers,* 4:235. For Morris's writing this draft, see Morris to Timothy Pickering, December 22, 1814, in Farrand, *Records,* 3:420; James Madison to Jared Sparks, April 8, 1831, in Farrand, *Records,* 3:499; Ezra Stiles, Diary (based on Abraham Baldwin's account), December 21, 1787, in Farrand, *Records,* 3:170.

12. For Morris's biographers and why they failed to focus on his maneuverings, see the Postscript.

13. In the spray of small details that scattered the floor debates over the final four days, one additional issue marginally affected the presidency. In previous drafts, the U.S. treasurer was to be appointed jointly by Congress, which raised and appropriated the funds the treasurer was supposed to guard. John Rutledge, though, wanted the president, not Congress, to choose the treasurer, and Gouverneur Morris instantly agreed. Morris's reasoning was a bit strange: Congress would do a better job of overseeing an officer who had been appointed by somebody else. Throughout the convention, Morris had argued that the president should be chosen by someone other than Congress to achieve more independence; now he was saying an independent appointee could be more closely scrutinized. Although his argument made no sense, it further revealed Morris's stance: the executive should receive all powers the convention was willing to give it. Rutledge's motion prevailed, not for Morris's reasons, but for consistency, since most similar appointments now lay with the president.

CHAPTER SIX: SELLING THE PLAN

1. Mason to Jefferson, May 26, 1788, in Mason, *Papers,* 3:1045.

2. Ibid., 991–92; *DHRC,* 8:43–45 or 13:348–50.

3. Mason, *Papers,* 3:1001–5; *DHRC,* 8:46.

4. Washington, *Diaries,* 5:186; *DHRC,* 13:243.

5. Washington to Mason and Mason to Washington, October 7, 1787, in Mason, *Papers,* 3:1001, 1004–5.

6. Madison to Washington, September 30, 1787, in *DHRC,* 8:27 or 13:275; Washington to Madison, October 10, 1787, in ibid., 8:49 or 13:358–59. For the publication of Mason's "Objections," see ibid., 13:346–48.

7. Washington to Henry, Harrison, and Nelson, September 24, 1787, in ibid., 8:15.

8. Washington to Knox, October 15, 1787, in ibid., 56–57; and Washington to Stuart, October 17, 1787, in ibid., 69.

9. Hamilton to Washington, November 10, 1787, Madison to Washington, November 18, 1787, Washington to Stuart, November 30, 1787, and Washington to Madison, December 7, 1787, in ibid., 152, 167–68, 181–82, 193–94, 224.

10. Washington, *Writings,* 26:483–96.

11. Mason's "Objections," in *DHRC,* 8:45 or 13:350; Washington to Stuart, November 30, 1787, in ibid., 8:193.

12. Washington to Madison, December 7, 1787, in ibid., 8:224; Washington to Stuart, November 30, 1787, in ibid., 193.

13. Donald to Jefferson, November 12, 1787, in ibid., 155.

14. Ibid., 197, 216, 276–78.

15. Douglas Southall Freeman, *George Washington: A Biography* (New York: Scribner's Sons, 1951), 6:119.

16. Ibid., 125; Madison, *Notes,* September 17.

17. Grayson to William Short, November 20, 1787, in *DHRC,* 8:150; Lee to Randolph, October 16, 1787, in ibid., 61.

18. John G. Roberts, "An Exchange of Letters Between Jefferson and Quesnay de Beau-

repaire," *Virginia Magazine of History and Biography,* April 1942, 134–42; Virginius
Dabney, *Richmond: The Story of a City* (Charlottesville: University Press of Virginia,
1990), 40–44.

19. Mason to Martin Cockburn, May 26, 1774, in Mason, *Papers,* 1:190.

20. *DHRC,* 9:963–64.

21. For Robertson's note taking, see ibid., 902–6.

22. Ibid., 962.

23. Ibid., 1045, 1063.

24. Ibid., 1051, and 10:1476.

25. Herbert J. Storing, ed., *The Complete Anti-Federalist* (Chicago: University of Chicago
Press, 1981), 5:196, 4:277, 3:129.

26. *DHRC,* 10:1378–79.

27. Storing, *Complete Anti-Federalist,* 5:196.

28. John DeWitt, Dissent of the Minority of the Convention of Pennsylvania, and Federal Farmer, in ibid., 4:26, 3:162, 2:304.

29. Ibid., 3:129, 89–90.

30. Madison, *Notes,* September 15.

31. *DHRC,* 10:1376.

32. The amendments can be found in the respective volumes of *DHRC,* in *The Bill of
Rights: A Documentary History,* ed. Bernard Schwartz (New York: Chelsea House,
1971), vol. 2, or by searching the Web site of Yale Law School's Avalon Project for
"ratification" plus each particular state.

33. New York also tried to close a worrisome loophole. In case of death or incapacity of
both the president and the vice president, Congress was empowered to appoint their
successors, but nowhere was it stipulated that these would serve only for the *remainder*
of a four-year term. To solve this, they proposed there must be a presidential election
every four years.

34. *DHRC,* 9:822, 10:1547–50.

35. Ibid., 10:1373–75.

36. Ibid., 1373; Madison, *Notes,* May 31; Storing, *Complete Anti-Federalist,* 2:115, 5:168. Cato
is believed to have been either Governor George Clinton or Abraham Yates (*DHRC,*
13:255).

37. *DHRC,* 10:1376. Although creating a method for popular elections would have presented great political challenges, it would not have been impossible at the Federal
Convention. (See chapter 5, note 7.) After the convention, however, the difficulties
in negotiating compromises addressing the issues mentioned in this paragraph were
greatly magnified; coming up with a politically viable alternative within the state ratifying conventions *was* nearly impossible.

38. Ibid., 2:566–67.

39. Madison, *Notes,* September 4, 6, and 7; *DHRC,* 13:341.

40. Madison to Washington, April 16, 1787, in Madison, *Papers,* Congressional Series,
9:384–85.

41. Madison, *Notes,* September 7, 8, 12, 14, and 15.

42. On February 24, 1815, Morris wrote to W. H. Wells, "I was warmly pressed by Hamilton to assist in writing the Federalist, which I declined" (Farrand, *Records,* 3:421).

43. Hamilton, *Papers,* 4:185–86.

44. Madison, *Notes,* September 7 and July 17.

CHAPTER SEVEN: THE LAUNCH

1. Washington to Pierce, January 1, 1789, and Washington to Madison, January 2, 1789, in Washington, *Papers,* Presidential Series, 1:227, 229; editorial comment, in ibid., 2:152–53; Washington to Henry Lee, September 22, 1788, in Washington, *Writings,* 30:97–98.

2. The draft Washington sent to Madison was originally composed by David Humphreys, his longtime aide, then copied and edited by the presumed author. Both the draft and the final speech, with editorial explanation, appear in Washington, *Papers,* Presidential Series, 2:152–77.

3. Maclay, *Journal,* 9–12.

4. Ibid., 24–29, 34–36; *Senate Journal,* 1:23–25, Library of Congress, American Memory, A Century of Lawmaking for a New Nation, http://memory.loc.gov/ammem/amlaw/lwej.html; *Annals,* 1:331–37; Stuart to Washington, July 14, 1789, in Washington, *Papers,* Presidential Series, 3:199.

5. Henry Knox to Washington, May 13, 1789, in Washington, *Papers,* Presidential Series, 2:289–94.

6. Washington to Adams, May 10, 1789, in ibid, 245–47; Washington to Madison, May 12, 1789, in ibid, 282; and Washington to David Stuart, July 26, 1789, in ibid., 322–23; Forrest McDonald, *The Presidency of George Washington* (Lawrence: University Press of Kansas, 1974), 26. See also Washington to Catharine Sawbridge Macaulay Graham, January 9, 1790, in Washington, *Papers,* Presidential Series, 4:552.

7. Washington, *Papers,* Presidential Series, 2:165.

8. *Annals,* 1:473–78.

9. Ibid., 479–82.

10. Ibid., 514–15, 574, 544.

11. Ibid., 558, 599. The full debate extends from page 473 to 599. The following Monday, the House returned to the issue from a slightly different perspective. The vote to make the secretary of foreign affairs removable by the president implied congressional authority to make such a decision; this made many members uneasy, for they had argued that this was a matter of constitutional interpretation, not a grant by Congress. So, in its stead, they substituted a convoluted motion that implied the power already existed within the Constitution, and this motion passed by approximately the same margin (ibid., 599–608).

12. Maclay, *Journal,* 111–16. Thirty-five years later, William Harris Crawford stated (not from firsthand evidence) that Washington "at an early period of his administration" had "gone to the Senate with a project of a treaty to be negotiated, and been present at their deliberations upon it. They debated it and proposed alterations, so that when Washington left the Senate chamber he said he would be damned if he ever went there again." James Monroe, present during Crawford's telling of this story, said that some eighteen months after the forming of the government he had gone to the Senate and heard that "something like this had happened." These tales do not reliably depict what happened on August 22 and 24, 1789, but they do speak to the legacy of what transpired. (James Hart, *The American Presidency in Action, 1789: A Study in Constitutional History* [New York: Macmillan, 1948], 96, citing *The Memoirs of John Quincy Adams* [Philadelphia: J. B. Lippincott, 1876], 6:427.)

13. The removal debate was not forever settled. In 1867, Congress passed the Tenure of Office Act, which prohibited a president, without consent from the Senate, from removing key executive officers who had been appointed by a previous president. This was specifically intended to shift control over Reconstruction from President Andrew Johnson, a foe to the radical Republicans who controlled Congress, to Secretary of War Edwin Stanton, their ally. Although the act remained in force for twenty years, it was not effective. Johnson removed Stanton anyway, for which he was impeached, but the Senate acquitted him. Subsequent presidents in those years found ways around the Tenure of Office Act, affirming their control over removal. In 1926, while ruling on a similar law, the Supreme Court declared in *Myers v. United States* "that the Tenure of Office Act of 1867, insofar as it attempted to prevent the President from removing executive officers who had been appointed by him by and with the advice and consent of the Senate, was invalid."

14. Charles C. Thach, *The Creation of the Presidency, 1775–1789* (Baltimore: Johns Hopkins Press, 1922), 157–59. Adding to the confusion was a clause in Article II, Section 2 authorizing the president to "require the Opinion, in writing, of the principal Officer in each of the executive Departments, upon any Subject relating to the Duties of their respective Offices." On the one hand, this would seem to imply presidential authority over executive officers, but opponents of presidential removal could argue the reverse. Why would the framers grant this one very specific authority if they had intended the president to have absolute control over other officers, his alleged underlings, in all matters?

15. Washington to the U.S. Senate, August 22, 1789, in Washington, *Papers,* Presidential Series, 3:521–25.

16. Maclay, *Journal,* 128–31.

17. Washington to Morris, October 13, 1789, in ibid., 4:176.

18. Washington, *Diaries,* 5:452–53, 460–97. For a map of the tour, see Washington, *Papers,* Presidential Series, 4:200–201.

CHAPTER EIGHT: WASHINGTON AND THE CHALLENGE
TO TRANSCENDENT LEADERSHIP

1. Maclay, *Journal,* 174.

2. Washington, *Papers,* Presidential Series, 4:543–46.

3. Hamilton, "Report on the Public Credit," January 9, 1790, in Hamilton, *Papers,* 6:65–168.

4. Hamilton, *Papers,* 6:99; Franklin to James Parker, March 20, 1750 (or 1751), in Franklin, *Papers,* 4:119.

5. Maclay, *Journal,* 189, 194.

6. Ibid., 177.

7. Randolph to Washington, February 12, 1791, in Washington, *Papers,* Presidential Series, 7:337.

8. Jefferson to Washington, February 15, 1791, in ibid., 352.

9. Washington to Hamilton, February 16, 1791, in ibid., 357.

10. Madison to Washington, February 21, 1791, in ibid., 395.

11. Hamilton to Washington, February 23, 1791, in ibid., 425, 429, 430.

12. For Hamilton's personal meeting with Washington, see ibid., 452.

13. Richard H. Kohn, "The Washington Administration's Decision to Crush the Whiskey Rebellion," *Journal of American History* 59, no. 3 (December 1972): 584; Washington, *Writings*, 34:28–37.

14. Washington to Graham, January 9, 1790, in Washington, *Papers*, Presidential Series, 4:552.

15. Washington to Burgess Ball, September 25, 1794, in *George Washington in the Ohio Valley*, ed. Hugh Cleland (Pittsburgh: University of Pittsburgh Press, 1955), 369–71; Washington, *Writings*, 34:37.

16. James Roger Sharp, *American Politics in the Early Republic: The New Nation in Crisis* (New Haven, Conn.: Yale University Press, 1993), 76; Hamilton, "Defense of the President's Neutrality Proclamation," in *The Pacificus-Helvidius Debates*, ed. Morton J. Frisch (Indianapolis: Liberty Fund, 2007), 3.

17. Frisch, *Pacificus-Helvidius Debates*, 1.

18. Madison to Jefferson, June 19, 1793, in Sharp, *American Politics in the Early Republic*, 77.

19. Hamilton, "Pacificus Number 1," in Frisch, *Pacificus-Helvidius Debates*, 12–13.

20. Jefferson to Madison, July 7, 1793, in Madison, *Papers*, Congressional Series, 15:43; Frisch, *Pacificus-Helvidius Debates*, 54.

21. Madison, "Helvidius Number 1," in Frisch, *Pacificus-Helvidius Debates*, 59–63.

22. Ibid., 63–64. Ironically, later writers who treat Hamilton's views in *The Federalist* as definitive expositions of the Constitution rather than arguments in favor of the Constitution also treat his Pacificus essays as explanations of what the Constitution really means, even though in this instance the views of Publius and Pacificus are diametrically opposed.

23. Madison, *Notes*, June 1 and August 6.

24. Ibid., September 7.

25. Ibid., August 17.

26. Hamilton, "Pacificus Number 1," 13.

27. *Senate Executive Journal*, April 19, 1794, Library of Congress, American Memory, A Century of Lawmaking for a New Nation, 152, http://memory.loc.gov/ammem/amlaw/lwej.html.

28. The full treaty appears in Samuel Flagg Bemis, *Jay's Treaty: A Study in Commerce and Diplomacy* (New Haven, Conn.: Yale University Press, 1962), 442–84.

29. Thomas J. Farnham, "The Virginia Amendments of 1795: An Episode in the Opposition to Jay's Treaty," *Virginia Magazine of History and Biography*, January 1967, 84–85.

30. In the nine-day period leading up to its final decision, it received 104 petitions containing 17,400 signatures urging a vote one way or the other. By this time, Federalists had been able to mobilize support among the educated and politically active mercantile class, and slightly more than half the petitions favored the treaty (Sharp, *American Politics in the Early Republic*, 129, 132).

31. Len Travers, *Celebrating the Fourth: Independence Day and the Rites of Nationalism in the Early Republic* (Amherst: University of Massachusetts Press, 1997), 88–106.

32. Jefferson to William Branch Giles, December 31, 1795, in Jefferson, *Papers*, 28:566.

33. For Hamilton's authorship of Washington's Farewell Address, see Hamilton, *Papers*, 20:168–83, 264–88, 294–303. While the introductory and concluding sections drew on Madison's draft, the heart of the address, which concerned policy issues, was largely Hamilton's doing. When Hamilton presented both a reworked draft of Madison's and

Washington's authorship and one he had written himself, Washington chose Hamilton's original.

34. *Aurora General Advertiser,* July 22, 1795; Hamilton, *Papers,* 18:471–72, 485–88, and 20:42; Ron Chernow, *Alexander Hamilton* (New York: Penguin, 2004), 489–91.

35. Documents from the Democratic-Republican Societies that Washington decried are collected in *The Democratic-Republican Societies, 1790–1800: A Documentary Sourcebook of Constitutions, Addresses, Resolutions, and Toasts,* ed. Philip S. Foner (Westport, Conn.: Greenwood Press, 1976). Washington's Farewell Address can be accessed through the Web site of Yale Law School's Avalon Project, http://avalon.law.yale.edu/18th _century/washing.asp.

36. Ames to Oliver Wolcott, September 26, 1796, cited in Alexander DeConde, "Washington's Farewell, the French Alliance, and the Election of 1796," in *Political Parties in American History,* vol. 1, *1789–1828,* ed. Winfred E. A. Bernhard (New York: G. P. Putnam's Sons, 1973), 160.

CHAPTER NINE: SYSTEM FAILURE

1. Hamilton to Wilson, January 25, 1789, in Hamilton, *Papers,* 5:248.

2. Madison, *Notes,* September 4.

3. After revealing to Wilson his plan to "throw away" seven or eight votes, Hamilton elaborated. "Under this impression I have proposed to friends in Connecticut to throw away two to others in Jersey to throw away an equal number & I submit it to you whether it will not be well to lose three or four in Pennsylvania" (Hamilton to Wilson, January 25, 1789, in Hamilton, *Papers,* 5:248–49). He then added, "Your advices from the South will serve you as the best guide," suggesting the network of communication on strategizing for the election extended wider yet. Hamilton also communicated on this matter with Theodore Sedgwick in Massachusetts, James Madison in Virginia (the two were still allies at that point), and no doubt Federalist colleagues in New York (ibid., 236, 247, 250–53).

4. Richard P. McCormick, *The Presidential Game: The Origins of American Presidential Politics* (New York: Oxford University Press, 1982), 41.

5. James Roger Sharp, *American Politics in the Early Republic: The New Nation in Crisis* (New Haven, Conn.: Yale University Press, 1993), 149 (Wolcott and Troup letters); Hamilton to King, May 4, 1796, in Hamilton, *Papers,* 20:158.

6. Sharp, *American Politics in the Early Republic,* 156.

7. Hamilton to ——, November 8, 1796, in Hamilton, *Papers,* 20:376–77.

8. John Adams to Abigail Adams, December 26, 1793, in *My Dearest Friend: Letters of Abigail and John Adams,* ed. Margaret A. Hogan and C. James Taylor (Boston: Massachusetts Historical Society, 2007), 345; Sharp, *American Politics in the Early Republic,* 160.

9. Jefferson to Adams, December 28, 1796, and Jefferson to Madison, December 17, 1796, in Jefferson, *Papers,* 29:235–37, 223.

10. Sharp, *American Politics in the Early Republic,* 162.

11. Jefferson to Madison, January 1, 1797, in Jefferson, *Papers,* 29:247–51; John Adams to Abigail Adams, December 12, 1796, in Adams, *Works,* 1:496.

12. Gordon Wood, *Empire of Liberty: A History of the Early Republic, 1789–1815* (New York: Oxford University Press, 2009), 213–15.

13. Stanley Elkins and Eric McKitrick, *The Age of Federalism* (New York: Oxford University Press, 1993), 535.

14. Jefferson to Edward Rutledge, December 27, 1796, in Jefferson, *Papers,* 29:232.

15. Jefferson, *The Anas,* in Jefferson, *Writings,* 1:415; Adams, *Works,* 9:286.

16. Jefferson to Rutledge, June 24, 1797, in Jefferson, *Papers,* 29:456–57.

17. Kentucky and Virginia Resolutions, Avalon Project, Yale Law School, http://avalon .law.yale.edu/18th_century/kenres.asp and http://avalon.law.yale.edu/18th_century/ virres.asp.

18. Hamilton, *Papers,* 22:4–5, 17–19.

19. Ibid., 9.

20. Washington to Adams, September 25, 1798, in ibid., 14–15.

21. Adams to Washington, October 9, 1798, in ibid., 15; *Senate Executive Journal,* July 2, 1798, Library of Congress, American Memory, A Century of Lawmaking for a New Nation, http://memory.loc.gov/ammem/amlaw/lwej.html.

22. William Heth to Hamilton, January 14, 1799, in Hamilton, *Papers,* 22:415; Sharp, *American Politics in the Early Republic,* 209; David McCullough, *John Adams* (New York: Simon & Schuster, 2001), 485.

23. Adams, *Works,* 9:291; Sharp, *American Politics in the Early Republic,* 179. Abigail Adams, protective of her husband, was perhaps more forthright in her advocacy of the Sedition Act than John. Before the bill was passed, responding to a wave of personal attacks issued by Benjamin Franklin Bache, she wrote, "In any other country Bache & all his papers would have been seized and ought to be here, but congress are dilly dallying about passing a bill enabling the President to seize suspicious persons, and their papers." Then, after the bill was passed and Congress had adjourned, she commented, "Their last deeds may be marked amongst their best, an Alien Bill a Sedition Bill and a Bill declaring void, all our treaties and conventions with France" (Elkins and McKitrick, *Age of Federalism,* 879n29).

24. Thomas L. Purvis, *Revolutionary America, 1763 to 1800,* Almanacs of American Life Series (New York: Facts on File, 1995), 102–3, 124–25.

25. McCormick, *Presidential Game,* 60.

26. Edward J. Larson, *A Magnificent Catastrophe: The Tumultuous Election of 1800* (New York: Free Press, 2007), 78–80; *Annals,* 10:33, 47 (January 24 and February 14). The original bill, before being amended, awarded the final slot to the chief justice of the Supreme Court. All actions on the bill at various dates, taken from the *Annals of Congress,* are collected in *The Presidential Counts: A Complete Official Record* (New York: D. Appleton, 1877), 414–34.

27. *Annals,* 10:49, 51 (February 20 and 24).

28. Ibid., 126–46 (March 28). Note that the supremacy of the states in determining the manner of selecting electors would be severely modified by the Fourteenth Amendment, but at the time, according to Article II, Section 1 of the Constitution, states held exclusive power in the matter.

29. Ibid., 146 (March 28).

30. Larson, *Magnificent Catastrophe,* 80–83; *Aurora,* February 19, 1800.

31. Hamilton, *Papers,* 24:444–52; Larson, *Magnificent Catastrophe,* 62–65; McCormick, *Presidential Game,* 60–62.

32. Hamilton to Jay, May 7, 1800, in Hamilton, *Papers,* 24:464–67.

33. Ames to Christopher Gore, March 5, 1800, and Sedgwick to Rufus King, December 12, 1799, cited in Larson, *Magnificent Catastrophe,* 84.

34. Hamilton, *Papers,* 25:169–234.

35. Jedediah Morse to Oliver Wolcott Jr., October 27, 1800, quoted in Hamilton, *Papers,* 25:178.

36. Elkins and McKitrick, *Age of Federalism,* 741–43.

37. Hamilton to Oliver Wolcott Jr., December 16, 1800, and Hamilton to Theodore Sedgwick, December 20, 1800, in Hamilton, *Papers,* 25:257, 270.

38. Sedgwick to Hamilton, January 10, 1801, in ibid., 311.

39. Jefferson to Monroe, February 15, 1801, in Jefferson, *Papers,* 32:594.

40. McKean to Jefferson, March 19, 1801, quoted in Sharp, *American Politics in the Early Republic,* 269. This is McKean's re-creation of a letter he wrote to Jefferson during the heat of the crisis. Monroe's role is also discussed in ibid., 268–71. Bayard to John Adams, February 19, 1801, in Larson, *Magnificent Catastrophe,* 266.

41. For a listing of presidential vetoes in the first century under the Constitution, see Edward Campbell Mason, *The Veto Power: Its Origin, Development, and Function in the Government of the United States* (Boston: Ginn, 1890). Although the threat of the veto was present from the start, the first three presidents shied from its use; Washington vetoed only two bills, Adams and Jefferson none.

CHAPTER TEN: JEFFERSON STRETCHES THE LIMITS

1. Hamilton to James Bayard, January 16, 1801, in Hamilton, *Papers,* 25:319–20.

2. Jefferson, *Papers,* 1:21 (*Summary View*), 415–32 (Declaration of Independence), and 359–60 (draft for Virginia Constitution).

3. Jefferson to Marquis de Lafayette and Jefferson to Baron von Steuben, March 10, 1781, in ibid., 5:113, 120; Jefferson to House of Delegates, May 28, 1781, in ibid., 6:28–29; Michael A. McDonnell, *The Politics of War: Race, Class, and Conflict in Revolutionary Virginia* (Chapel Hill: University of North Carolina Press, 2007), 410–11, 462–65. *Notes on the State of Virginia,* in *Basic Writings of Thomas Jefferson,* ed. Philip S. Foner (New York: Willey, 1944), 132, 137.

4. Jefferson, "Draught of a Fundamental Constitution for the Commonwealth of Virginia," in Jefferson, *Papers,* 6:298–99.

5. Jefferson to Adams, November 13, 1787, in ibid., 12:351; and Jefferson to Madison, December 20, 1787, in ibid., 12:439–40.

6. Jefferson, "Opinion on the Powers of the Senate Respecting Diplomatic Appointments," April 24, 1790, in ibid., 16:378–79.

7. For the context of the arguments over Washington's proclamation of 1793, see chapter 8. For Jefferson's and Hamilton's arguments within Washington's cabinet, see ibid., 27:411–12.

8. Jefferson to James Monroe, March 21, 1796, in ibid., 29:42. Jefferson included the president, who could sign or veto a law, as a branch of the legislature.

9. Jefferson to Madison, March 27, 1796, and November 26, 1795, in ibid., 51, and 28:539–40.

10. Ibid., 33:134–35, 148–52. Contemporary quotations, cited by the editors, are from Margaret Bayard Smith.

11. Jefferson to Monroe, March 7, 1801, and Giles to Jefferson, March 16, 1801, in ibid., 208–9, 311.

12. Jefferson to Monroe, March 7, 1801, in ibid., 209; Jefferson to Nicholson, May 13, 1803, in Jefferson, *Writings,* 10:389.

13. Jefferson to Henry Knox, March 27, 1801, in Jefferson, *Papers,* 33:466. See also ibid., 172–73, 436–37, 460–61, 555, 663.

14. Jefferson to Benjamin Rush, March 24, 1801, in ibid., 437.

15. Ibid., 36:63.

16. Jefferson to Benjamin Rush, December 20, 1801, in ibid., 178; Cutler to Dr. Torrey, February 27, 1802, in *Life, Journals, and Correspondence of Rev. Manasseh Cutler,* ed. William Parker Cutler and Julia Perkins Cutler (Cincinnati: Robert Clarke, 1888), 2:87, quoted in James Simon, *What Kind of Nation: Thomas Jefferson, John Marshall, and the Epic Struggle to Create a United States* (New York: Simon & Schuster, 2002), 164. For Jefferson's behind-the-scenes influence in Congress, see Robert M. Johnstone, *Jefferson and the Presidency: Leadership in the Young Republic* (Ithaca, N.Y.: Cornell University Press, 1978), 130–53; Forrest McDonald, *The Presidency of Thomas Jefferson* (Lawrence: University Press of Kansas, 1976), 38–41; Simon, *What Kind of Nation,* 200.

17. Morris to Hamilton, June 13, 1788, in Hamilton, *Papers,* 5:7; Morris, "Notes on the Form of a Constitution for France," in Sparks, *Gouverneur Morris,* 3:481–500; for dating this document, see *The Diary and Letters of Gouverneur Morris,* ed. Anne Carey Morris (New York: Charles Scribner's Sons, 1888), 1:484. Even allowing for the differences between France and the United States, Morris's French constitution shows an extreme preference for executive authority. "It is essential to the free exercise of the executive power, that the chief be inviolable," he wrote. The monarch would be "hereditary in the male line, in the order of primogeniture," and he would have exclusive power to make war, conclude peace, and control all foreign policy. The king would appoint not only his council and ministers but also members of the Senate. Morris's only nod to republican government was the National Assembly, which would represent the nation and share legislative authority with the Senate and the king. Even within this three-way partnership, Morris made clear which partner was supreme: "The style of the laws shall be, 'The King, by common consent with the Senate and the French Nation, orders that, &c.' But the style of the laws which levy imposts shall be, 'The nation [National Assembly] grants to the King for the necessities and honor of the State the imposts, which the Senate has consented to, and which his Majesty accepts, to be employed for the objects designed by the people in granting them.'" We can safely infer from this work that Morris failed to grasp the depth of the French Revolution already under way, that he believed a strong executive was key to a strong state, and that in 1787 he had modified his natural inclination for top-down rule to suit the particular "habits and manners" of the United States, with its demand for a republican government. Regardless of the change in venue, the pro-executive tilt of Morris's French constitution sheds light on his relentless push to free executive authority in the United States from the control of Congress. In his mind, dominance by the legislature provided a path to tyranny, which he believed was evidenced by the French Revolution. Under the unicameral French system, he wrote in 1792, with

monarchical power faded and without an upper house of the legislature, the Assembly was "under no control except some paper maxims and popular opinion." "The People or rather the Populace, a thing which thank God is unknown in America," he added, were "flattered with the idea that they are omnipotent." The fears he had originally voiced about the American Revolution back in 1774—"The mob begin to think and to reason. Poor reptiles: it is with them a vernal morning, they are struggling to cast off their winter's slough, they bask in the sunshine, and ere noon they will bite"—were to his horror realized in France (Morris to Rufus King, October 23, 1792, in Sparks, *Gouverneur Morris,* 2:241).

18. Madison, *Notes,* August 23; *Annals,* 11:77, 92.
19. Jefferson to Morris, March 6, 1801, in Jefferson, *Papers,* 33:201.
20. Jefferson to Abigail Adams, September 11, 1804, in Jefferson, *Writings,* 11:51.
21. R. W. Carrington, "The Impeachment Trial of Samuel Chase," *Virginia Law Review* 9, no. 7 (May 1923): 489; Jefferson to Nicholson, May 13, 1803, in Jefferson, *Writings,* 10:390. The complete proceedings of Chase's impeachment trial appear in *Annals,* 14:81–676. A vivid description of the trial setting in the Senate chamber is on page 100. Chase's remarks to the Baltimore jury are on pages 673–76.
22. Jefferson, *Works,* 10:346–56.
23. Jefferson to Giles, April 20, 1807, in ibid., 383–88.
24. Jefferson to Hay, May 26 and 28, June 2, 5, 12, 17, 19, 20, and 23, August 7 and 20, and two letters dated September 7, 1807, in ibid., 394–409.
25. Jefferson to Hay, June 2, 1807, in ibid., 396–97.
26. Jefferson to Hay, June 12, 1807, in ibid., 398.
27. Jefferson to Hay, September 4, 1807, in Jefferson, *Writings,* 11:360; Seventh Annual Message to Congress, October 27, 1807, in Jefferson, *Works,* 10:523–24.
28. Jefferson to James Pleasants, December 26, 1821, in Jefferson, *Works,* 12:214.
29. Jefferson to Livingston, April 18, 1802, in ibid., 9:364.
30. Gallatin to Jefferson, January 13, 1803, and Jefferson to Gallatin, January [n.d.], 1803, Henry Adams, ed., *The Writings of Albert Gallatin* (Philadelphia: J. B. Lippincott, 1879), 1:111–15.
31. Jefferson to Dickinson, August 9, 1803, in Jefferson, *Works,* 10:29; Jefferson to Breckinridge, August 12, 1803, in ibid., 5–7.
32. Jefferson to Breckinridge, August 18, 1803, Jefferson to Paine, August 18, 1803, Jefferson to Madison, August 18, 1803, Jefferson to Lincoln, August 30, 1803, in ibid., 7–10.
33. Jefferson to Nicholas, September 7, 1803, in ibid., 10–11.
34. Ibid., 3–8.
35. Jefferson to Gallatin, July 12, 1808, in Jefferson, *Writings,* 12:83.
36. Gallatin to Jefferson, December 18, 1807, quoted in Johnstone, *Jefferson and the Presidency,* 266.
37. *Annals,* 17:50–52, 1217–23.
38. Ibid., 2870–74.
39. Jefferson to Gallatin, May 6, November 13, and December 7, 1808, in Jefferson, *Writings,* 12:52–53, 194, 209.
40. Jefferson to Gallatin, July 29 and September 9, 1808, in ibid., 109, 160; Leonard W. Levy, *Jefferson and Civil Liberties* (Cambridge, Mass.: Belknap Press, 1963), 130–31.

41. Levy, *Jefferson and Civil Liberties*, 131–32.

42. Ibid., 126–30, 133–34.

43. Jefferson to Gallatin, August 11 and December 28, 1808, in Jefferson, *Writings*, 12:122, 221; Levy, *Jefferson and Civil Liberties*, 125.

44. *Annals*, 19:1798–804.

45. Jefferson to Gallatin, May 6, 1808, in Jefferson, *Writings*, 12:52.

46. Jefferson to J. B. Colvin, September 20, 1810, in ibid., 418–22.

47. Some historians and legal scholars argue that the executive vesting clause, because it is unqualified, is more sweeping than the legislative vesting clause, which is qualified: "All legislative Powers herein granted shall be vested in a Congress." This argument ignores both the extreme imbalance in specific powers granted, heavily weighted in Congress's favor, and the elastic "necessary and proper" clause that concludes the grants of congressional authority and has no parallel in the executive grant. Further, a qualification is implicit in the very nature of executive authority, "to carry into execution the national laws" that are passed by the legislative branch—this is the wording of the general grant of executive authority in the early drafts, only to be supplanted by a list of specific grants in the Committee of Detail's report. In the absence of any elastic clause, the final list of executive powers can easily be construed as exhaustive; so said Jefferson and Madison in the 1790s, in any case. This remains a reasonable reading of the Constitution, although historically it has lost out. All this is to say that the presence of two words in the legislative grant that do not appear in the executive grant does not in itself signify any great preference for executive power over legislative power, as is often suggested.

48. There is one respect in which the power of the presidency arguably contracted rather than expanded: its relationship with the judiciary, which culminated in judicial review. The Constitution did not stipulate who was to have the final say on the constitutionality of laws and executive actions, and Jefferson and future presidents had good reason to contend that the oath they took to "preserve, protect and defend the Constitution" implied it was their responsibility to interpret the Constitution as well. Today, though, we assume the Supreme Court, not the president, is the final arbiter, and the notion that any particular body outranks the presidency can plausibly be seen as a diminution of his authority, as originally construed.

EPILOGUE: THEN AND NOW—TRANSLATIONS

1. Washington, *Diaries*, 5:461–62.

2. Some scholars, reading history backward, claim that this democratic thrust was implicit within the Constitution and that the framers favored democracy as we know it today. (See Akhil Reed Amar, *America's Constitution: A Biography* [New York: Random House, 2005].) They do so by ignoring key historical contexts. The absence of federal property qualifications for the franchise, which some claim was a reflection of democratic principles, was actually a political necessity. Any attempt to impose such uniform standards would have created a host of troublesome problems, such as how to count (or not count) slaves. The absence of property qualifications for national office-holders, allegedly another democratic move, was also a political necessity because of the dissimilarity among state economies; further, it was not deemed necessary, for the framers assumed that only men of means would ever be considered for such positions.

The direct election of House members, truly a democratic element, met the minimum standard for republican government, but the framers ensured that no other federal officeholders would be elected by the people. Instead of insisting that presidential electors be chosen by the people, they left the matter in the hands of state legislatures; this was a states' rights issue, not a democratic one. In sum, the Constitution itself did not "pull . . . America toward a populist presidency," in Amar's words (152); later events did, and as they did, they subverted the basic intentions of the framers. Mass campaigning and pandering to voters, hallmarks of modern democracy and a "populist presidency," were anathema to the men who wrote the Constitution. Such phenomena they would view as signs of decay, the beginning of the end of true republican government. Gouverneur Morris, when recalling the mood among the framers, later wrote, "History, the parent of political science, had told them, that it was almost as vain to expect permanency from democracy, as to construct a palace on the surface of the sea" (Morris to Robert Walsh, February 5, 1811, in Farrand, *Records,* 3:418).

There is one respect in which the Constitution was indeed democratic, but this did not pertain specifically to the presidency. The ratification process called for conventions in each state to legitimate the proceedings in an uncontestable fashion. Here, the framers remained true to the basic premise of popular sovereignty: only the people themselves had the right to establish a constitution. Even this move, though, was motivated in part by the need to bypass state legislatures, which had good reasons to oppose the new Constitution because it usurped the authority of state governments and therefore the political power of each state legislator.

3. "There are a number of us in the caucus now pushing back very hard on our leadership. Who knows where they'll end up, but maybe we can take enough Ds with us to make them uncomfortable and to make them stick with making the president act like a Democrat." Peter DeFazio (D-Ore.), interviewed on MSNBC, April 11, 2011.

4. Garry Wills, *"Negro President": Jefferson and the Slave Power* (Boston: Houghton Mifflin, 2003), 5–6, 234; Leonard L. Richards, *The Slave Power* (Baton Rouge: Louisiana State University Press, 2000), 9, 42; William W. Freehling, *The Road to Disunion* (New York: Oxford University Press, 1990), 1:147.

5. Wills, *"Negro President,"* 6–8; Richards, *Slave Power,* 9; Douglas Southall Freeman, *George Washington: Patriot and President* (New York: Charles Scribner's Sons, 1954), 6:343–48.

6. Adams to John Taylor, April 15, 1814, in Adams, *Works,* 6:456–57.

7. Ames to Christopher Gore, March 5, 1800, cited in Edward J. Larson, *A Magnificent Catastrophe: The Tumultuous Election of 1800* (New York: Free Press, 2007), 84.

POSTSCRIPT: WHY THE STORY HAS NOT BEEN TOLD

1. Even when specifically focusing on Morris's views and impact, scholars studying the presidency at the Constitutional Convention who do not take a narrative approach have missed Morris's maneuverings. See, for example, Donald L. Robinson, "Gouverneur Morris and the Design of the American Presidency," *Presidential Studies Quarterly* 17, no. 2 (Spring 1987): 319–28. (This bicentennial issue, titled *The Origins and Invention of the American Presidency,* also featured separate articles on the influence of Madison, Wilson, Hamilton, Washington, and Adams.)

Although most studies eschew the narrative form, not all do. One of the classics in this field, Charles Thach's 1923 *The Creation of the Presidency, 1775–1789* (repr., New York: Da Capo Press, 1969), was based loosely on a narrative construction, and this led Thach to observe that Morris was "the real floor leader of those attached to the idea of the independent executive" (99). Even so, Thach's focus on Morris's intellectual positions led him to overlook the actual dynamics of Morris's floor leadership. After analyzing at some length Morris's impressive speech on July 19, he failed to mention that those words caused the convention to reverse its earlier preference for a single term, seven-year president chosen by Congress, only to return to that default mode a few days later. Similarly, because he focused on positions to the exclusion of procedures, Thach missed Morris's maneuverings of August 24 and 31 that sent the selection of the president back into committee. Subsequent studies, following Thach, have declared Morris a "floor leader" without demonstrating what that entailed. His speeches are quoted but his actions overlooked. One such work, William B. Michaelsen, *Creating the American Presidency, 1775–1789* (Lanham, Md.: University Press of America, 1987), agrees with Thatch's "real floor leader" assessment and notes in particular that Morris "took things into his own hands" by bringing up presidential selection in the Committee of Eleven (Michaelsen, with other modern commentators, calls it the Committee on Remaining Matters). By organizing his brief work around twelve subject heads ("presidential selection," "Impeachment," "Veto Power," etc.), however, he misses the narrative thread that would reveal Morris's machinations.

One recent study that does treat the debate on selection of the president as a dynamic process and therefore takes note of Morris's "omnipresence" is William H. Riker, "The Heresthetics of Constitution Making: The Presidency in 1787, with Comments on Determinism and Rational Choice," *American Political Science Review* 78, no. 1 (March 1984): 1–16. As the title suggests, Riker's narrative supports his "heresthetic" analysis (a term Riker coined), which is intended to reveal how political actors reframe debates to break apparent deadlocks and achieve their preconceived ends. Riker's protagonist in this case is Gouverneur Morris—"ever the opportunist and an exceptionally adroit parliament man"—but as Gerry Mackie observes in *Democracy Defended* (New York: Cambridge University Press, 2003), Riker's argument is essentially reductionist, forcing the narrative into the narrow confines of his structural model. While Riker gives credence to Morris's strategic maneuvering, he does so mechanistically, failing to allow for the organic evolution of Morris's own thoughts or give much credence to the meaningful philosophic argumentation at the convention. Further, because both Riker's presentation and Mackie's rebuttal are framed in such technical terms, their debate has done little to advertise Morris's role in shaping presidential selection. A more accessible treatment, which highlights the small-state/large-state theme discussed by both Riker and Mackie, is Shlomo Slonim, "The Electoral College at Philadelphia: The Evolution of an Ad Hoc Congress for the Selection of a President," *Journal of American History* 73, no. 1 (June 1986): 35–58. While Slonim's narrative approach allows him to uncover the basic outline of the elector compromise, he does not dig deeply into the strategies and political maneuvering that breathe life into the tale, and he therefore underplays Morris's role.

2. Morris's recent biographers, none of whom give Morris sufficient credit for his dynamic role in restructuring the presidency, include William Howard Adams, *Gou-*

verneur Morris: An Independent Life (New Haven, Conn.: Yale University Press, 2003); Richard Brookhiser, *Gentleman Revolutionary: Gouverneur Morris, the Rake Who Wrote the Constitution* (New York: Free Press, 2003); James J. Kirschke, *Gouverneur Morris: Author, Statesman, and Man of the World* (New York: Thomas Dunne Books, 2005); Melanie Randolph Miller, *An Incautious Man: The Life of Gouverneur Morris* (Wilmington, Del.: ISI Books, 2008). Of these writers, only Miller takes any note of Morris's participation in the Committee of Eleven's restructuring of the presidency, and even she does not disclose Morris's maneuverings on July 19 and August 24 and 31, or in fashioning the committee's reversals of the working draft. While Kirschke, following Thach, states that Morris "was the floor leader of the drive for a strong and independent chief executive" (187), he does not provide a narrative of what that floor leadership entailed.

3. Notable general narratives of the Constitutional Convention include, in reverse chronological order, Richard Beeman, *Plain, Honest Men: The Making of the American Constitution* (New York: Random House, 2009); David O. Stewart, *The Summer of 1787: The Men Who Invented the Constitution* (New York: Simon & Schuster, 2007); Carol Berkin, *A Brilliant Solution: Inventing the American Constitution* (New York: Harcourt, 2002); Thornton Anderson, *Creating the Constitution: The Convention of 1787 and the First Congress* (University Park: Pennsylvania State University Press, 1993); Christopher Collier and James Lincoln Collier, *Decision in Philadelphia: The Constitutional Convention of 1787* (New York: Reader's Digest, 1986); Catherine Drinker Bowen, *Miracle at Philadelphia: The Story of the Constitutional Convention* (Boston: Little, Brown, 1966); Clinton Rossiter, *1787: The Grand Convention* (New York: Macmillan, 1966).

4. Rossiter, *1787*, 248; Jack Rakove, *Original Meanings: Politics and Ideas in the Making of the Constitution* (New York: Alfred A. Knopf, 1996), 76; Beeman, *Plain, Honest Men*, 252.

Index